WALTER BENJAMIN AND THE MEDIA

The Spectacle of Modernity

JAEHO KANG

polity

First published in 2014 by Polity Press

Polity Press
65 Bridge Street
Cambridge CB2 1UR, UK

Polity Press
350 Main Street
Malden, MA 02148, USA

ISBN-13: 978-0-7456-4520-9
ISBN-13: 978-0-7456-4521-6(pb)

A catalogue record for this book is available from the British Library.

Typeset in 10.75 on 14 pt Janson Text by
Servis Filmsetting Ltd, Stockport, Cheshire
Printed and bound in Great Britain by Clays Ltd, St Ives plc

For further information on Polity, visit our website: www.politybooks.com

WALTER BENJAMIN
AND THE MEDIA

Theory and the Media

To Junghee Ryu and Kisoo Kang

CONTENTS

ABBREVIATIONS

ACKNOWLEDGEMENTS

This is a small book, but there is a large number of people I would like to thank.

A great debt is owed to the students at the New School and at SOAS who have participated over the years in my classes on the critical theory of media. Their exhaustive curiosity and radical imagination have provoked this book to engage more with politics of contemporary media culture. I am also very grateful to my mentors and *Doktorväter* for their guidance, support and encouragement throughout: John Thompson, Nick Couldry, Axel Honneth, Gyuhwan Seo, the late David Frisby, the late Miriam Hansen, Elihu Katz, Daniel Dayan, Jeffrey Goldfarb, Andrew Arato and Patrick Baert. I hope that my debt to and respect for their insights are evident throughout this book. Thanks are also due to my friends and colleagues who made intellectual contributions to this work: Paolo Carpignano, Vinayak Chaturvedi, Lawrence Hamilton, Noah Isenberg, Troels Degn Johansson, Andreas Kalyvas, Sungdo Kim, Robert Kirkbride, Claus Krogholm,

Shannon Mattern, Marcos Nobre, Dominic Pettman, Martin Roberts, José Rodrigo Rodriguez, Sanjay Ruparelia, Barry Salmon, Martin Saar, Nidhi Srinivas, Erik Steinskog, Sam Tobin, and McKenzie Wark. Bernadette Boyle deserves special mention for her help with meticulous proofreading in preparing the manuscript in every state. Parts of the chapters appeared in the following journals: *Constellations*, *Theoria*, and *International Journal of Politics, Culture and Society*. I thank them for the permission to use.

I would especially like to express my gratitude to Graeme Gilloch. Since we first met in a café near the University of Frankfurt in 2001, he has rigorously encouraged me to pursue the topical issues we discussed and helped elaborate my rough ideas at every stage of their development. Without his friendship, this book would not have been possible. I am deeply grateful to Jeesoon Hong for many years of understanding, patience and encouragement. I also wish to thank my sisters, Moonhee and Jinhee for their understanding and support especially over the past few years.

This book is dedicated to my parents, Junghee Ryu and Kisoo Kang, for their endless generosity, patience and understanding.

1

INTRODUCING DR BENJAMIN

THERE AND THEN, HERE AND NOW

Key Works
'Curriculum Vitae (I)' (1925)
'Curriculum Vitae (VI): Dr Walter Benjamin' (1940)

In September 1940, on the Franco-Spanish border, Walter Benjamin, aged just 48, committed suicide. At that time, the media world that we know today was only in embryonic form: few people had telephones; television was in its infancy as a technology; in terms of film, the age of the silent screen was fresh in the memory and the use of colour still something of a novelty; the printed word, of newspapers, magazines and journals still predominated, while radio had emerged as its main electronic rival. For his generation, the 'wireless' had an altogether different meaning. Some seventy years later, we live in a globalized world dominated by electronic communications of all kinds: mobile technologies, information and communication technologies (ICTs), satellite channels, instant global telecommunications, blogs, social networking sites, tweets, palm-held instant Internet access pads and pods. What, then, can Benjamin's writings tell us about our own twenty-first-century world of ubiquitous digital media? What kind of challenges and questions might they pose for readers today, for whom instant communication across the globe, instant access to information, instant downloads, gaming graphics, 3D, HD, massively multiplayer online role-playing games (MMORPGs), live broadcast TV events from most distant parts of the world, and omnipresent advertising are such an integral part of everyday life that we scarcely notice them, let alone think about them?

In this book I want to argue that despite his living in a different media age, Benjamin's writings are still fundamental to the task of critically analysing the global mediascape of the present. There are two main reasons for this: first and foremost, because what Benjamin was concerned with was the close relationship between the media and capitalist modernity; and secondly, because he foregrounded the intimate intersections of technological innovations and the transformation of human senses and experiences, links that have certainly intensified in the seventy years since his untimely death.

I first became interested in Benjamin's writings about media as a post-graduate student. Several years later, rereading his central texts on this theme in the process of writing this book, I was struck by the enduring relevance of Benjamin's analysis for our contemporary mediascape. For example, Benjamin was one of the few early thinkers who critically challenged conventional perceptions of media as mere technical devices to disseminate messages to a receiver. Moreover, I recognized the powerful sense of political engagement found in Benjamin's media writings as he sought to explore their socio-economic and political circumstances and consequences. Although there are many debates around these issues, for me Benjamin's insights show him to be indebted to his working within the historical materialist tradition of Karl Marx, and that he is a profound, often melancholic, critic of capitalist modernity and its catastrophic inhumanities, injustices and inequalities. Benjamin's work was always geared to the possibilities of communication for human emancipation, not in some naive way that sees modern media as enabling tools – a kind of technological development – but rather as part of his abiding concern with regulating and harmonizing the complex and convoluted interplay between human beings, technology and nature.

It would be true but a little harsh to describe Benjamin himself as a 'failed' academic. He was never an academic if by this we mean a paid employee of an educational institution of higher learning. He never held a university post. When he was obliged to withdraw his *Habilitationsschrift* (post-doctoral thesis) from consideration by the examining committee in 1923, his hopes of obtaining a professorship were ended. As we will see later, his thesis was deemed unreadable, unintelligible and unacceptable by the great and good of the German academic establishment, whose names are now long forgotten or best forgotten. Whether intentional or not, Benjamin's abrupt and unceremonious exit from the university system enabled him, or forced him, into a different way of life and certainly a different kind of writing – not the 'fat books' or 'weighty tomes' that he so scorned, but rather all manner of essays, reviews and other miniatures destined for the feuilleton section of newspapers, magazines, journals and periodicals that were to serve as the pre-eminent site of his literary activity. The newspaper, rather than the lecture theatre, was to be his main setting for communicating his ideas and thoughts. True, when in Paris in the 1930s, he spent many hours on his labour of love, *The Arcades Project*, burrowing away in the archives in the Bibliothèque Nationale, in exemplary scholarly fashion; but it is also true that he continually referred to the cafés he frequented in Berlin, Paris and elsewhere as key loci for his own intellectual production. We might like to think of Benjamin as a kind of forerunner of those who sit with their laptops and lattes in our metropolitan coffee shops hooked up by wi-fi connections today.

So let me introduce Dr Benjamin in a number of different guises, not so much as academician, a lone scholar hiding in dusty library reading rooms, poring over arcane obtuse materials destined for the most exclusive elite intellectual readers, but rather as a politically engaged critic whom we are going to encounter in a number of different circumstances, historical moments, life situations and unlikely production sites.

Benjamin was officially stateless from 1939 but, much earlier than that, he was already embraced as a 'left-wing outsider'. From the spring of 1934 onwards, he relied on a monthly stipend of 500 francs from the Institute of Social Research in New York and constantly argued with publishers over fees. Even in this desperate situation as intellectual refugee, he remained unaffiliated to any academic institutions or political parties. He was a member neither of the Institute of Social Research nor of the Communist Party. Yet, this marginal position did not dissuade him from playing the role of public intellectual. For example, in 1935, Benjamin attended the first International Writers' Congress, a gathering that sought to unite communist and socialist writers against the fascist regimes. At a café in Paris on 22 June 1935, Benjamin gave a talk on his essay 'The Work of Art in the Age of Its Technological Reproducibility', an event organized by the Paris Defence League of German Authors. In the midst of political turbulence, Benjamin was invited by the Institute for the Study of Fascism to give a lecture on the relationship between literary form and politics, a lecture that later came out as a seminal essay, 'The Author as Producer'. His article 'The Letter from Paris' was published in *Das Wort*, a Moscow-based journal, in 1936. This publication was recognized by the Gestapo and resulted in the revocation of Benjamin's German citizenship. Benjamin never had an office, a private space, in any sense. He was always present in a public space: he read in libraries; wrote in cafés; and gave talks in book shops. He was a public man and the public space of the city was his work-space.

Without wishing to sentimentalize or romanticize Benjamin's life, it is nevertheless part of the attraction of his writings that they emanate from outside the university system, beyond academy, and from the margins not the mainstreams. He was never an insider. In what follows, I want above all to try to convey a sense of Benjamin as a writer of energy and excitement, of political engagement and transgression, as a thinker preoccupied with cutting-edge technologies, new generations, and new political formations and possibilities. His ideas were new in his time and remain inspirational for us here and now. Benjamin, then, was a writer of the topical, of *modernité*. It is what makes him of both his time and ours. So, let us become acquainted with Benjamin in the form of four figures: the student activist; the journalist; the media practitioner; and the media critic.

FIGURING BENJAMIN

Key Works

'Experience' (1913)

'The Metaphysics of Youth' (1913–14)

'The Life of Students' (1914–15)

'On the Program of the Coming Philosophy' (1918)

'The Concept of Criticism in German Romanticism' (1919)

'Outline for a *Habilitation* Thesis' (1920–21)
'Letter to Florens Christian Rang' (1923)
'Main Features of My Second Impression of Hashish' (1928)
'Diary from August 7, 1931, to the Day of My Death' (1931)
'The Destructive Character' (1931)
'Experience and Poverty' (1933)
'Berlin Childhood around 1900' (1938)

The Student Activist

Benjamin was born in 1892 into an upper-middle-class secular Jewish family in Berlin, yet interestingly his schooling was far from typical for a child of this background. Instead of attending the Gymnasium, he was sent in 1905 to a progressive boarding school in Haubinda in rural Thuringia, where he joined the left-liberal wing of the Youth Movement led by Gustav Wyneken (1875–1964), a prominent German educational reformer. The school reform programme advocated by Wyneken instilled a life-long preoccupation with radical pedagogy and the possibilities of alternative education systems for young people. At that time, the period just prior to the First World War, Benjamin's adolescence was, like so many others of his generation, marked by the generational clash between the sterile conservative bourgeois world of the Prussian Empire and the progressive radical youth movement desperately seeking new possibilities and opportunities at the dawn of the twentieth century. It was a time still dominated by old hierarchies, by traditional social mores, and long-established patterns of privilege and deference. This was a world of suffocating bourgeois manners and prejudices, of triumphant German militarism and Imperial ambition. It was a social and political order that for many of the brightest young people was increasingly anachronistic and reactionary. It was to be swept away in the horrors of the Great War from 1914 to 1918.

In 1912, Benjamin travelled to the German–Swiss border to enrol at the University of Freiburg in Breisgau, where he began studying philosophy. A year later, he was back in Berlin, attending lectures by the famous sociologist Georg Simmel (1858–1918). Simmel's sociological analysis of commodity culture and contemporary urban life, epitomized in his *The Metropolitan and Mental Life* (1903) and *The Philosophy of Money* (1907), provided Benjamin with an enduring theoretical ground upon which a critical examination of commodity culture and modern human experience could be elaborated and elucidated. Nevertheless, for a student like Benjamin who was seeking an alternative model of intellectual and political practice, 'the university simply is not the place to study' (C, 72) and, indeed, might be actively injurious in that it might be 'capable even of poisoning our turn to the spirit' (C, 74). As president of the Berlin Free Students' Association (FSA), Benjamin was more actively involved in the student movement than in his university classes. One of his first publications, an essay entitled 'Educational Reform: A Cultural Movement', appeared in 1912 in *Student and School Reform*, a magazine published by the FSA in Freiburg. His paper demanding the new conception of the university was presented at a student conference in Weimar in 1914. It is of vital importance to recognize that the metaphysical themes (such as the nature of language, communication and experience) explored in his early essays (such as 'Metaphysics of Youth', 'The Religious Position of the Youth' and 'Experience and Poverty') are part of Benjamin's philosophical reflection on concrete socio-political issues stemming from his active engagement with the student movement. In these essays Benjamin attributed the limitations and failings of the German education system to the hierarchical relationship between professor and student, conceived as it was as one between master and apprentice, between the powerful and the powerless, a relationship based then on old ideas of one-way communication between s/he who speaks and s/he who listens. Radical pedagogical practice that shaped Benjamin's own schooling convinced him that communication is by no means and should never be reduced to a 'one-way street' but must always involve mutual and communal activity. The aim of education is less akin to the conveyance of information or knowledge from an authoritative teacher to a passive student than it is to an active engagement with collective communication as reciprocal interaction. In opposition to those conventional Enlightenment pedagogic principles that dominated the German public education system at the turn of the century (and that are probably still powerful in most countries today), Benjamin saw education and entertainment as complementary rather than incompatible processes. Benjamin's leitmotif with respect to communication, education and entertainment is the imperative to challenge all forms of established power, orthodoxy and authority, be it of conventional knowledge, of the text, of the teacher as master, of institutions, including the university, and of prevailing political power.

The Journalist

Upon the completion of his studies, Benjamin started to think about his future profession and, despite his disdain for university as institution, he decided to pursue an academic career with the hope of becoming 'a philosophical literary critic': 'The goal I had set for myself has not yet been totally realized, but I am finally getting close. The goal is that I be considered the foremost critic of German literature' (Letter to his close friend, Gershom Scholem (1897–1982),

20 January 1930; C, 359). Having narrowly avoided con-
scription into the German army, Benjamin relocated to the
University of Bern, Switzerland, where he worked on his
doctoral dissertation examining the philosophical foundation of the early Romantic theory of criticism ('The Concept
of Criticism in German Romanticism', published in 1920).
In a letter of 1918 to his friend, Ernst Schoen (1894–1960),
Benjamin expressed his uncertainty regarding an academic
career: 'I do want to get my doctorate, and if this should
not happen, or not happen yet, it can only be the expression
of my *deepest* inhibitions' (C, 125). It is not entirely clear to
what extent or how seriously Benjamin envisioned himself as
a professor.

After a brief period with his father's antique business in
Berlin, during which time Benjamin imagined the possibility
of a career as a seller of antique and rare books, Benjamin
returned to academia and worked on his *Habilitationsschrift*
on German Baroque Trauerspiel (mourning drama) in the
period between May 1924 and early April 1925. It was sub-
mitted for consideration in May 1925 to the professor of
literary history at Frankfurt University, then to the professor
of aesthetics, and finally was passed along to members of the
philosophy faculty, including Max Horkheimer (1895–1973),
then a young member of the faculty and later to the director of the Institute of Social Research. This work explored a
particular form (or idea) of post-medieval German theatre,
which Benjamin argued gave expression to the melancholy,
creaturely condition of a god-forsaken human world.
Incomprehensibility was the common assessment by the
examiners of the thesis, which incorporated no less than 600
quotations from the most obscure sources. Rather than facing
the embarrassment of outright failure, Benjamin heeded the
informal recommendation of the university authority and
withdrew his submission from consideration, thus ending

any chance of an academic post in the German university system of the Weimar Republic. Yet, it was perhaps a lucky escape for him (and for all those who admire his work so much). He himself expressed a sense of relief at the outcome and there is no reason to think that this was not genuine: 'All in all, I am glad. The Old Franconian stage route following the stations of the local university is not my way' (C, 276). A few years later in 1928, his withdrawn thesis was published under the title, *The Origin of German Mourning Drama* [*Ursprung des deutschen Trauerspiels*]. Contrary to the negative response from the German academic system, his book instantly received wide critical attention and a number of positive reviews in literary circles in both Germany and France.

Instead of becoming an academic, Benjamin became increasingly engaged with forms of journalistic writing, involving reviews, essays and other short pieces aimed at a mass readership, types of writings and readerships treated with some scorn by academic elites and mandarins. His collection of aphorisms and fragments, *One-Way Street*, appeared in the same year as *The Origin of German Mourning Drama*, but could not have been more different in design, conception and tone. With the sensational photomontage cover designed by Sasha Stone, a Dadaist, *One-Way Street* constituted and attempted to articulate a new and alternative mode of intellectual practice and to develop Benjamin's own innovative literary criticism. The essential feature of this distinctive and pioneering intellectual practice was to be the capturing and documentation of the topicality of everyday metropolitan life. The task of the critic was to record and show the here and now. Current events, developments in culture, new forms of entertainment, excerpts from everyday life, fragmentary insight into existential conditions of capitalist modernity – all these were captured by means of aphorisms, jokes, literary fragments, reviews of books, pen portraits of cityscapes both near and far, interviews and other textual elements. All these fragments were gathered and composed into patterns, mosaics, constellations, and shot through with humour, irony and critical scorn for established and conventional forms, genres, critics and writers, so-called intellectuals and politicians. As we will see, such practices were carried over into his unfinished (or unfinishable) project on the nineteenth-century Paris arcades, a project that was conceived in the mid 1920s and was not so much a reconstruction of the past as a rendering of the meaning of the contemporary. In this vein, Benjamin's intellectual practice might be understood under the term 'correspondent', that is to say, one who writes in a way that corresponds to the imperatives of their time. His writings involved urgent, short, sharp and pointed sentences, jagged lines with which to puncture the pretentions and pomposity of the complacent pseudo-intellectual bourgeois circles of Weimar culture. In this journalistic form, he wrote not only for his own time but for ours as well. This is correspondence more akin to an urgent message in a bottle than a long-winded letter.

Benjamin's multifaceted work – as a reviewer and interviewer, editor and translator – was centred on various journals and newspapers based not only in major western European cities such as Frankfurt (i.e., *Frankfurter Zeitung*), Berlin (*Die literarische Welt*) and Paris (*Le Monde*) but also in eastern European cities like Moscow (*Die Kreatur* and *Das Wort*) and Prague (*Prager Tageblatt*). Characterizing Benjamin as a figure of misfortune and melancholy perhaps underestimates his success as a journalist. For example, during his visit to Berlin, the French novelist, André Gide (1869–1951), gave an exclusive two-hour interview to Benjamin in January 1928. He also interviewed other notable literary figures of the time such as Julien Green (1900–1998), Marcel Jouhandeau (1888–1979), Emmanuel Berl (1892–1976) and the Surrealists Louis Aragon (1897–1982) and Robert Desnos (1900–1945).

Founding his own journal was Benjamin's persisting hope. During the 1920s it nearly came to fruition when he was commissioned by a publisher to edit a new periodical of literary and philosophical criticism. The title he proposed was *Angelus Novus* (New Angel), echoing the title of a small painting by Paul Klee that he owned. In his inaugural editorial piece, 'Announcement of the Journal Angelus Novus', Benjamin announced that 'the vocation of a journal is to proclaim the spirit of its age', exploring contemporary cultural politics, drama and religion. Benjamin may have been able to put a brave face on his academic failure with the Trauerspiel piece, but there was no hiding his bitter disappointment when, following various disputes and financial problems, the publisher pulled out and *Angelus Novus* was never published.

A second and equally unsuccessful attempt to publish his own journal was made in close collaboration with Bertolt Brecht (1898–1956) in the early 1930s. Benjamin and Brecht shared the view that bourgeois forms of art and culture had been subject to meltdown in the face of the new mass media. The rise of new forms of art necessitated equally innovative types of criticism corresponding to the rapid development of communication technologies. The proposed title of this second journal, *Krise und Kritik* [*Crisis and Criticism*], indicated their fundamental insight into the collapse of traditional aesthetic practices and categories. Benjamin and Brecht planned to include contributions from a wide range of prominent left-oriented cultural critics and writers such as Georg Lukács (1885–1971), Karl Korsch (1886–1961), Siegfried Kracauer (1889–1966), Theodor W. Adorno (1903–1969) and Alfred Döblin (1878–1957). Yet again, the plan was not realized due to financial difficulties as well as editorial disagreement between Benjamin and Brecht.

There was one third and final attempt by Benjamin to publish his own journal, but this was made in very different circumstances. While interned as a detainee in Chateau de Vernuche in 1939, Benjamin sought to collaborate with one or two other camp inmates to produce a publication, less as a way of developing intellectual practice, more as a means to distract himself and to survive in the conditions of the camp.

The Media Practitioner

Benjamin was a media practitioner before he was a media theorist. Not only was he a journalist, working on newspapers and magazines, but he also became actively involved in radio broadcasting in the late 1920s and early 1930s, a period when the German radio industry was rapidly expanding and the popularity of radio as a new mass medium reached its peak. Unlike other German intellectuals, who mainly devoted themselves to theoretical discussion of the possibilities of radio, Benjamin took a key role in broadcasting itself, sometimes as a director, sometimes as a presenter, and sometimes as a scriptwriter. Even though his involvement with radio broadcasting was prompted by his desperate need for money, his engagement with the medium was pioneering. Radio was regarded by many German intellectuals as a debased form of 'mass' communication. Benjamin's broadcasting output did not involve high literary or intellectual programming (unlike that of some of his contemporaries) but was rather one of the most scorned areas of popular culture, namely, children's programmes.

Benjamin was aware that the possibilities of a new public culture would never arise from declining high art but only from within the centre of new 'mass' cultural industries such as radio and film. In the mass media, he saw new opportunities to go beyond the tired education system founded on Enlightenment principles and to find potential answers to the pedagogic questions that had preoccupied him since his days in the youth movement. As a media practitioner, Benjamin was in a position to create not so much a theory of pedagogic practice but actual programmes that combined education and entertainment for young audiences. Benjamin came to see radio broadcasting as a possible mediated public sphere in which he could take on the role of, and serve as, a public intellectual. As we will see in chapter 3, Benjamin's radio broadcasting spans a diverse range of styles, forms and themes, including travel writings, book reviews, cultural histories (e.g., the history of toys) and letter collections. His trip to Moscow between December 1926 and February 1927 was publicized through his radio talks ('Young Russian Writers') and diaries ('Moscow Diary'). After the Nazis seized power in 1932, left-oriented and Jewish directors and producers were dismissed from the stations. Benjamin was among the first to go. He left his radio practice in Berlin and took up exile in Paris.

The Media Critic

The last incarnation of Benjamin's intellectual practice involves his attempt to create a new model of criticism. Benjamin recognized that the new age of mass media necessitated a reconceptualization of the task of the critic, in which aesthetic categories and judgement are unmasked as, and subordinated to, the political. In a letter to Scholem, he stressed a new form of criticism was required: 'The problem is that literary criticism is no longer considered a serious genre in Germany and has not been for more than fifty years. If you want to carve out a reputation in the area of criticism, this ultimately means that you must recreate criticism as a genre' (C, 359). In the course of the 1930s, Benjamin endeavoured to develop an alternative form of criticism corresponding to the changing nature of communication, focusing on the most radical experiments in art, media and politics. These would be his most distinctive and famous contributions to media theory and remain the subject of fierce debate even today. Benjamin's writings on photography, film, radio, theatre and audiences are often seen as his original studies of aesthetics and politics. These writings were inspired by a number of encounters and experiences. Brecht's active adaptation of technological advancements also prompted Benjamin to consider the precise material condition of intellectual and cultural practices. In the works of varied avant-garde movements such as Surrealism, Bauhaus and Russian experimental film-making, Benjamin perceived a new moment of European intellectual life, which took cognizance of the rapidly developing technological apparatus of media and cultural production. As we will see in chapter 4, in these movements, Benjamin saw the final demise of the humanistic Enlightenment project and the not yet fully formed, recognizable emergence of a new revolutionary collective subject. The role of the media critic was seen as a harbinger of revolutionary politics and a radically transformed cultural sphere in which the mass public were to take centre stage as distracted – yet critical – spectators.

CONFIGURING BENJAMIN

Key Works

'An Outsider Makes His Mark' (1930)

'Review of Kracauer's *Die Angestellten*' (1930)

'Bert Brecht' (1930)

'Exchange with Theodor W. Adorno on the Essay "Paris, the Capital of the Nineteenth Century"' (1935)

'Exchange with Theodor W. Adorno on "The Paris of the Second
Empire in Baudelaire"' (1938)

While the failure of his *Habilitationsschrift* certainly meant
that Benjamin was to remain an outsider in terms of the
German academic system, it is also true that he was able to
engage with and forge connections with a number of other
intellectuals, writers and artists. He was very much a part of
the Weimar intellectual scene and cultural *milieu*, if for no
other reason than that his position as a freelancer obliged
him to cultivate a substantial and wide-ranging network of
colleagues from whom he was able to obtain commissions.
Being financially 'independent', living as a literary producer,
required the maintenance of close and continuous relations
with editors, publishers and other journalists. We should be
reluctant to accept the romantic notion of Benjamin as some
kind of lone scholar, cut adrift from academy, producing
works of genius in isolation, bereft of friends and colleagues.
To survive by means of his own typewriter throughout the
1920s and 1930s would have been inconceivable without
well-placed colleagues and friends such as Ernst Schoen,
who was at *Südwestdeutscher Rundfunk* and instrumental in
Benjamin's brief radio career, and Siegfried Kracauer, who
was an editor, first in Frankfurt and then in Berlin, with the
Frankfurter Zeitung.

I want to suggest that Benjamin's thought can be located
in terms of a number of competing philosophical, literary
and cultural influences that were at work throughout his
life. One way of understanding these currents is to think of
them in terms of four of his closest friends/associates, each
of whom exerted a kind of gravitational pull on Benjamin,
drawing him towards, but never wholly or exclusively into,
their intellectual orbit.

The first and most enduring of these forces of attraction

was that of his closest friend, the mathematician and Judaic scholar, Gershom Scholem. While it is not always clear who is influencing whom in Benjamin's relationship with Scholem, it is widely recognized that Scholem played an absolutely fundamental role in stimulating and encouraging Benjamin's life-long fascination with Judaic mystical and messianic traditions.[1] From his earliest writings on themes such as language, experience and naming, to his very last work, the 1940 thesis, 'On the Concept of History', Benjamin draws upon and reworks Judaic theological and cabbalistic motifs in highly original and provocative ways, questioning secular and rationalistic worldviews. In terms of language for example, as we will see in chapter 2, Benjamin is keen to refute the idea of words and names as arbitrary signifiers of their referents and instead posits the necessary, now lost, perfection of language as Adamic naming. The arbitrariness in the relation between words and things that is the mark of, for example, Saussurean semiological linguistics, is for Benjamin not the condition of language as such but only of fallen human language. One of the most distinctive and enigmatic aspects of Benjaminian thought is this curious preoccupation with what may seem to us today obscure and arcane theological categories and concepts.

The second main influence would be Theodor W. Adorno. Adorno was Benjamin's key contact at the Institute of Social Research in Frankfurt, their friendship having developed from the mid 1920s, and their correspondence contains some of the most important discussions shaping Benjamin's key texts during the 1930s: for example, 'The Work of Art in the Age of Its Technological Reproducibility', and 'The Paris of the Second Empire in Baudelaire'. Adorno draws Benjamin away from Scholem's theologically inspired themes and more to those in the German philosophical traditions of idealism and materialism, especially Marxist dialectics. Adorno insisted on a sceptical attitude to the notion of totality, and emphasized the notion of mediation as a way of conceptualizing the complex relationship between the economic infrastructure of society and its cultural and aesthetic manifestations.[2] For example, works of art were not to be understood as mere reflections of the prevailing forces of production but rather to involve manifold levels of mediation and transformation. Benjamin did not share Adorno's negative perception of mass media, Hollywood cinema and popular music, but instead set out to find revolutionary moments and possibilities in developing new technological apparatus. As I have already suggested, Benjamin worked in and for the very cultural industries (radio and newspapers) that Adorno was so quick to denounce as betrayals of art, culture and the Enlightenment.

Indeed, Benjamin's critical understanding of mass culture and media is much closer to that of the third figure, namely Siegfried Kracauer. Kracauer was highly interested in the phenomenology of the city, the concrete manifestations of everyday life, and popular entertainment. Kracauer also demonstrated a redemptive concern with the reconstitution of this everyday world, recovering it from what he saw as a state of modern spiritual homelessness, of absence of meaning. Kracauer's own writings in the 1920s and 1930s portray a bleak vision of modernity that has lost the notion of the transcendent, but that nevertheless retains the promise of a new and privileged proximity to the world of things through the prosthetic work of the film camera. A disciple of Simmel's cultural and urban sociology, Kracauer shared with Benjamin a preoccupation with the minutiae of the modern metropolis and the sensitive appreciation of both its positive and negative moments.[3] Benjamin saw Kracauer as a kind of prototypical revolutionary rag-picker, and therefore as an important and innovative model for his own textual practices ('Review of Kracauer's Die Angestellten' (SW2, 355–7)).

The last of my four key figures influencing Benjamin is the famous playwright Bertolt Brecht. Brecht's 'crude thinking' and didactic Marxist approach were curiously appealing to Benjamin, who came to see so-called epic theatre as a key demonstration of notions of pedagogy, communication, distraction and interruption, as a pause in which dramatic or political situations are suddenly laid bare, recognized and become decisive ('Bert Brecht', SW2, 365–71). This structure of momentary illumination and political mobilization inspires Benjamin's notion of the dialectical image, his key historiographic principle for *The Arcades Project*. Much to Adorno's dismay, Brecht's own brand of revolutionary proletarian pedagogy and politics also became important to Benjamin in terms of his concern with collective experience, the formation of a new political subject, and the task of ideology criticism, and many of Brecht's central motifs are theoretically reworked in Benjamin's late writing in the 1930s.

So, how might one characterize these four formative influences working on Benjamin? We see:

(1) Judaic theology and mysticism (Scholem);
(2) the German philosophical tradition, notions of critique in aesthetic theory, fragmentation, the avant-garde and modernism (Adorno);
(3) quotidian urban experiences and film (Kracauer); and
(4) notions of revolutionary pedagogy, class struggle and political praxis (Brecht).

In short, we might say that Benjamin's work exists at the crossroads of the four Ms: messianism, modernism, metropolitanism and Marxism. To these, I want to add a fifth M, namely, *media critique*.

In this book, I am going to use the term 'media critique' to characterize the essential features of Benjamin's distinctive account of the media and experience, an account that reflects the crisis of criticism in an age in which the various media were becoming mass phenomena. The new forms of media technology appearing in the early twentieth century, coupled with the emergence of radical avant-garde artistic movements pioneering experimental techniques and practices, called into question established notions of art, literature, taste and aesthetics. This period of cultural transformation created new challenges and possibilities and in particular led to a crisis of bourgeois literary criticism. Witnessing the collapse of bourgeois literary culture, Benjamin sought to develop a new kind of critical practice and engagement corresponding to the new world of media culture.

Benjamin's media critique involves a critical appreciation of media 'aesthetics', a term widely – yet equivocally – used in the field of art history and film theory. It is imperative that in Benjamin's work, 'aesthetics' does not designate part of a theory of fine art that seeks to identify the essence of beauty in a work of art; rather, it delineates a study of perception and the senses in connection with a certain form of technology. Notably, *aisthētikos*, the Greek epistemological root of aesthetics, refers to a study of the human sensorium. Benjamin's concern with film is less akin to a textual interpretation of the filmic representation and narratives than to a critical analysis of the cinematic reception process involving multiple intersections of technology, image and body. He outlines a key theoretical issue of this intersection thus: 'Film, by virtue of its shock effects, is predisposed to their form of reception. In this respect, too, it proves to be the most important subject matter at present, for the theory of perception, which the Greeks called aesthetics' (SW3, 120). Benjamin's media critique asks a more specific question of a changing nature of perception: To what extent can media technology expand the possibility of aesthetic experience, retrieve the alienated and fragmented human sensorium and thereby reorganize the new subject? His media critique aims to grasp the changing nature of perception and the constructive role of media for a new mass public.

As we will see later, media critique also entails Benjamin's unique idea of 'critique', reflecting a crisis of communication and of criticism. Benjamin was not a conventional media 'theorist'. He did not view the media as a structural or institutional system; nor did he endeavour to offer a functional analysis of communication technologies by means of a mathematical or quantitative methodology. Rather, he approached the media from a non-functionalist perspective and examined the interplay between various modes of communication technology and diverse forms of human experience from his own unique perspective of materialist anthropology. Benjamin rightly understood the need to explore the media not only within the prevailing political and economic contexts of capitalist modernity, but also in relation to the transformation of the public sphere and, not least, in relation to the reconfiguration of human perceptions and faculties.

We should remember that Benjamin's arguments are innovative and contentious. This is what makes them so interesting. He may not provide us with clear-cut answers, but many of the questions and issues he grapples with – the role of technologies, bodily experiences, the organization of space, attention and distraction, communication and information – are ones that preoccupy us still in our own age of digital technology. This is why we still need to read and understand his work some seventy years after his death.

CHAPTER OVERVIEW

This book seeks to provide a detailed reconstruction and analysis of Benjamin's media critique. It shows how

Benjamin critically analysed the profound impact of various modes of communication technology on capitalist modernity, in particular, how media shaped human experience, commodity culture, urban space and politics. Four key themes are identified and these form main chapters: the crisis of communication; mediated storytelling; technological reproducibility; and the media city. Each chapter seeks to bring out Benjamin's account of the relationship between specific media of communication (books, newspapers, radio, photography and cinema) and corresponding forms of experience.

In chapter 2, I will examine the crisis of communication in terms of the demise of bourgeois literary culture and the public sphere. I explore how Benjamin links the decline of storytelling with the development of the information industry in Europe in the nineteenth century.

Chapter 3 focuses on Benjamin's media practice in terms of his engagement with radio broadcasting. It will show how in his own programmes for children and others he experimented with contemporary theoretical issues (e.g., education, entertainment, and a new form of storytelling via electronic mass media).

Chapter 4 examines Benjamin's best-known essay, 'The Work of Art in the Age of Its Technological Reproducibility', in considerable detail. It looks closely at key themes of cinematic experience such as the demise of aura; the optical unconscious of the photographic image; and shock, distraction and tactility. Benjamin's analysis of art and politics will clarify the complex dimension of political spectacle and the formation of a new public in the age of modern media.

Chapter 5 traces the theoretical relevance of Benjamin's magnum opus, *The Arcades Project*, for our understanding of modern media in relation to the metropolitan cityscape. This chapter also identifies some of the methodological implications of Benjamin's analysis of communication technology and urban space for media studies.

In the conclusion I look to appraise Benjamin's media critique by means of brief comparisons with more recent media and social theorists. In so doing, I hope to clarify Benjamin's distinctive contribution to contemporary media studies and help readers further develop their own critical inquiry.

2

THE CRISIS OF COMMUNICATION
AND THE INFORMATION INDUSTRY

The modern newspaper is a product of city life; it is no
longer merely an organ of propaganda and opinion, but a
form of popular literature.[1]

– Robert Park (1923)

INTRODUCTION

In the early twentieth century, most European metropolises
such as London, Paris and Berlin were witnessing the rapid
growth of mass media, including popular magazines, newspapers and radio. The burgeoning of the publishing industry
and of daily newspapers was captured by the literati in association with the looming crisis of literature and intellectual
activity. Their primary responses to the impact of mass
media, whether lamentations over the death of high literature
or the enthusiastic greeting of a new era of popular culture,
converged in the crisis of the bourgeois culture, focusing
in particular on the novel, hitherto the prevailing literary

form. For Benjamin, literature's ongoing crisis was not an entirely new phenomenon but was rooted in a much deeper process of transformation: the meltdown of bourgeois forms of communication. His extensive study of European modernism, in particular of the French poet Charles Baudelaire (1821–1867), was an attempt to investigate the crisis of the novel within the development of urban capitalist culture and communications technology.[2]

The primal question Benjamin poses is why modern readers find lyric poetry difficult to read. Unlike his contemporary literary critics, Benjamin sought answers that were directed towards the changing material conditions of bourgeois literature and the alienation of modern readers' experiences from lyric poetry: 'One wonders how lyric poetry can be grounded in experience [*einer Erfahrung*] for which exposure to shock [*Chockerlebnis*] has become the norm' (SW4, 318). Even in the middle of the nineteenth century, before the emergence of electronic media, lyric poetry was already regarded as an obsolete literary genre, giving rise to critical concerns about the demise of literature as a whole. Benjamin's analysis of the crisis of the literary public sphere unpacks the dynamics of the information industry in high capitalism. The discrepancy between bourgeois literature and urban experience was the topical issue that had preoccupied Benjamin's thought since his initial encounter with French avant-garde movements – the surrealism of the mid 1920s – a thought that came to be realized in his work *One-Way Street* (1928). This chapter examines Benjamin's unique approach to the transformation of bourgeois forms of communication, focusing on the 'communicability of experience' [*die Mitteilbarkeit der Erfahrung*] (SW3, 145), a key concept underpinning Benjamin's thought on the crisis of experience. In this chapter, I shall examine three main questions:

(1) How does Benjamin's comparative analysis of oral and visual culture explain the dynamic of the rise of modern society?
(2) What is the impact of the information industry on literary practice in the nineteenth century?
(3) How can we assess the technical attributes of intellectual activity that are bound up with mass media via an analysis of Benjamin's account of journalism and the literary practices of radical intellectuals?

STORYTELLING AND THE CRISIS OF THE NOVEL

Key Works
'On Language as Such and on the Language of Man' (1916)
'The Task of the Translator' (1921)
'The Crisis of the Novel' (1930)
'Doctrine of the Similar' (1933)
'On the Mimetic Faculty' (1933)
'The Storyteller: Observations on the Works of Nikolai Leskov' (1936)

The unprecedented scale of technological warfare and the development of weapons of mass destruction during the First World War led Benjamin to recognize the profound changes in the nature of modern experience and to locate the question of the communicability of experience at the centre of his investigation. He asks: 'Wasn't it noticeable at the end of the war that men who returned from the battlefield had grown silent – not richer but poorer in communicable experience?' (SW3, 143–4). Technological warfare led to the dramatic rupture of the continuity and quality of experience and the ability of people to impart that experience both socially and individually. In the shadow of the Great War, it became evident that past experiences had been lost, had failed to assimilate to daily life, resulting in the fragmentation, dislocation and disorientation of our experiences. Although the depreciation in the quality of experience was conspicuous during the war, this was in fact the result of the long-term process of civilization.

The notion of experience is one of the principal elements in Benjamin's thinking, that is, 'the true focal point of his analysis of modernity, philosophy, of history and theory of the artwork'.[3] Benjamin challenges two philosophical traditions on the notion of experiences: the overly rational version of *Erfahrung* (outer social experience, as presented by Immanuel Kant) and the alleged immediacy and meaningfulness of *Erlebnis* (inner lived experience, as presented by Wilhelm Dilthey). By analysing the historical and technological condition of experience, he tries to avoid the shortcomings embedded in conventional dichotomies between *Erfahrung* and *Erlebnis*.[4] The crisis of experience, represented as the atrophy of experience and the decline in our subjective capability to discern it (and express it in the way that the soldiers did after the war), is bound up with particular historical and material conditions of communication.

> Historically, the various modes of communication have competed with one another. The replacement of the older relation by information, and of information by sensation, reflects the increasing atrophy of experience. In turn, there is a contrast between all these forms and the story, which is one of the oldest forms of communication. (SW4, 316)

Likewise, Benjamin attempts to differentiate between two patterns in the transformation of communication: the shift from oral to visual communication and from storytelling to the modern information and entertainment industries. These historical shifts are compared throughout Benjamin's analysis of the relation between communication and the human sensory apparatus: listening versus seeing; speaking versus writing; unmediated communication versus mediated communication; and the assimilated collective experience versus the isolated individual experience. The contrast between oral and visual culture is stressed in his analogy of the storyteller and novelist.

'The Storyteller: Observations on the Works of Nikolai Leskov', published in October 1936, investigates the end of storytelling as a historically parallel phenomenon to the decline of aura (Benjamin's letter to Adorno of 4 June 1936, ABC, 140). Using the Russian fiction writer as 'a masterful storyteller', Benjamin identifies four distinctive attributes of storytelling in the context of the crisis of modern communication.

First, storytelling, 'the oldest and most artisan form of communication', is distinguished from other forms of communication by its orality. While over time depicting local events and traditions, as well as journeys and travels, storytelling is emblematic of oral culture, in which the storyteller's experience is communicated directly by word of mouth, and from generation to generation. The story itself is always fully present to the group of listeners and repeatable but not completely replicable or, in Benjamin's terminology, 'reproducible'. Storytelling's useful value is the second essential feature, a value that is closely connected to the everyday life of a community. It represents a form of communication that hinges upon the exchange of practical knowledge, such as peasants' exchange of agricultural know-how. The essence of this communication, therefore, lies in its 'wisdom' and 'truth', as embedded in tradition. Third, the stories brought by travellers from afar or from long-established traditions mark the distinctive spatio-temporal attributes of storytelling. The ancient storyteller is characterized as one of two types: 'the settled tiller of the soil', bound up with time, and

'the trading seaman', with space (SW3, 144). The validity of storytelling lies in its longevity or perpetuity, which
relies upon continuity between the experience of the teller
and the listener. Tradition functions as the medium, rendering the transmissibility of a story possible. Fourth, a shared
collective experience is underlined. The communal feature
of storytelling is firmly distinguished from other modes of
communication because it necessitates the 'assimilation
of experiences' between storyteller and listeners, a process
acquired by mutual companionship. This exchange of experience takes place between the collective listener and the
storyteller via face-to-face interaction.

Benjamin's emphasis on the assimilation of collective
experience precipitated by the immediacy of communication may seem to resemble the traditional assertion made by
such ancient Greek philosophers as Socrates and Plato. They
ascribed 'true' communication to verbal expression and
denounced literacy, fearing it would affect human faculties
such as mimesis and memory. These ancient philosophers
praised dialogue as the most effective means of communication for teaching and learning, while accusing the nascent
writing culture of impairing the appreciation of meaning. For
instance, Plato went on to exclude poets from his ideal republic because these new poets arose from a new chirographically
styled poetic world by outmoding conventional poetic formulation.[5] Unlike that shown in Platonic tradition, Benjamin's
view on storytelling as a prototypical mode of communication
involves more physiological aspects of orality precipitated by
three key elements: language, mimesis and memory.

Language

In his essay, 'On Language as Such and on the Language of
Man', written over the summer of 1916, Benjamin contrasts

two views of communication: the magical and the instrumental. On the one hand, he endeavours to unravel a 'redemptive appropriation of language's mystery',[6] and on the other hand he tries to free language from 'the instrumental view' that conceives it as no more than a means or vehicle of transmission.[7] At this early stage, while studying the philosophy of language developed by Johann Georg Hamann (1730–1788) and Wilhelm von Humboldt (1767–1835), the young Benjamin becomes interested in delving into the metaphysical nature of absolute experience. Approaching language from its mythical and theological aspects, Benjamin sums it up thus: 'What does language communicate? It communicates the mental being corresponding to it. It is fundamental that this mental being communicates itself *in* language and not *through* language' (SW1, 63). For him, the perception of language merely as mediation or transmission is a fundamental problem for the idealist view on language. The instrumental use of language (or the 'semiotic view') fails to grasp 'degrading language to a mere tool and reifying itself as a barrier to true reality'.[8]

Benjamin's insight into language is concerned less with the 'content' of communication and what is meant or transmitted than with 'the way' the experience is communicated. In his effort to move beyond the instrumental view of language, he regards storytelling as a primal form of communication, in which the entity of communication is not simply understood as 'the content of the story', but as the storyteller's unmediated total experience. The distinctive feature implicit in storytelling is its capacity to facilitate companionship between audiences, which is attained through corporeal actions like listening and speaking. Benjamin underscores the onomatopoetic attributes of language, ascribing the crisis of modern communication to the mediation of written language. The rise of visual communication, exemplified by the birth of the novel, marks the shift from the sensuous, ono-matopoetic nature of language to the semiotic, non-sensuous character of writing and reading. While storytelling pertains to a sensory mode of communication, the novel reflects the semiotic and instrumental nature of language. He calls, however, neither for the restoration of the pure quality of language nor for the absolute silence advocated by some modernist writers such as Samuel Beckett (1906–1989).[9] In Benjamin's view, neither the instrumental nor the magical uses of language can provide the solution to the crisis of communication. He draws more attention to how modern communications technologies can call up multisensory com-munication, as exemplified in a primal oral culture.

Mimesis

The crisis of experience also marks the atrophy of mimesis. The concept of mimesis (from the Greek *mimeisthai*) usually refers to the perfection, representation or imitation of the real world, or of nature. To emphasize the aspect of delib-erative behaviour, Benjamin tends to use the term mimesis or, frequently, mimetic faculty. Benjamin believes the most vital feature of mimesis to be, not imitation or mimicry, but a communicative correspondence between the object and the subject and between nature and perception. For instance, a child at play does not merely 'imitate' an aeroplane or a rock. The child tries to 'become' an aeroplane or a rock. The members of the Frankfurt School tend to associate the decline of an authentic experience of art and literature with the predominating power of science and technology. In their radical critique of the Enlightenment, both T.W. Adorno and Herbert Marcuse identified that the increas-ing process of abstraction stemming from the subjugation of nature in modern science has brought about the decline of mimesis. Like Adorno and Marcuse, Benjamin distances his speculation on mimetic faculty from Platonic or Aristotelian ideas of imitation or aesthetic verisimilitude of works of art. Benjamin's idea of mimetic faculty draws on 'a wider range of anthropological, psychological, sociobiological, and language-philosophical strands of mimesis'.[10] It is crucial, as Hansen aptly highlights, that Benjamin's mimetic faculty should involve 'not a category of representation but a relational practice', that is, 'a process, comportment, or activity of producing similarities' and 'a mode of access to the world involving sensuous, somatic, and tactile forms of perception and cognition'.[11] What Benjamin established through the theory of mimesis is that his idea of communication is less akin to the reflection or mediation of the objective world than to the reciprocal correspondence between nature and the perceptual body.

In the fragments 'On the Mimetic Faculty' (1933) and 'Doctrine of the Similar' (1933), Benjamin places a particular emphasis on the fact that the mimetic faculty has atrophied over time in the historical and technological context of modern industrial society: 'The direction of this change seems determined by the increasing fragility of the mimetic faculty. For clearly the perceptual world [*Merkwelt*] of modern man contains only minimal residues of the magical correspondences and analogies that were familiar to ancient peoples' (SW2, 721). Yet, unlike the Greek ancient philosophers, he does not call for the restoration of magical correspondences between the storyteller and the audiences who were familiar with the primal oral culture. Rather, he is more interested in seeking the way to restore the weakened mimetic faculty with the help of new communications technologies.

Memory

The decline of mimesis in modern industrial society is also bound up with the degeneration of memory. Remembering has been a key feature of storytelling since ancient times. The transmissibility of the story from generation to generation relies profoundly on the power of memory of both storyteller and listeners and is grounded in the assimilation of collective experience. As Henry Bergson (1859–1941), the French philosopher, argues in his seminal work, *Matière et Mémoire* (1911), memory is actualized in bodily sensations. Benjamin, influenced by Bergson's thought on memory, conceives memory in storytelling as involving multiple senses like touch, sound and smell. In Benjamin's view, Marcel Proust, the French novelist, puts Bergson's ahistorical account of experience to the test under the material conditions of modern society. The sociological aspects of Proust's work, in particular, *À la recherche du temps perdu* [*In Search of Lost Time*], captured Benjamin's attention: 'Proust's analysis of snobbery, which is far more important than his apotheosis of art, constitutes the apogee of his criticism of society' (SW2, 243). Grounding Bergson's placement of experience not in 'nature' but in 'memory', Proust formulates two types of memory: voluntary and involuntary.

According to Proust, on the one hand, voluntary memory is uniform memory in the service of the intellect, which reproduces only the impressions of the past that were consciously, attentively and intelligently acquired. On the other hand, involuntary memory involves physiological, emotional, affective and neurological dimensions. Proust's emphasis on the role of involuntary memory is well exemplified in the moment of the madeleine in *In Search of Lost Time*. The narrator's conscious attempts to recall his childhood at Combray prove futile; but the taste of a madeleine dipped in tea vividly brings the past back to him. By this moment, Proust shows that the past is somewhere beyond the reach of the intellect and present in certain material objects or fragments. In *The Arcades Project*, Benjamin reveals his intention of making use of Proust's description of awakening, 'the critical moment in the reading of dream images' (AP, 912). As this event epitomizes, and McCole describes, the distinctive sign of Proust's involuntary memory, comprising spontaneous, trivial, instantaneous, pre-verbal and sensory experience, rests in the 'fleeting correspondence through which a present sensation evokes an earlier, lost experience'.[12] Benjamin draws attention to the fact that Proust, in resurrecting his own childhood, identifies a means by which the figure of the storyteller might be restored to the present generation. From the perspective of the decline of the communicability of experience, the scope of involuntary memory is narrowly restricted to isolated and privatized individual memory in the metropolitan environment and its constitutive role in forming collective subjectivity is increasingly replaced by modern technology.[13] The birth of printing technology symbolized the decline of storytelling, which necessitated multisensorial and collective communication. The consequent widespread availability of the book provided the conditions for the dominance of single-sensory communication in modern society.

It is the novel, 'the dominant epic form of modern times', that accelerates the loss of these core characteristics of storytelling. The storyteller and his memories are disrupted by 'modern temporality – of Newtonian time, of the novel'.[14] Benjamin emphasizes the destructive impact of printing on oral culture by underlining Alfred Döblin's comment: 'The book spells the death of real languages. The most important, creative energies of language elude the epic author who only writes' (SW2, 300). Of course, by 'real language' Benjamin means the physiological multisensory dimensions embedded in storytelling. The industrialization and popularization of the book replaced the social constitutive role of tradition with the print media. At a social level, the shift from storytelling to the novel is bound up with the disintegration of community, the transition from a collective community to an individualist social structure, from *Gemeinschaft* to *Gesellschaft*, in Ferdinand Tönnies' terminology, involving the loss of direct personal contact and the spread of abstract and formalized relations. This transition represents the predominance of visual communication. Many media theorists, most notably Marshall McLuhan, commonly characterize modern society as the Gutenberg Galaxy, the ocular-centric epoch based on printing technology.[15] According to this view, the dominance of optical perception was rendered possible only by virtue of the development of printing technology and printed materials and the resultant propagation of public literacy.[16] Anticipating these later media theorists, Benjamin's essay, 'The Crisis of the Novel' (1930), a review of Alfred Döblin's novel *Berlin Alexanderplatz* (1929), analyses the relationship between storytelling and the modern novel in a way similar to, yet more nuanced than, McLuhan's analysis. Benjamin draws a sharp contrast between the two modes of communication by highlighting the distinctive characteristics of the subjects of communication: the storyteller and the novelist, and the change from the collective audience to the solitary reader. Benjamin links the emergence of the modern novel to the increasing prominence of a new social subject, the middle class in the period of the growth of industrial capitalism.

It took the novel, whose beginnings go back to antiquity, hundreds of years before it encountered in the evolving middle class those elements that were favourable to its flowering. With the appearance of these elements, storytelling began to recede very gradually into the archaic. True, in many ways it took hold of the new material but was not really determined by it. (SW3, 147)

The novelist writes for the privatized subject, who is no longer bound together with other members of society through communal ties, but remains connected only through increasingly complex and rationalized communication media. The novelist is truly a 'solitary, silent person', having cut himself off from people and from what they do.[17] It was private citizens and members of the middle class who began to play the main role in both the writing and reading of the novel, at the very heart of which lay personal moral psychology. From the titles of a cluster of famous European novels – *Don Quixote*, *Tom Jones*, *David Copperfield*, *Jane Eyre*, *Jude the Obscure*, *Anna Karenina*, *Madame Bovary* and *Père Goriot*, to name a few – one can see that the novel of the early modern period privileges individuality, reflecting the isolation of private experience.

Benjamin's account of the rise of the novel is linked to the radical cultural criticism of Western society via the Hungarian writer and Marxist philosopher Georg Lukács (1885–1971).[18] It was in the mid 1920s that Benjamin became interested in the Marxist theory of art and literature, especially the theory of ideology and commodity fetishism, through Lukács' influential work, *History and Class Consciousness* (1923). His seminal literary work, *Theory of the Novel* (1920), served as a significant backdrop to Benjamin's social criticism of the bourgeois culture in the context of the rise of industrial society. In *Theory of the Novel*, Lukács places the novel as the emblem of modern culture in an age of 'transcendental homelessness' in which the totality of life is no longer apparent. Lukács' pessimistic description of modern culture is influenced by the German classical sociologist, Max Weber (1864–1920), who analogically likens the necessity of rationalization and bureaucratization to an 'iron cage'; an analogy that illustrates the fact that in a rationalized yet fragmented and individualized society, life's meaning has become problematical and incomprehensible.[19] The novel, for Lukács, is the aesthetic form most appropriate to this soulless and sordid bourgeois civilization. Lukács' famous description of the novel as a form of 'transcendental homelessness' refers to the situation resulting from the breakdown of the totality of life, in which the *Gemeinschaft* underpinning the oral transmission of traditional rules is shattered. As for many German intellectual mandarins of the time, including Oswald Spengler and Thomas Mann, some of whom were conservative reactionaries or radical leftists, Benjamin's critical analysis of the bourgeois culture shares some elements with Lukács' somewhat romantic criticism of capitalist culture. Yet, there are crucial differences. In Benjamin's view, while the collective experience acquired through tradition and storytelling is more closely associated with the transformation of historical and social experiences, the novel's subjective experience implies the private and individual experience. Lukács' belief in the redemptive role of the novel in retrieving the totality of life does not offer a convincing explanation of *how* the integration of society can be achieved in a situation where the core of experience is profoundly fragmented, isolated and subjective. Lukács' romantic view pays little critical attention to the material conditions of the collapse of the foundations of bourgeois modes of communication. Without relying upon either the romanticist call for redemption or the teleological perspective of history, Benjamin tries to uncover material conditions for the new subject articulated by communication technology. At this point, Benjamin substantially diverges from conventional humanist thinkers (such as Spengler and Mann) and romanticist idealists (including Lukács). Benjamin founds a new logic of literary practice that begins the growth of a new social subject in the transition to a new mass culture bound up with the information industry.

THE NEWSPAPER AND THE INFORMATION INDUSTRY

Key Works
'Journalism' (1927)
'A Critique of the Publishing Industry' (1930)
'The Newspaper' (1934)
'The Paris of the Second Empire in Baudelaire' (1937–8)
'On Some Motifs in Baudelaire' (1940)

The Rise of the Information Industry

Benjamin's analysis of the ascendancy of the information industry reflects the developing stages of the capitalist system. Whereas the emergence of the novel was accompanied by the rise of the new middle class at the beginning of industrial capitalism, the rapid growth of the newspaper was indicative of the predominance of the middle class and the culmination of the expansion of mass media in the advanced capitalist system. In Benjamin's view, the rise of the information industry is penetratingly linked to the differentiation of social classes and the masses.

> On the other hand, we can see that with the complete ascendancy of the middle class – which in fully developed capitalism has the press as one of its most important instruments – a form of communication emerges which, no matter how ancient its origins, never before decisively influenced the epic form. But now it does exert such an

influence. And ultimately it confronts storytelling as no less of a stranger than did the novel, but in a more menacing way; furthermore, it brings about a crisis in the novel. This new form of communication is information. (SW3, 147)

The rapid growth of the publishing industry in the early nineteenth century was a decisive factor that accelerated the industrialization of literary practice. In contemporary communication studies, the concept of information as distinct from knowledge is linked with the post-industrial character of capitalism in the mid twentieth century.[20] However, the notion of information in Benjamin's work is employed in the particular historical context of the rise of the newspaper and publishing industries in nineteenth-century Europe. As an integral component of early industrial society, information is a new form of communication and a type of report that 'conveys an event or a happening *per se*', the pure essence of the thing, and, unlike a story, is not assimilated into everyday life or tradition (SW4, 316). Benjamin derives the key features of information from the notion of gossip, which was widely used in the nineteenth century. Gossip was a type of news spread through cafés, salons and the boulevard. Within literary circles, the notion of information was used to mean a valueless story or piece of knowledge. In a somewhat pejorative sense, information is utilized by Benjamin to reflect only quantified experience deprived of the profundity of life.

Central to this critical insight into the rise of the information industry is the fact that, despite noticeable increases in the amount of information, over time knowledge as a whole has become poorer in quality. Benjamin underscores this: 'Every morning brings us news from across the globe, yet we are poor in noteworthy stories. This is because nowadays no event comes to us without already being shot through with explanations. In other words, by now almost nothing that happens benefits storytelling; almost everything benefits information' (SW3, 147–8). In the early twentieth century, the liberal views in newspapers were not linear and focused their emphases on different topical issues. On the one hand, those philosophers in the tradition of pragmatics, such as John Dewey (1859–1952) or George Herbert Mead (1863–1931), conceived information to be 'a genre of self-denial and the story of self-indulgence'.[21] On the other hand, those theorists more closely linked with the earlier study of political communication, such as Walter Lippmann (1889–1974) and Harold Lasswell (1902–1978), hailed the propagation of information by mass media as the strong development of public opinion and deliberative democracy.[22] Unlike his contemporary liberal thinkers, Benjamin had already pointed out the malfunction of the information industry and the danger of the production of public opinion. It is noteworthy that Benjamin, a high literary critic, attributed the deterioration of language and the degradation of the novel to the newspaper: 'It is virtually impossible to write a history of information separately from a history of the corruption of the press' (SW4, 13). This is a primary symptom of the rapid atrophy of the communicability of experience. His dismissive view of the function of the information industry is contrary to the core principle of the Enlightenment tradition, which links increasing levels of knowledge with the progress of civilization. In their ideological criticism of the culture industry, Horkheimer and Adorno reveal the destructive feature of the Enlightenment as mass deception.[23] In a similar vein, Benjamin uncovers the paradoxical consequences of the development of the information industry, yet goes further to tackle the issue of the profound atrophy of quality of social experience and communication in modern industrial society. While storytelling drew its validity from the wisdom of tradition bestowed upon it by the ancients, information lays claim only to prompt verifiability. Information is grounded in 'newness, brevity, clarity, and, above all, lack of connection between the individual news items' (SW4, 316). The momentary nature of information reflects the key features of modern industrial society, involving its fragmented, instantaneous and ephemeral nature. Thus, information does not become part of tradition and is not assimilated with daily life. Likewise, reading the newspaper accelerates 'the de-contextualized' empty experience in a modern big city, that is, the hollow consumption of commodities by the urban middle class.[24]

The Decline of Bourgeois Public Spheres

Benjamin's writings on the disintegration of bourgeois culture illustrate how intellectual work became subjugated to the information industry during the Second French Empire from 1852 to 1870, the Imperial Bonapartist regime of Napoleon III (the nephew of Napoleon I), leading to the collapse of the literary field. Gravitating towards mass media such as periodicals, journals and magazines, high literary culture began to alter dramatically. Benjamin introduced the issue of the intersection of the media and urban culture by focusing on the rapid growth of the newspaper industry, its penetrating effect upon Parisian café life, and the resulting decline of the bourgeois public sphere. It is Jürgen Habermas who locates the notion of the public sphere in the centre of the discussion of media, bourgeois culture and deliberative democracy. Habermas' groundbreaking work, *The Structural Transformation of the Public Sphere* (1962), reassessed the crucial role of the periodical press in early modern Europe during the transition from absolutism to a liberal-democratic regime.[25] Analysing an arena in which political communication took place, this work illuminated the important contributions of the print media, as well as public spaces such as cafés and salons, to the articulation of public opinion and the construction of a rational and critical attitude to traditional society.

To some extent, Benjamin foreknows the constructive role of the bourgeois public sphere in the wake of the information industry in a more nuanced way than Habermas' perspective. Benjamin focuses on the role of the café as a kind of 'boulevard press', where the exchange of information and public discussion took place before the wide availability of the mass press, but, at the same time, as a public space where a new form of the affective, aesthetic communication is articulated by the popular, consumer culture.[26] When newspapers were still a luxury item, seldom bought, they were instead consulted by people who frequented the coffee-houses. The café, although by no means a nineteenth-century invention, became a fundamental institution of Parisian culture during the nineteenth century. The café represented the concrete expression and focus of 'sociability' – the heightened concern with public affairs and the desire for dynamic interchange with others – unleashed by the French Revolution.[27]

Benjamin also links the meltdown of the bourgeois culture with the impact of the marketization and commodification of information in the public sphere. He attributes three pivotal innovations to the dramatic changes in the newspaper industry: the decrease in the cost of subscriptions to newspapers, the increase in advertising, and the growing importance of the serial novel in the feuilleton section (the part of European newspapers devoted to light fiction and reviews of general entertainment) (SW4, 13). Soon after the rapid rise in the number of large printing presses, newspapers came to need advertising revenue in order to offset the lower subscription rates demanded as circulation and competition increased. The liberal legislation introduced in France in July 1828 made dailies and periodicals accessible to a much wider readership. These changes resulted in newspapers being burdened with certain financial obligations, and developing a new strategy based on advertising and mass circulation. For Benjamin, nothing illustrates better the relationship between the cost of subscription and advertising than a piece from a popular magazine of the time: '"What will we do to cover the new expenses?" demanded the newspapers. "Well, you will run advertisements", came the response' (AP [U9,1], 585). In Benjamin's view, the emergence of newspaper advertisements was pivotal to changes in the relationship between technology, market and public. Consequently, what had been a quarter page now became a poster to accommodate the many necessary advertisements, and had to be seen by as large a number of subscribers as possible if the newspaper were to remain competitive.

Following these significant innovations in the newspaper industry, and with the introduction of the electronic telegraph, 'news of accidents and crimes could now be obtained from all over the world' (SW4, 14). Individuals began to take advantage of the reduced price of newspapers, which now covered not only a wider range of information than any other source, but also published stories much sooner after the event. These innovations discouraged private citizens from visiting cafés and public spaces like squares in order to receive and exchange information, and thus accelerated the privatization and isolation of individuals. The newspaper industries tried to appeal to a wide spectrum of these new readers, regardless of their private opinions or political viewpoints. This encouraged the shift of the function of the newspaper from a public forum for serious political debate to an entertainment space filled with mere gossip and cultural information. The information industry came to be one with the sensational entertainment industry.

The commercialization of the information industry also accelerated change in the nature of literary practice in the bourgeois literary fields of the nineteenth century. Benjamin focuses particular attention on the development of the feuilleton. The newspaper, Benjamin emphasizes, completely subsumed literature by publishing fiction in serial form. It even appropriated the novel: the impact of serialization on the status of the author is closely examined via a focus on the cases of Alexandre Dumas and Eugène Sue, two of the most popular French writers of the 1840s (SW4, 14/ AP [U8a,3], 585). The essay 'The *Flâneur*' in 'The Paris of the Second Empire in Baudelaire' begins to reveal the close tie between the author and the market: 'Once a writer had entered the marketplace, he looked around as if in a panorama. A special literary genre has captured the writer's first attempts to orient himself. This is the genre of panoramic literature' (SW4, 18). As we will see in chapter 5, the panorama here represents the prototype of the modern entertainment industry, in which the main attributes of perception lie in the shock experience and the distraction of collective spectatorship. In the context of the growth of sensational popular literature, Benjamin emphasizes significant differences in the human sensory apparatus that result from reading the novel in an attentive, as opposed to a distracted, manner. The German philosopher, G.W.F. Hegel (1770–1831), once remarked that 'reading the morning paper is a sort of realistic morning prayer'. This suggests that, in the early days, the experience of the newspaper was grounded upon regular and daily attentive contemplation much like praying. Even by the mid nineteenth century, however, reading a mass-circulated newspaper is associated with forms of experience that seem quite unlike praying. As Berman identifies, the market expansion led not only to 'the diversification of the literary public' but also to 'the depersonalization and objectification of social relations' articulated by literary institutions and 'the desubjectification of writing'.[28] In the newspaper, the readers' perception is less akin to 'devoting' themselves to a story than to 'shopping' as a consumer. The serialized novel is not intended for a man of letters in his private space; it appeals to the public readers on the streets of a big city. The traditional form of the book itself began to alter. In big-city literature, 'the inconspicuous, paperback, pocket-size volumes' began to appear for sale on the street (SW4, 18). Attitudes towards the book also changed in accordance with its social status. The newspaper-reading public came to regard literature as 'an instrument of entertainment, animation, or the deepening of sociability' (SW2, 290). As fees paid to feuilleton contributors increased, rising to two francs per line, for instance, 'authors would often write as much dialogue as possible so as to benefit from the blank spaces left in the lines' (AP [U9a,1], 586). Benjamin's analysis of the changing status of the author in the period following the emergence of the feuilleton underlines the decline of the man of letters, that is, the death of the novelist. In an age when newspapers subsumed literature, fame, or rather success, became 'obligatory', and was no longer the 'optional extra' it had formerly been: 'In an age when every wretched scrap of paper is distributed in hundreds of thousands of copies, fame is a cumulative condition. Quite simply: the less successful the writer, the less available his works' (SW2, 145). Benjamin demystifies literature, and disperses the aura surrounding the bourgeois literary public sphere, by showing literature to be nothing more than a commercial mass product. Likewise, in Benjamin's view, the growth of feuilletonism in the literary arena accelerated the integration of literature and the publishing industry.

The Flâneur in the Mediated Public Sphere

Benjamin's famous account of the flâneur focuses primarily on the rise of a new social subject, endowed with new modes of perception, set against the backdrop of a period of rapid growth in urban commodity culture. The concept of the flâneur was established by writers such as Baudelaire and Emile Zola in the nineteenth century and is first and foremost the nineteenth-century stroller on the city street and the dawdler in shops. Benjamin's interest in flânerie was deeply influenced by his close friend and collaborator, Franz Hessel. He describes the most significant features of flânerie as follows:

> *Flânerie* is a kind of reading of the street, in which faces, shop fronts, shop windows, café terraces, street cars, automobiles and trees become a wealth of equally valid letters of the alphabet that together result in words, sentences and pages of an ever-new book. In order to engage in *flânerie*, one must not have anything too definite in mind.[29]

Although it has various nuanced meanings and applications, a core feature of flânerie is a new form of behaviour and perception involving observation of spectacle, the spectacle created by new urban space and media technology. The active communication of serial observations is inextricably linked with the rise and establishment of urban consumer space and the entertainment industry. This urban spectacle provides the noble yet commodified public space to which the flâneur devotes himself, a metropolitan space in which Baudelaire's poetry is born. For Benjamin, Baudelaire possessed real insight into the true situation of a man of letters in the age of the information industry, standing and looking at himself in the marketplace. It is noteworthy that Benjamin utilized the flâneur as a model of (among other things) the journalist in the period of the information industry. From his early writing onwards, Baudelaire had no illusions about the world of art. With an understanding of the real prospects of a man of letters, no wonder Baudelaire frequently described such authors, including himself, as 'whores'. Benjamin was very impressed by Baudelaire's speculation on the commodified author, and used this as the basis upon which he built the edifice of his critical account of the decline of the educated middle class. Here, Benjamin illustrates that a writer becomes merely a literary worker and a wordsmith; the notion of the creative genius is wholly undermined, and the true nature of the writer is made brutally apparent.

Notably, Benjamin conceives of journalism as 'the social base of flânerie' (AP [M16,4], 446). Herein lies the distinctive aspect of Benjamin's phenomenological analysis of the intersection of metropolitan life, media and the urban subject. The journalist-flâneur is an urban spectator or the 'physiognomist' of urban life, one who regards the metropolitan space as an entertaining spectacle as well as a text. Baudelaire characterizes Paris as a 'gastronomy of the eye', and the flâneur as 'a kaleidoscope endowed with consciousness' (SW4, 328). The rise of consumer culture enabled the flâneur to appear as a new social figure in a public space by providing him with visual amusement. As we will see in chapter 5, while the existence of the flâneur on the street could be linked to the growth of the commodity space exemplified by areas such as arcades, his decline was accelerated by rapid urban planning, that is, the Haussmannization of the Paris street, as well as the rise of the mass consumer culture generated by department stores.

This figure of the flâneur also coincides with that of the detective (personified in, for example, the Chevalier C. Auguste Dupin) and the invisible observer in the stories of the American poet and editor, Edgar Allan Poe (1809–1849), such as 'The Murder in the Rue Morgue' (1841), 'The Mystery of Marie Roget' (1842), 'The Purloined Letter' (1844) and 'The Man of the Crowd' (1840). The journalist, the flâneur and the detective share the attribute of being hunters in a jungle-like metropolitan city. Benjamin lends particular emphasis on the way in which the journalist, like the flâneur, strolls among the crowd: 'the skill and nonchalance which the flâneur displays as he moves among the crowds in the streets and which the journalist eagerly learns from him' (SW4, 322).

Both Baudelaire and Benjamin find the prototype of the journalist-flâneur's way of seeing in two French caricaturists: Constantin Guys (1802–1892) and Honoré Daumier (1808–1879). It is not coincident that Baudelaire draws attention to the fact that Guys' snapshot images of the Crimean War appeared in one of the most widely circulated English journals, *The Illustrated London News*. Baudelaire remarks that he has been able to 'read' a 'detailed account of the Crimean campaign which is much preferable to any other that I know'. Praising Guys as 'the painter of modern life',[30] Baudelaire states that: 'anyone who is capable of being bored in a crowd is a blockhead. I repeat: a blockhead, and a contemptible one' (SW4, 19). For Baudelaire, Guys' images confirm his delineation of modernity as 'the transitory, the fugitive, and the contingent'.[31]

While Guys characterizes the bourgeois public as 'harmless' and 'perfect bonhomie' from a melancholic view, Daumier illustrates the everyday urban life in a more satirical way. For Baudelaire, Daumier is 'one of the most important artists', not only in the field of caricature, but in 'the whole of modern art', who is able to respond to the daily requirement of amusing the public.[32] In Benjamin's view, it is Daumier who finally provides the urban physiognomist images serialized in the daily newspapers, which the public can access on an unprecedented scale. These new readers 'the bourgeois, the business-man, the urchin and the housewife all laugh and pass on their way, as often as not – what base ingratitude! – without even glancing at his name.'[33] Daumier is 'the creator of Ratapoil – the Bonapartist lumpenproletarian' (AP [b1,9], 741), providing the images that are neither aggressive nor bitter, but poisonously cheerful to the newspaper readers.

It is imperative to see that the journalist-flâneur, exemplified as Guys and Daumier, acts not merely as an observer or a decipherer, but instead has a more sophisticated role as a producer of literary and journalistic texts. The crucial difference lies in the fact that the journalist's observation is basically associated with the production of a text, while the flâneur's visual pleasure is with the consumption of that text. Paradoxically, the journalist undermines the flâneur by providing mediated flânerie in a media space like the newspaper. A city dweller experiences the urban spectacle captured through the journalist's eye. This mediated flânerie invokes, not the attentive watchfulness of the observer, but distracted reading for information and the urban spectacle.[34]

Benjamin's account of the journalist-flâneur also focuses on his commodity-status in the marketplace of the literary industry: a writer-cum-commodity. In the age of high capitalism, the journalist, who observes the city and reads it as a text, cannot be free from the market and must produce and sell his information as a commodity. Then, finally, he becomes a commodity himself. The journalist is the prototype of the salaried flâneur, standing between the writer and the advertiser.[35] The difference between the literary man and the journalist lies only in their different perception. The journalist already recognizes his commodified status as a writer, while the literary man is still reluctant to sell himself (even though he is doomed to sell eventually). The journalist as an analogical figure of the commodified flâneur is congruent with the figure of 'the sandwich-man', who walks the streets with advertisements hanging on his body as 'the last incarnation of the flâneur' (AP [M19,2], 451). When the flâneur himself becomes commodified, the end point of flânerie is reached; the journalist is completely transformed into a commodity and, as such, becomes part of the endless series of spectacle of the city.

THE INTELLECTUALS IN THE AGE OF MASS MEDIA

Key Works

'Surrealism: The Last Snapshot of the European Intelligentsia' (1929)

'Left-Wing Melancholy' (1931)

'Karl Kraus' (1931)

'The Present Social Situation of the French Writer' (1934)

'The Author as Producer' (1934)

Karl Kraus

While Benjamin's study of Baudelaire addresses the profound impact of the information industry on the bourgeois literary sphere, his account of the Austrian journalist and satirist Karl Kraus (1874–1936) is devoted to a particular issue: the detrimental influences of journalistic practice on language. At the centre of the essay lies Benjamin's longstanding interest in the theory of language, yet the essay also reveals the political and economic dimensions of journalism and the formation of public opinion in capitalist society. Benjamin considered the essay 'Karl Kraus', which appeared in four instalments in the liberal newspaper *Frankfurter Zeitung* in 1931, to be one of his most important works. Karl Kraus founded and edited the journal *Die Fackel* [*The Torch*] from 1899 until shortly

before his death in 1936.[36] Through his radical journalistic
practice, Kraus vigorously attacked the destructive influence
of the press on Viennese cultural life at the turn of the century. For Kraus, the Viennese journalism is grounded upon
'dilettantism and corruption' (SW2, 350). The corruption of
literary and cultural criticism derives from the coalescence
of the commercialized press and the politics of interest. In
his radical view, the Viennese newspapers were nothing but
instruments working to manufacture public opinion and
consent, primarily in accordance with the wishes of the state
authorities and secondarily in the interests of financial and
economic corporations. The ownership of the press by individual entrepreneurs controlled and distorted the editorial
policy and hindered the growth of independent critics. In
his satirical poem, Kraus unravels the pressing situation of
the press and undermines any credibility or integrity of the
information:

The Journalist
What paper has yet
Sought news to present?
The headline is set –
Go, find the event!

Benjamin agrees with Kraus' radical criticism that from
the outset newspaper production was deeply interwoven
with the commercial value of information as well as political interest in power, summing it up thus: 'The newspaper
is an instrument of power. It can derive its value only from
the character of the power it serves; not only in what it represents, but also in what it does, it is the expression of this
power' (SW2, 440). Since Walter Lippmann's pioneering
study of propaganda and public opinion in 1922, we can see
now that the fundamental problem of 'the manufactured

consent' in the media-saturated society derives from the
mediation itself between events, information and public
perception. In Europe at a similar period, Benjamin draws
more attention to Kraus' radical criticism of the interplay
between public opinion and degeneration of language. Here,
Benjamin goes on to challenge the core foundation of liberal democracy that is predicated upon the formative role
of public opinion under the rubric of objective information
flow and informed participation of all free citizens. In *One-
Way Street*, Benjamin underlines that 'opinions are to the
vast apparatus of social existence what oil is to machines: one
does not go up to a turbine and pour machine oil over it; one
applies a little to hidden spindles and joints that one has to
know' (SW1, 444). In Benjamin's view, Kraus demonstrates
that public opinion played a pernicious role in depriving the
individual of authentic language and critical judgement and
in integrating him/her into the establishment.

> The very term 'public opinion' outrages Kraus. Opinions
> are a private matter. The public has an interest only in
> judgments. Either it is a judging public, or it is none. But
> it is precisely the purpose of the public opinion gener-
> ated by the press to make the public incapable of judging,
> to insinuate into it the attitude of someone irresponsible,
> uninformed. (SW2, 433)

The widespread notion of public opinion in political and
literary discourse at the time is indicative of the damaging
impact of the press on the relationship between private and
public spheres. For Kraus, the objective newspaper is illusory,
disguising the interest-oriented transmission of news under
the rubric of neutrality, public accountability or impartiality.
Moreover, and this is the point that Benjamin emphasizes,
the newspaper led to the de-subjectification of language and

writing in the name of 'objectivity'. Kraus' criticism shows
that information and public opinion come to be depersonal-
ized and objectified forms of language. In Benjamin's view,
Kraus' critique of public opinion is linked to his opposition
to the distinction between personal and objective criticism
as such. Journalism formulates opinion 'in the name of taste'
(SW2, 407), divesting readers of their capability of judging
and destroying criticism. Benjamin emphasizes that Kraus
never puts forward an opinion and never offers an argument
that does not engage his whole personality: 'For opinion
is false subjectivity that can be separated from the person
and incorporated in the circulation of commodities' (SW2,
439). Benjamin's contrasting of opinion with critical judgement represents the disparate status of the journalist and the
critic. The journalist tends to separate opinion from judgement under the rubric of objectivity; that is, a writer 'who
has little interest either in himself and his own existence, or
in the mere existence of things' (SW2, 434). The journalistic usage of language has many ornamental features and only
constitutes an empty phrase de-contextualized from everyday
life. Like the whore concerned only with 'mere sex' without
human contact, the journalist transmits information to the
reader in exchange for money. In contrast, a critic helps readers judge and form their own independent ideas. Benjamin
contends that: 'it is quite meaningless to learn the opinion of
someone about something when you do not even know who
he is. The more important the critic, the more he will avoid
baldly asserting his own opinion' (SW2, 548). Benjamin's
perception of the task of the critic derives from his unique
idea of immanent criticism, a criticism that he had continued
to elaborate since his doctoral dissertation, 'The Concept of
Criticism in German Romanticism' (1919), aiming to unfold
and fulfil the incomplete meaning of the work of art.

Later in the essay, criticizing the discrepancy between

Kraus' radical practice and his reactionary theory of language, Benjamin substantially distances himself from Kraus. Benjamin was not satisfied with the fact that Kraus' radical critique of public opinion eventually served to protect the authentic private sphere from the public arena. Benjamin pinpoints that Kraus is overly preoccupied with the preservation of the private sphere from outside 'evil'. The conservative aspects of Kraus' critique of the press are, in Benjamin's view, rooted in his mythic understanding of language. Kraus attributes the corruption of language to the inevitable processes resulting from the discrepancy between language and nature. In Benjamin's view, Kraus' perspective on language is nothing more than 'a Platonic love of language' (SW2, 453) and is devoid of sociological insight. Kraus is a 'warrior against the corruption of language' but at the same time 'merely one of the epigones that live in the old house of language' (SW1, 469). In contrast to Kraus' naturalist view of language, Benjamin focuses on the social and political conditions of communication.[37] Benjamin's criticism of a rationalist perspective on language underscores the myth of the logo-centric approach to language that only metaphysically constitutes linguistic subject and the possibility of pure communication. Hence, for Benjamin, journalism can only be understood as 'the expression of the changed function of language in the world of high capitalism' (SW2, 435). For Benjamin, Kraus endeavoured in vain to reverse the corruption of language. Kraus was a journalist armoured with a critical spirit but not the intellectual engaged in changing the social and political conditions of communication.

Intellectual Practice in an Age of Mass Media

From 1931 onwards, the year when he wrote the Kraus essay and National Socialism became the dominant political power in Germany, Benjamin became noticeably more concerned with political issues, drawing greater attention to the intersection of mass media and intellectual practice. Benjamin's analysis of the impact of the media on the role of intellectuals involves highly political and ideological contexts during a period of political turmoil. However, in his view, successful intellectual practice could be achieved not by the improvement of political or ideological propositions but by the progressive adaptation of communication technology. Benjamin investigates contemporary intellectual activity, from left-wing radicals via the Surrealists to Brecht, with particular reference to the technologization of writing and the rise of the new public through polytechnical education. Benjamin's essay 'Left-Wing Melancholy' appeared in 1931 in the social-democratic periodical *Die Gesellschaft* [*The Society*], after it was rejected by the liberal newspaper *Frankfurter Zeitung*. In this essay, Benjamin points out that left-wing literary works are still deeply rooted in classical humanist ideas such as individual freedom and authentic creativity; ideas that were articulated in the age of the Renaissance. Benjamin accuses left-radical writers, such as Kurt Tucholsky (1890–1935), Walter Mehring (1896–1981) and Erich Kästner (1899–1974), of touching the surface level superficially and of providing commodities for the publishing industry, rather than weapons against the class struggle. Despite their allegedly radical critique of bourgeois culture at the forefront of artistic movements, Benjamin insists, their writings consist of nothing more than 'sensationalism', as they protect 'the status interests of the middle stratum – agents, journalists, heads of departments' (SW2, 424). The readers of such publications are distinguished from those of the daily newspaper. Newspapers or 'the new magazines' are read by people 'who are excluded from higher education' and 'who have lost their faith in education' (SW2, 653). In

fact, it is the left-wing publications that appeal to the afflu-
ent and have a decimating, petty bourgeois character. They
are 'mournful, melancholy dummies who trample anything
and anyone in their path' (SW2, 426). As an extension of his
criticism of degenerate journalistic practice, the resemblance
between the literary work of left-wing radicals and the ornamental functions of journalistic writing is underscored:
'Their function is to give rise, politically speaking, not to
parties but to cliques; literarily speaking, not to schools but
to fashions; economically speaking, not to producers but to
agents' (SW2, 424). The left-wing radicals are nothing but
'the decayed bourgeoisie's mimicry of the proletariat' (SW2,
424), whose idiosyncrasy derives from the romantic and
humanistic view commonly held by conventional middle-
class intellectuals. In Benjamin's radical view, they naively
underestimate the subjugating power of an established social
and cultural system on individualized intellectuals, and
eagerly overestimate their relative independence or incorpo-
ration in such a system.

Turning away from left-wing melancholy, Benjamin
begins to be preoccupied with the work of the Surrealists,
who represent one of the most radical European avant-
garde movements, which tries to integrate alienated social
areas of life, politics and art by utilizing the advanced communications technologies. Surrealism is one of the first
aesthetic practices that challenge the conventional dichotomy of rational/myth, consciousness/unconsciousness, the
real/the unreal, and nature/civilization. In combining the
dialectic of myth and urban experience, the Surrealists want
to unpack the subversive – yet uncultivated and barbaric
– energies embodied in mundane everyday life. The
Surrealist experiments with the technologization of writing
oppose conventional humanist literary practice as rationalist approach to language and communication. Benjamin

finds that their writings cannot be grasped in a traditional sense of art and literature. By creating 'demonstrations, watchwords, documents, bluffs, forgeries' (SW2, 208), they destroy the foundations of bourgeois literary culture, which are grounded upon rational, cognitive communication. The new conditions of intellectual activity brought about by the newspaper led Benjamin to draw more attention to the technological dimensions of literary practice. In the short piece 'The Newspaper', Benjamin succinctly illustrates the ways in which the corruption of writing has been intensified and maintained by the commercialization of information. 'The reader's impatience' (SW2, 741) was reproduced for new excitement every day and pseudo-participation of the readers was intensified. The newspaper editorial offices introduced new columns for readers' questions, opinions and even protests, spaces in which readers were able to voice their own opinions and desires. His analysis illustrates the extent to which newspapers brought about the pseudo-democratization of information by readers' participation and became an arena of 'literary confusion' rather than rational communication. Yet, unlike his contemporary conservative cultural critics, among them Karl Kraus, Benjamin unravels a dialectical factor hidden in the newspaper's disruptive function. 'For as writing gains in breadth what art loses in depth, the separation between the author and the public – a separation that journalism maintains in a corrupt way – starts to be overcome in an admirable way' (SW2, 505). In his view, the newspaper's function in assimilating unselective readers has produced 'unintended consequences'. It weakens the sizeable substantial barrier between writers and readers and further decimates 'the conventional distinction between genres, between writer and poet, between scholar and popularizer' (SW2, 772). The everyday lives of ordinary people are described, reported and presented to the public

by means of newspapers. Benjamin calls this transformation
the 'literarization of the conditions of living' (SW2, 742).[38]
In Soviet journalism, Benjamin saw a particular example of
how polytechnic education could lead to intellectual specialization. His account of 'literarization of the conditions
of living' is, however, not restricted to the Soviet case.
Rather, it represents one element of Benjamin's broader
account of the impact of communication technology on
forms of cultural life. The prominent feature of 'technological civilization' in Benjamin's thought is bound up with the
'levelling of culture', that is, the erasing of the old boundaries between high and low culture:

> The dismantling of the old, hierarchical spheres of soci-
> ety had just been completed. This meant that the noblest
> and most refined substances had often sunk to the bottom,
> and so it happens that the person who can see more deeply
> can find the elements he really needs in the lower depths
> of writing and graphic art rather than in the acknowledged
> documents of culture. (SW2, 255)

The emergence of the public as writers signifies that writing
is no longer an esoteric inspirational activity but a popular
cultural practice, and literary competence is now based, not
on 'specialized training', but on 'polytechnical education',
and becomes 'public property' (SW2, 742). The growth and
propagation of blogging and the Internet literature in recent
years, to exemplify only a few, demonstrate how writing
itself has been an everyday cultural practice for the masses,
that is, the public authors. Benjamin does not regret this
divergence; instead, he reveals the newly configured conditions of communication and shows how newspapers broaden
the horizons of collective cultural and literary practices. The
meltdown of the bourgeois literary public sphere also led to

the rise of the new media space in which the masses prove to be a multiple social agency as consumers, spectators, the public and even the journalists themselves.

Bertolt Brecht: An Aesthetic Engineer

In the age of newspapers, when the public becomes the writer, the intellectual becomes 'a producer', that is, a literary or aesthetic 'engineer' (SW2, 780), a figure Benjamin finds in the German playwright and poet Bertolt Brecht. Benjamin met Brecht for the first time in May 1929, a meeting arranged by Asja Lacis (1891–1971), a Latvian Bolshevik theatre director and Benjamin's lover. For Benjamin, who was becoming more interested in the Marxist theory of art and literature, Brecht represents a German successor to the tradition of literary decadence who combines the French modernist spirit and the new socialist culture of Soviet Russia. Benjamin characterizes Brecht as a writer who 'transforms him from a supplier of the productive apparatus into an engineer who sees it as his task to adapt this apparatus to the purposes of the proletarian revolution' (SW2, 780).[39] The essay, 'The Author as Producer', based on the lecture he prepared but never presented at the Institute for the Study of Fascism in Paris in April 1934, reconsiders the activities and tasks of the intellectual within the highly technological culture. This essay shows how Benjamin fully employs the notion of technique to go beyond the conventional dichotomy between form and content in the discussion of art (SW2, 770). Benjamin reformulates two facets of the question of ideology and aesthetic quality as one of the technical natures of the work of art.

> Rather than asking, 'What is the attitude of a work *to* the relations of production of its time?' I would like to ask,

'What is its position *in* them?' This question directly concerns the function the work has within the literary relations
of production of its time. It is concerned, in other words,
directly with the literary *technique* of works. (SW2, 770)

Benjamin's aim here is to argue that the position of a work
of art cannot be recognized without critical consideration
of its relation to such mass media as newspapers and radio.
In parallel with the transformation of the reader, the status
of the author begins to change in a more technical sense:
that is, its character comes to be that of the 'engineer'. The
central problem of the widely accepted concept of 'the intellectual' derives from its humanistic orientation, which fails
to consider the position of intellectuals in the process of
information production. As an extension of his critique of
public opinion, Benjamin criticizes those intellectuals who
try to help forge public opinion from a neutral position.
The intellectual activity of the prominent German writer
Alfred Döblin (1878–1957) was singled out. For Benjamin,
Döblin's concept of the intellectual differs little from the
dominant concept of a free-floating intellectual and is bound
up with a person defined by his 'opinions, attitudes or dis-
positions' (SW2, 773).[40] This kind of understanding only
locates the intellectual 'beside' the proletariat, assuming
the place of a 'benefactor, of an ideological patron' (SW2,
773). Instead, Benjamin places intellectuals 'in' the process
of production. Benjamin opposes the instrumentalist view of
language, technology and the media, and in a similar way
he criticizes those attitudes of the intellectuals who adopt
communication technology only as the instrument or tool.
As the detrimental impact of newspapers on the journalist
shows, in the age of mass media, the intellectual no longer
has the privileged status of exclusively supplying intellectual
products; rather, the intellectual should be able to employ

and utilize media technologies; that is, 'to re-function' communication technology. 'Re-functioning' here indicates that
intellectual activity should fully adopt current technological advancement, which in essence repositions the political
tendency of the author: 'technical progress is for the author
as producer the foundation of his political progress. In
other words, only by transcending the specialization in the
process of intellectual production ... can one make this
production politically useful' (SW2, 775). The role of the
intellectual as polytechnic engineer reflects his emphasis on
communication technology over aesthetic ideas. Aided by
the development of technological conditions for 'polytechnic
education', it becomes increasingly possible for the public
to become writers, reporters and editors. The relationship
between intellectuals and technology becomes more intimate and leads them to master technology. By presenting
Brecht, not as an artist, but as an engineer, Benjamin intends
to underscore less his political ideology than his enthusiastic adaptation of technological advancement into art, which
Brecht calls 'functional transformation' [*Umfunktionierung*]
of communication technology (SW2, 774). Benjamin's
interest in Brecht's theatrical practice, primarily the epic
theatre, arises less from its political content than from its
concomitant technical advancements.

Benjamin's marked emphasis on the technological attributes of intellectual practice, however, does not mean that
he totally rejects the role of the intellectual in criticizing
ideology, which serves to maintain dominant and unequal
social relations. What Benjamin here emphasizes is the fact
that the conditions of intellectual activity in the age of mass
media have rapidly changed and the form of intellectual practice, therefore, should reflect these changes. The model of
the intellectual aims to show *how* this might be achieved. In
the new mediated public sphere, where intellectual practice

is bound up with communication media, the possibility of mass public participation has increased at an unprecedented rate. The intellectual encountering various media should therefore not consider the media simply as a means of transmitting his ideas, but as the source of formulation, projection, transformation and the reproduction of ideas. In the age of mass media, the primary activity of the intellectual could be regarded as a struggle for technological re-function.

CONCLUSION

Benjamin's analysis of the information industry reveals how the development of the newspaper and publishing industries accelerated changes in the early literary field, eradicating the autonomous status of the author, subjugating literary work to the commodity market and rendering obsolete traditional categories such as genius, creativity and authenticity. Benjamin's examination of the rise of the information industry is mainly concerned with print culture. In arguing that 'information' has been replaced by 'sensation', he intends to stress that technological civilization is entering into another stage of communication. By means of this analysis, Benjamin develops his account of the impact of electronic media on contemporary social and political changes.

These are the points I have tried to make in this chapter:

(1) We have examined in detail Benjamin's argument that, ever since the serialization of the novel in the feuilleton, intellectual work has rapidly become subjugated to the information industry. By focusing on the relationship between authors and the publishing industry, Benjamin chronicles the transformation of the writer from the figure of the flâneur to that of the journalist.

(2) The journalist is the information hunter and the detec-

tive in the jungle-like metropolis; he observes the city, reads it as a text, sells his story as a commodity, which then, finally, becomes a commodity itself.

(3) Drawing upon Benjamin's analysis of the unexpected consequences of the newspaper, we have discussed his critique of the outdated concept of the intellectual, which is limited by its association with European humanism. Benjamin identifies changing conditions created by the media with opportunities for, and sites of, struggle and contestation. These consist of reversals and plays *within* the apparatus of ideological reproduction. The media may be re-engineered for the purpose of counter-hegemonic practice.

Of course, some elements of Benjamin's account of the newspaper cannot be applied to an examination of contemporary media space generated by the Internet without careful consideration of their historical and technological contexts. It seems quite naive and overly optimistic, for example, that Benjamin should see the rise of a new public as collective author in the Soviet press of the early revolutionary period. He overestimates the autonomous aspects of socialist public spheres as much as he underestimates the bureaucratic and propagandist functions of the Soviet media. Despite such limitations, however, Benjamin's account of the primal history of the information industry back in the nineteenth century makes a number of significant contributions to our understanding of mediated public spheres. For instance, Internet-mediated communication has produced new types of mediated interaction and accelerated the democratization of knowledge and information on a gigantic scale in terms of 'collective intelligence' as Pierre Lévy calls it.[41] Wikipedia and the GNU Project are good contemporary examples. It should be reiterated that Benjamin is aware

of the dangerous possibility of manipulating public opinion. The key issue is related to how the enormous amount
of information can be assimilated into people's daily experiences. The Internet has also led not only to the socially
networked media space but also the privatization of experience, reproducing the phantasmagoria of the isolated space
and the socially disconnected individual. Social network
sites like Facebook have multiple functions. The electronic
screen plugged into the network becomes the 'primary
window' through which the world is experienced, in much
the same way as, in Benjamin's account, the drawing room
is the centre of spectacle for the petite bourgeoisie during
the Second Empire. Here, Benjamin's analysis of the nineteenth-century information industry has particular relevance
to the formation of mediated experience in the age of the
Internet. At a time when the death of the conventional newspaper industry is being widely discussed, Benjamin's insight
into the rise of public writers as an unintended consequence
of the development of newspapers is particularly relevant to
our understanding of the replacement of conventional newspapers run by trained journalists with the citizen journalists
and public newspapers emerging through various forms of
Internet communication, such as blogospheres and social
media. What Benjamin really wants to reveal via his analysis
of the information industry is the fact that the masses are
no longer the passive consumers of the information market
or inert spectators of the entertainment industry; rather they
are the active producers of information, the aesthetic crea-
tors of the new media art, the authors of their own lives in a
media space equipped with ever more advanced communication technology, and the consumers of their own lives via
social media. They are the new intellectuals, or 'smart mobs'
as Howard Rheingold hails, to re-function communications
technologies for their own aims.[42]

3

RADIO AND MEDIATED
STORYTELLING

INTRODUCTION

Benjamin was actively involved in radio broadcasting in the late 1920s and early 1930s when radio was rapidly emerging as a new medium in Europe and the US following the telegraph and the telephone. Since the Berlin Vox record company had broadcast the first German radio programme on the evening of 29 October 1923, the number of subscribers in Germany increased rapidly from 100,000 in 1924 to over four million in 1932.[1] When the Nazi regime came to power in 1933, half of all households were 'wirelessly' connected via their own radio equipment and almost the entire population was able to listen to Hitler's address in real time. Not unlike any previous encounter with new technologies, a speaker at the World Radio Convention of 1938 assuredly declared: 'Of all the miracles this age has witnessed, radio is the most marvellous. It has taken sound, which moved with leaden feet, and given it to the wings of morning. We are now like gods. We may speak to all mankind.'[2] The voice of technologically created gods quickly turned out to be the one of formidable dictators, especially in Germany and Italy. In the summer of 1934, while staying with Brecht in a farmhouse in Skovsbostrand, Denmark, Benjamin wrote to his friend Scholem about his encounter with Hitler's voice through radio: 'Thus, I was able to listen to Hitler's Reichstag speech, and because it was the very first time I had ever heard him, you can imagine the effect' (BSC, 130). Until the arrival of the television in 1940 marked the end of an era of radio, this medium had to a great extent changed the underlying structure of communication relating to the forms of high art such as literature and theatre and the way of political mobilization. Benjamin was one of the few intellectuals who closely observed these pivotal transformations and the new possibilities brought about by the new electronic media, while being engaged practically with the production of radio broadcasting.

It was probably at the beginning of 1925 that Benjamin first revealed his intention of working in radio. He described his plans to Scholem in a letter dated 19 February 1925: 'For the time being, I am keeping an eye open for any opportunities that may arise locally, and finally have applied for the editorship of a radio magazine' (C, 261–2). Despite the failure of this application for a part-time supplementary job, by 1929 other opportunities had arisen to present his work on the radio. This was made possible by Ernst Schoen (1897–1973), Benjamin's old friend and the artistic director of *Südwestdeutscher Rundfunk* (Southwest German Radio) in Frankfurt. It was the most avant-garde broadcaster in the Republic and promoted programmes featuring new music by the composers Ernst Krenek (1900–1991) and Paul Hindemith (1895–1963) with introductory lectures by T.W. Adorno and political radio plays by Bertolt Brecht. The station also pioneered live sports event coverage. Benjamin was not the only intellectual to be deeply involved in discussions about radio's impact on art and politics in the period; others were engaged in similar debates. Significantly, however, Benjamin was also an actual practitioner of radio and took a key part in broadcasting as a director, a presenter and a radio playwright. Benjamin, unlike many of his contemporaries, directed his own radio programmes and read his own scripts. He had, according to his contemporaries, 'a pleasant voice'.[3] His frequent broadcasts were among the most popular programmes of the day, and won large audiences. He proved to be a successful co-ordinator of his own radio plays and was one of the top ten radio presenters in Frankfurt and Berlin during the period of the Weimar Republic.

Benjamin made his debut at the microphone of a radio station on 23 March 1927, through a talk entitled 'Young Russian Writers', in a series called 'The Great Metropolises'. This took place shortly after Benjamin's two-month trip to Moscow between 6 December 1926 and 1 February 1927.[4] Two years later, he began to make radio broadcasts (lectures and readings) more regularly. He directed continuously, mainly for *Berliner Rundfunk* (Berlin Radio) and Southwest German Radio, and by 1932 had produced around eighty-six of his own programmes. However, at this point in time, the Nazis dismissed any left-oriented directors and producers at the stations and subsequently Benjamin's radio work was brought to an end. In comparison to his considerable involvement in radio broadcasting, Benjamin wrote relatively little of direct relevance to the issue of radio-mediated communication. In his essays and fragments, mostly unpublished in his lifetime, Benjamin offers a working commentary on his five-year involvement with radio broadcasting and gives a perceptive insight into the potential of new mass media in the turbulent period of the Weimar Republic, marking not only the cultural transition from literary high art to mass culture but also the noticeable political shift from parliamentary democracy to fascism. In reconstructing and analysing Benjamin's numerous scripts, radio plays and relevant writings on theatre, in this chapter we will focus on three key issues:

(1) What are the new possibilities of communication brought about by radio?
(2) What are the distinctive features of the audience in radio broadcasting?
(3) What are the main aspects of Benjamin's media pedagogy in relation to new communication technologies?

TOWARDS A CRITICAL SOCIOLOGY OF THE AUDIENCE

Key Works
'Conversation with Ernst Schoen' (1929)
'Reflections on Radio' (1931)
'Theatre and Radio: The Mutual Control of Their Educational Program' (1932)
'Two Types of Popularity: Fundamental Reflections on a Radio Play' (1932)
'On the Minute' (1934)

Media as Mass Education Machine

Many Weimar intellectuals were drawn to radio's enormous potential for transmitting information beyond the restriction of distance to huge numbers of listeners instantaneously and simultaneously.

For 450 years people have been printing books, which is nothing other than the multiple reproduction of thoughts

and their effect . . . The public nature of this type of art presents it with new and particular tasks. There was a courtly
art for the court, the poetry of mastersingers for the rich
artisans of the cities, a bourgeois art for the bourgeoisie –
now there will have to be an art for nine million.[5]

Music was also radically transformed by the advent of radio.
When radio began to broadcast classical music performed
in a studio, it seemed to offer a powerful tool for the disintegration of the old opera- and concert-going public.
With advancements in gramophone technology and the
rapid increase in the broadcasting of music, listeners in the
Weimar Republic became increasingly accustomed to elec-
tronically mediated music.[6]

In the wake of the new communication condition, radio
became the converging space where new technological
imagination collided with the old cultural forms. Bertolt
Brecht was one of the most experimental artists who eagerly
attempted to integrate the noble – yet uncertain – technical
features of radio into his theatrical practice. He conceived
radio as being a substitute for old forms of the bourgeois
public spheres such as theatre, opera, concerts, lectures,
café music, local newspapers and so forth. Opposing the
restricted and one-sided transmission of radio, Brecht argues
in his essay 'Radio as an Apparatus of Communication' that
its objectives should not centre on distribution, but instead
aim for communication.[7] The radio, Brecht claims, should be
the 'finest possible communication apparatus in public life, a
vast network of pipes'.[8] Despite his emphasis on communication, it is not clear to what extent Brecht differentiates the
communicative function of radio from its function of transmission. This widely shared instrumental view of radio is
typified in Ernst Schoen's description of radio as 'a gigantic
machine for mass education' (SW2, 584–5). Despite being

aware of radio's potential to access the masses and to prompt education, Benjamin criticizes those commentators who fail to grasp fully its potential for mutual communication. For Benjamin, radio is a completely new medium without a 'classical age behind it', constituting a different level of communication from print media, not only quantitatively but also qualitatively.

> Radio – and this is one of its most notable consequences – has profoundly changed this state of affairs. Thanks to the technological possibility it opened up – that of addressing countless numbers of people simultaneously – the practice of popularizing developed beyond a well-intentioned philanthropic effort and became a task with its own types of formal and generic laws, a task as different from the older practices as modern advertising is from the attempts of the nineteenth century. (Media, 403–4)

Foremost, radio propels the transition from a conventional form of 'knowledge education' to a 'training for critical judgement' (Media, 396). Those who conceive the role of the information-transmission of radio tend to confine radio within 'the instrument of a vast public-education enterprise'. For Benjamin, this instrumental view fails to grasp the rise of a new media environment that requires completely new principles of pedagogy. The instrumentalist view of radio communication restricts the role of radio to the traditional Enlightenment ideas of education, which delivered knowledge to the masses by means of 'lecture series, instructional courses, large-scale didactic events' (Media, 397). In Benjamin's view, radio needs to throw off the shackles of the instrumentalist approach to education from the Enlightenment perspective.

Witnessing the enormous function of German radio

broadcasting in mobilizing social and political movements, Benjamin came to investigate the dangerous effect of radio on the audience's ability for critical judgement. The period of the 1920s and 1930s was characterized by state-controlled stations, the upsurge of National Socialism, and its intention of using radio as a means of political propaganda. In August 1929, Benjamin and Schoen decided to work together on an article about the dangers of contemporary radio. Benjamin's critical approach to radio is made explicit in a letter to Schoen of 4 April 1930. In this letter, Benjamin outlines thirteen theses they intended to develop in the article, including: the trivialization of radio as a consequence, in part, of the failure of the liberal press; the crude political agitation and demagogy of the press; the politicization of radio; the censorship of poetical works; the dominance of bureaucratic limitations in radio; corruption in the changing relationship between radio and the press; the role of the radio magazine and so on (GS II-3, 1497–9). It is apparent that these theses hold topical issues in the present period in conjunction with the impact of media on the crisis of democracy. Unfortunately, this broad plan was never realized. Yet, from his theses, we can recognize how Benjamin's radio project grapples with the inevitable link between the instrumentalist view of communication and the rise of fascism and an undiscovered potential for the fulfilment of the essential attributes of interactive communication, such as assimilation of experience. Obviously, new electronic forms of communication made possible by radio are no longer rooted in face-to-face interaction and overcome spatial differences. Radio appears to be a truly 'mass' media, representing the interests of the mass audiences in an altogether new way: 'The masses it grips are much larger; above all, the material elements on which its apparatus is based and the intellectual foundations on which its programming is based are closely intertwined in the interests of its audience' (SW2, 584).

Radio's primary attribute, according to Benjamin, is constituted by a communicative interaction between the practitioner and the listener. In his essay 'Reflections on Radio', Benjamin claims that the failure to realize radio's potential has perpetuated the fundamental separation between practitioners and the public, a separation that is at odds with its technological basis, that is, contemporary radio has failed to 'authenticate itself by taking advantage of its own forms of technology' (SW2, 543), or to utilize fully its technological potential to create in the public a new expertise. Benjamin locates his approach in terms of 'the sociology of the audience', urging a rethink of the interplay of radio and audience on multiple levels (Media, 405).

First of all, Benjamin's sociology of the audience identifies the subjective dimension of radio communication to be its individuality in urban culture: 'The radio listener is almost always a solitary individual; and even if you were to reach a few thousand of them, you are always only reaching thousands of solitary individuals. So you need to behave as if you were speaking to a solitary individual – or to many solitary individuals, if you like, but in no case to a large gathering of people' (Media, 407). The distinctive feature of radio communication from the solitary reader of the novel lies in its de-spatialized – yet simultaneous – collective experience.

Secondly, the sociology of the audience is interested in how, in the new media space created by radio, the conventional relationship of communication has been reformulated. The boundary between the culture of the expert and the masses is blurred, just as the one between the presenter and the audience has intertwined, but on a much bigger scale: 'In short, the radio play in question seeks the most intimate contact with the latest research on the so-called sociology of the audience. It would find its strongest confirmation in its ability to capture the attention of both the expert *and* the layman, even if for different reasons' (Media, 405). Rather than transforming the mass audiences into experts, radio with its unrestrained development of a consumer mentality converts its audiences into 'dull, inarticulate masses' and creates a public that has 'neither yardsticks for its judgements nor a language for its feelings' (SW2, 543).

Thirdly, Benjamin's sociology of the audience prioritizes the formal and technical aspects of radio communication over its content or subject. 'The technical and formal aspects of radio' indicate specific features of actual broadcasting such as the voice, the diction, the language and the form of narration. The reason for the contemporary failure to arouse the interest of the masses, leading to audience 'sabotage' (that is, 'their switching off'), was wrongly thought by most radio managers and media critics of the period to result from the remoteness of the subject matter. A programme's subject and content may initially keep the audience listening for a while before they make up their minds whether or not to switch off the radio. Occasionally, even programmes that might seem totally irrelevant can hold the listener spellbound. Benjamin therefore asserts that it is the failure of 'the formal and technical side of the broadcast' that so frequently makes even the most potentially interesting programmes unbearable for the listener (SW2, 544). In his own broadcast, Benjamin strives to improve the technical aspects of radio communication by presenting serious literary commentaries and lectures interspersed with background music and sound effects. With regard to this point, it should be noted that a number of Benjamin's famous essays were originally written for radio broadcast. The unique character of these essays derives not from their content but from their style, that is, their non-discursive and non-analytic narration, through which Benjamin attempts to fulfil the potential of storytelling. His emphasis on the technical aspects of radio uncovers the materialist and formalist approach to communication in Benjamin's thought, an approach that is predicated upon his unique idea of the audience as participants of communication, not supplements but necessary components of the communication process. Benjamin conceives his own radio scripts to be a new literary genre specifically designed for radio broadcasting; that is, making stories more accessible to a greater number of listeners necessitates re-configuring literary texts with media technology and making them responsive to listeners' interests. To understand the distinctive aspects of Benjamin's formalist approach to radio, we need to take account of his own radio model (*Hörmodelle*), a model that he tries to differentiate from a conventional form of radio play (*Hörspiel*).

RADIO MODEL

Key Works

'Demonic Berlin' (1930)

'Myslovitz-Braunschweig-Marseilles: The Story of a Hashish
    Trance' (1930)

'Bert Brecht' (1930)

'Unpacking my Library: A Talk about Book Collecting' (1931)

'Franz Kafka: *Beim Bau der Chinesischen Mauer*' (1931)

'The Lisbon Earthquake' (1931)

'The Railway Disaster at the Firth of Tay' (1932)

Mediated Storytelling

As radio came to wield enormous power, particularly in the verbal arts, the radio play emerged as a new literary genre. This resulted from the call for an original radio-specific genre – that is, a literary text composed exclusively for radio. After the first German radio play was broadcast in 1926, this new genre became the dominant artistic form of radio broadcasting. Contributions were made by a number of famous writers and literary critics, including Alfred Döblin and Thomas Mann. It is notable that this genre became a major source of income for Weimar writers and intellectuals, in much the same way as the feuilleton had for popular novelists and critics during the growth of newspapers in nineteenth-century Europe. Yet, Benjamin's radio plays have received relatively little attention from the perspective of media compared with the exhaustive studies of his literary criticism and visual culture.[9] This partially results from the comment he made about his involvement in radio in his letter of 28 February 1933 to Scholem: 'As to your other requests for your archive, i.e. my works for the radio. Even I haven't been successful in collecting them all. I am speaking of the radio plays, not the series of countless talks, which [will] now come to an end, unfortunately, and are of no interest except in economic terms, but that is now a thing of the past' (C, 403–4). These cynical remarks should be understood in the context of his financial destitution during the period. In fact, his numerous radio scripts and reflections reveal how seriously Benjamin tested the nature of radio broadcasting for its grasp of the distinctive conditions of communication.

In Benjamin's view, the influence of radio as an electronic medium on literature is substantially different from the impact of the novel on storytelling or of books on oral communication. This shows in his unique approach to radio broadcasting: texts of radio plays must correspond to the specific technological qualities of the medium. To utilize technological potentials fully, the essential principles of storytelling are brought to the fore. On the one hand, his radio plays give pre-eminence to technique rather than to the subject matter, keeping that distance from sensational or popular drama radio plays. On the other hand, Benjamin's radio plays do not rely on explanation, which would necessitate analytical narration. The nature of storytelling lies not in explanation but in conversation, allowing for assimilation of the story into the audience's everyday life. It is worth noting that his radio plays draw on the approach of Herodotus, one of the first Greek storytellers, who used a technique of flat reportage in telling his ancient stories.

> Herodotus offers no explanations. His report is utterly dry. That is why, after thousands of years, this story from ancient Egypt is still capable of provoking astonishment and reflection. It is like those seeds of grain that have lain for centuries in the airtight chambers of the pyramids and have retained their germinative power to this day. (SW3, 148)

Between 1929 and 1932, Benjamin wrote some thirty radio plays for the two programmes, the *Jugendstunde* and the *Stunde der Jugend* (the children's or youth hour) broadcast by the radio stations in Berlin and Frankfurt, specifically aimed at young listeners. Each programme was delivered in the form of a twenty-minute talk or monologue. Benjamin's involvement with children's radio programmes is by no means coincidental. The notion of childhood is one of the major motifs in Benjamin's thinking from 1918 onwards, and is central to his account of the mimetic faculty. His interest in children's experiences led him to examine his own childhood and the children's culture of his time, motivated by his desire to change the socialization process in Germany. Benjamin's disdain for bourgeois pedagogic philosophy reflects his own involvement with the idealistic German Youth Movement. In Benjamin's account, childhood anticipates the creative and emancipatory relationships of a new social order. In his radical critique of education, 'the discipline the bourgeoisie demands from children is its mark of shame' (SW2, 205). Conversely, a new pedagogy aims to give children, particularly between the ages of four and fourteen, the fulfilment of their creative and emancipatory potential:

> Task of childhood: to bring the new world into symbolic space. The child, in fact, can do what the grown-up absolutely cannot: recognize the new once again. For us, locomotives already have symbolic character because we met with them in childhood. Our children, however, will find this in automobiles, of which we ourselves see only the new, elegant, modern, cheeky side. (AP [K1a,3], 390)

Understood thus, his emphasis on the intersection of childhood and mimetic faculty is not a Romanticist act of yearning for an idyllic past, but a social act of regeneration that is intended to lead to the affirmation of children's distinctive spaces such as 'kindergartens, youth groups, children's theatres, and outdoor groups' (SW2, 275). Benjamin's radio programmes involve his endeavour to engender a unique form of media space for children's aesthetic engagement through story.

Children's Radio

'The City of Berlin' was one of the main series that Benjamin produced for the children's programme, the scripts of which were later incorporated into his autobiographical essay, 'Berlin Chronicle' (1932) (one of which is later expanded and revised in 1938 under the title, 'Berlin Childhood around 1900' (SW3, 343–86)). In these essays (and probably in his programmes too), Benjamin brings to the fore varying cultural objects, urban spaces and fragmented images that are

interwoven with his childhood memory. Along with Imperial
Panorama, Victory Column, a corner of the Berlin streets,
sexual awakening and so on, the telephone located in the
hallway of his house plays a mediating role to excavate his
memory. 'The noises of the first telephone conversations' are
so vivid for Benjamin that they remain and 'echo differently'
throughout his life like 'nocturnal noises' (SW3, 349). Since
the arrival of the telephone in his house, the abrupt calls
from his schoolmates or the loud row between his father and
switchboard operators serve to disturb the private space of the
urban bourgeois family. However, for Benjamin, the noise
penetrating into his everyday life is no less than 'a newborn
voice' and even like his 'twin brother' (SW3, 349). Benjamin
in fact had a younger brother, Georg, who died later in a
Nazi concentration camp. By outshining middle-class private
ornaments displayed in the front rooms (for instance, 'the
chandelier, fire screen, potted palm, console table, gueridon
and alcove balustrade'), this 'apparatus' quickly comes to be a
harbinger of the arrival of modern space, a space that is constantly connected with the outside. The telephone prevails
like 'a legendary hero' who 'left the dark hallway in the back of
the house to make its regal entry into the cleaner and brighter
room that now was inhabited by a younger generation' (SW3,
349). While the telephone is bound up with a coming generation, radio is linked with the children's world. Benjamin
finds a noticeable affinity between the telephone and radio,
especially for children, that is, the function of solace via voice.

> For the latter [a young generation], it became a consolation
> for their loneliness. To the despondent who wanted to leave
> this wicked world, it shone with the light of a last hope.
> With the forsaken, it shared its bed. Now, when everything
> depended on its call, the strident voice it had acquired in
> exile was grown softer. (SW3, 349–50)

Benjamin's emphasis on the consoling role of voice for children stems from a mode of bedtime storytelling. It is no coincidence that his radio plays for children's programmes comprise a number of questions and jokes. While questions intend to invite young audiences' active participation, jokes unwind their strung attention. This indirect, non-discursive communication style, using the technique of storytelling, allows us to see how he treated his young listeners as equal partners in communication akin to adults. In these programmes, Benjamin tried to make particular use of the narrative form by providing stories that would be equally accessible, entertaining and interesting to young listeners. Benjamin uses various subjects and formats, finding themes in his personal collection of children's books, in daily newspapers, or in his own reminiscences. The city, for instance, is one of Benjamin's major subjects throughout his analysis of modernity. The main themes of his programmes can be outlined thus:

(i)   adventures, or strange characters;[10]
(ii)   swindlers and smugglers;[11]
(iii)   catastrophes from the ancient to the contemporary;[12]
(iv)   travel reports;[13]
(v)   a drug-induced trance;[14]
(vi)   fairy tale;[15]
(vii)   animal stories;[16] and
(viii) literary talk.[17]

The above topics are not chosen in an arbitrary way. Rather, in Benjamin's view, these kinds of subject could be most easily tailored to the acoustic media, and were best suited to the children's programme. For example, one of the most significant features of these plays is that when Benjamin presents stories concerned with magic or mythology, he does not consider them to be purely fairy tales or fantasies. Rather, he sees them, as the early Romanticists would have done, as a form of universal story.

It is imperative that the literary attributes of the 'essay' form are integrated into his plays; essay as a genre he considers to be a reflection of the fragmentation of modern life. Benjamin believes the essay's non-analytical narrative attributes are especially suited to the acoustic presentation of a literary talk in radio broadcasting. A significant characteristic of the essay is that of quotation, often used in full in his plays. In his radio broadcasting, Benjamin seeks to freeze the normal flow of events in life in order to subject them to an intensive process of critical scrutiny by means of the ample use of quotation. In his radio talks about literature, he always cites at length quotations from literary texts – whether a short story, a synopsis of a novel or a full-length newspaper report – aiming to bring the effect of interruption to the audience. For instance, in his radio lecture on Franz Kafka, Benjamin quotes and retells a Chinese legend in its entirety, observing that he will not interpret this story for the audience, rather letting them judge for themselves (SW2, 494–500). Benjamin's technique is less akin to the transmission of information than to the stimulation of the audience's imagination. In another example, he quotes an interview and the result of a survey, intending to elicit listeners' active participation in the same way that 'original sound' recording functions today.[18] Benjamin's own radio model indicates his effort to formalize a model that fully induces the audience's participation.

Radio Model

Against the transmission of the 'one-way-street' model of radio, Benjamin, in collaboration with the journalist Wolf

Zucker, develops an alternative radio broadcasting model on the basis of radio's technical and formal aspects of communication (GS IV-2, 628). Three key features of Benjamin's model can be identified.

(1) The Participatory Audience

Benjamin's model is primarily concerned with representing the listeners' interests and fostering their active participation. Benjamin characterizes the attributes of radio listeners as distinguished from readers of the novel and newspapers, or audiences of other modes of communication, such as theatre or cinema.

> We need only reflect that the radio listener, unlike every other kind of audience, welcomes the human voice into his house like a visitor. Moreover, he will usually judge that voice just as quickly and sharply as he would a visitor. Yet no one tells it what is expected of it, what the listener will be grateful for or will find unforgivable, and so on. This can be explained only with reference to the indolence of the masses and the narrowmindedness of broadcasters. (SW2, 544)

Thus, Benjamin's account of the communicative function of radio is based not on the wish to transmit 'knowledge' or 'information', but on the desire to help the audience members improve their capability of judging social and political reality. At this point, Benjamin seems to be highly optimistic about the audiences' receptive capability. In fact, by leading the listener to his/her own recognition, Benjamin's model tries to enable the audiences to train themselves and to acquire greater self-understanding. Benjamin's concept of 'training' diverges markedly from the Enlightenment-oriented understanding of 'education' in the sense that the subject and object of the education are the audiences themselves. Radio's formative role is to provide a space for the condition of training (SW2, 585). Listeners, in Benjamin's view, should not be considered to be indolent masses or passive consumers. Instead, they should be appealed to as 'experts' (SW2, 544). While Benjamin rarely attempts to explain how newspaper readers can obtain this expert status (or 'the distracted critics' in cinema to whom he refers in his later writings, as we shall see), he underscores the participatory role of the audience in his discussion of radio. Benjamin believes that each individual should be trained to become an informed, confident listener, able to recognize his own interests in society. While Benjamin censures those facets of the press that render 'the public incapable of judging' (SW2, 433), he necessitates the audiences' active engagement to realize the process of communication. Radio audiences are not passive receivers or, in his own terminology, 'the fifth wheel on the carriage of technology' (SW2, 585) but actual players and practitioners of broadcasting who actualize the communication process.[19]

(2) The Formalized Structure
Benjamin's radio model is intended to posit an exemplary instance of radio broadcasting. As such, the model is distinguished from the prevailing 'dramatic' forms of radio programme. In contrast, his model primarily involves a specific, formalized structure. This formality is evident in the method of instruction, and the standardized pattern that seeks to oppose correct examples and incorrect counter-examples of social behaviours drawn from typical everyday situations, such as 'school and education', 'the techniques of success', 'marriage difficulties' and so on (GS IV-2, 628). A discussion between the presenters and listeners takes place at the end of the programme.

In a typical structure, the narrator appears three times in a programme. At the beginning s/he makes the listener familiar with the programme's subject, and subsequently introduces the other actors who appear in the first part. The first part of the programme also includes the counter-example; that is, the course of action that is the least desirable of the two presented. The narrator returns after the conclusion of the first part and hints at the mistakes that have been made. He then introduces a new figure, who presents the alternative solution. At the end of the play, the narrator compares the incorrect course of action with the right one and draws out the morals of the story. Therefore, no radio model has more than four supporting voices: (1) the voice of the narrator; (2) another character who appears in both the first and the second parts; (3) the mistaken or foolish character in the first part of the play; and (4) the character presenting the preferable course of action (GS IV-2, 628).

With Wolf Zucker, Benjamin wrote three programmes based on the principles of this model. These were broadcast at South German Radio in the years 1931 and 1932. For instance, 'Pay rise? You must be joking!' (GS IV-2, 629–40) contrasts clumsy and skilful employees in negotiation with their boss. 'The boy never tells the truth' presents a ten-year-old boy who keeps on telling a small lie. 'Can you help me out until Thursday?' compares the actions of one foolish man, who asks his friend for money and receives a refusal, with the more intelligent and successful actions of another in the same situation (GS IV-2, 628). By means of his model Benjamin aims to construct a formal structure for radio, which best facilitates the audience's self-training for critical judgement.

(3) Dialogue with Invisible Listeners

Benjamin's alternative model also aims to maximize radio's potential in helping the audience play a decisive role in the conversation, aided by recording technology. According to this model, 'conversation' is understood as the technique most suited to radio broadcasting, having the particular purpose of abolishing the distance between the sender and the receiver. Radio presenters are like storytellers who 'tend to begin their story with a presentation of the circumstances in which they themselves have learned what is to follow, unless they simply pass it off as their own experience' (SW3, 149). He treats his listeners as equal conversation partners, calling them 'Dear Invisible Listeners' [*Verehrte Unsichtbare*] (SW2, 250), and presents his programme according to the pattern of everyday conversation. In one programme, Benjamin compares the role of the radio-presenter to that of the 'chemist'. In the opening lines of his programme 'The Lisbon Earthquake', he tells the audience:

> Have you ever had to wait at the drug store, watching a prescription being made up? The pharmacist measures out on a scale all the substances and powders that are needed for the finished medicine, using a finely calibrated set of weights, gram by gram or ounce by ounce. *I feel like a chemist when I talk to you over the radio.* My weights are the minutes, and I have to measure them out very accurately: so much of this and so much of that, if the final mixture is going to come out right. (SW2, 536, emphasis added)

This remark shows how acutely Benjamin is aware of the temporal nature of radio broadcasting. Unlike the literary product, the success of radio broadcasting hinges upon whether it can capture audiences' attention and participation in 'a given air time'. Time in the novel relates to the subjective and individual attribute, but the novel can be read again and again. However, time in the radio broadcast has a greater affinity with storytelling: it is collective but also a one-off. Benjamin underlines: 'So don't forget: adopt a relaxed style of speaking and conclude on the minute!' (Media, 407). It is unsurprising, therefore, that a number of Benjamin's radio scripts are repeated in the form of a conversation, through which Benjamin tries to create 'a state of relaxation': 'a state which the process of mutual assimilation requires' (SW3, 149). His enthusiasm with the dialogical attributes of radio is also evident in a discussion broadcast by the Frankfurt radio station on 9 May 1930, 'Recipes for Comedy Writers' (GS VII-2, 610–16). The discussion involved Wilhelm Speyer, the comedy writer, and Benjamin himself, who attempted to present his idea of literary criticism to a general audience. Benjamin's famous essay, 'Unpacking my Library: A Talk about Book Collecting', presented on 27 April 1931 in the early evening (SW2, 486–93), also exemplifies how Benjamin adapted the technique of conversation for the purpose of communicating with collective audiences.

SOME MOTIFS FOR MEDIA PEDAGOGY

Key Works

'A Glimpse into the World of Children's Books' (1926)
'The Political Groupings of Russian Writers' (1927)
'On the Present Situation of Russian Film' (1927)
'Moscow' (1927)
'Toys and Play' (1928)
'Program for a Proletarian Children's Theatre' (1928/9)
'A Communist Pedagogy' (1929)
'The Destructive Character' (1931)
'Theatre and Radio: the Mutual Control of their Educational
    Program' (1932)
'What is the Epic Theatre?' (1939)

Radio and Theatre

Despite its privileged position within German bourgeois culture, theatre in the Weimar Republic represented the disintegration of the bourgeois public sphere and became one of the key political spaces not only for the intellectuals and artists but also for the masses. The Weimar theatre served as a cultural space where new technology and radical artistic experiments energetically met. In his 1932 essay 'Theatre and Radio: the Mutual Control of their Educational Program', Benjamin elaborates a further problem engendered by the intersection of radio, the new communication technology and theatre, an emblem of traditional bourgeois culture. In his view, the competition between radio and the theatre might not be as marked as that between radio and the concert hall. The crisis of live music or concert-hall music is brought about by new technological inventions. Hence, as in radio, a new task of any old forms of art like theatre is to radically transform or 're-function' (*Umfunktionierung*) its form itself by eliminating the antithesis 'between performers and listeners' and 'between technique and content' (SW2, 775–6). Benjamin aims to change the way in which radio intersects aesthetic practices, in particular theatrical practices. Two theatrical experiments fire his imagination: the children's theatre movement in Russia and Brecht's epic theatre. Benjamin's writings on the theatre are usually recognized as being a supplement to, or a further explication of, Brechtian epic theatre. And indeed, Benjamin's essays on Brecht's epic theatre, written for a children's radio programme, show that his own thinking might often overlap with Brecht's experiment with didactic pedagogy and radio communication. However, although Benjamin's account of Brecht seems positive in this regard, his writings on epic theatre stand at some distance from Brecht's theory of theatre and radio. As we will see, if Benjamin's account of epic theatre is examined in conjunction with his radical programme for children's theatre, it becomes more apparent that Benjamin's account of theatrical movements contains distinctive understandings of the role of theatrical space in constructing a new form of media pedagogy. This demonstrates that Benjamin considers the theatre as a sensual public space for playing and privileges it over a rational public sphere for disciplinary education in the tradition of the Enlightenment. Benjamin's analysis of these theatrical movements reveals the fact that the conventional dichotomic relation of education, such as discipline and entertainment, is not incompatible.

The Epic Theatre

As a leading Weimar intellectual who enthusiastically engaged with this new technology, Brecht wrote original radio plays for children and working-class audiences and adapted his own pre-existing theatre plays for radio broadcasting. Given his strong emphasis on the educational and political function of art and radio, it seems likely that his theory of epic theatre was created with the purpose of making plays adaptable for radio transmission. Brecht himself illustrates this point quite clearly: 'Epic theatre, because it is made up of separate numbers, because of its separation of elements – the separation of image and word and of words and music – but particularly because of its didactic attitude, could provide a great number of practical hits for radio.'[20] When Benjamin and Brecht first met via an introduction by Asja Lacis in the summer of 1924 in Berlin, Benjamin was quite preoccupied with radio broadcasting. However, it is to some extent true that Benjamin focuses on the impact of radio on the theatre in a way that echoes Brecht's enthusiastic utilization of technology for the main contour of epic theatre.

Over the period of their 'very friendly relationship' between 1929 and 1931, they had a serious discussion about radio and the epic theatre, in addition to the topics afforded by Charlie Chaplin's films, which constructs 'the Brecht/Benjamin partnership'.[21] Brecht greatly encouraged Benjamin's efforts in radio and Benjamin gave his radio talk 'Bert Brecht' on Southwest German Radio on 24 June 1930. However, there are substantial differences between Benjamin's and Brecht's understanding of radio.

Two particular attributes of epic theatre prompt Benjamin's idea of a radio model: the adaptation of the montage technique developed in films, and its characteristically new attitude towards the mass audiences. Benjamin identifies two separate types of response to the theatre: the reactionary and the progressive. The reactionary response is represented by the theatre that exists as 'symbol and organic totality' and is aimed at the total work of art (*Gesamtkunstwerk*), typified by Wagner's operas (SW2, 584). When confronted with the development of communication media, traditional theatre can only offer 'live people'. Recruited as stage-extras, the masses function as the monumental, identifying themselves with the leader, the 'tragic hero'. This type of theatre's main principles are rooted in the *Gesamtkunstwerk* and, according to Benjamin, involve a 'hopeless competitive struggle' forced by new media and 'its position is a lost one' (SW2, 778). In contrast to theatrical illusion, epic theatre tries to adapt fully to the advancement of new media towards dramaturgic principles:

Not so that of a theatre that, instead of competing with newer instruments of publication, seeks to use and learn from them – in short, to enter into debate with them. This debate the Epic Theatre has made its own affair. It is, measured by the present state of development of film and radio, the contemporary form. (SW2, 778)

Benjamin is aware that Brecht's theory of the politicization of theatre corresponds to Brecht's strong claim for the secularization and de-aestheticization of art. Benjamin is especially interested in how epic theatre specifically deals with the problems of aesthetic reception in the age of such new media as radio and film, and how it can utilize communication technology in order to shatter the spectacular illusion over the audiences. Benjamin is fascinated by the fact that epic theatre takes a similar approach to the audience in adopting the principles of electronic media. Benjamin underlines key aspects of epic theatre on five levels in his essay, 'What is the Epic Theatre?' (SW4, 302–7).

(1) Epic theatre tends to deny Aristotelian catharsis, the purging of the emotions through identification with the destiny that rules the tragic hero's life. Hence, the fragmentation arising from epic theatre's use of montage stands in contrast to the organic totality of the *Gesamtkunstwerk*.

(2) Unlike traditional drama, epic theatre aims to arouse 'astonishment' (similarly, Eisenstein's montage effect seeks to awaken 'attraction') rather than 'empathy'.

(3) In much the same way as the mode of communication in storytelling, the audience of epic theatre 'collectively' follows the play in a 'relaxed' manner, unlike the isolated reader of a novel alone with his text. The audience is called upon to learn and to be challenged by the circumstances of the play.

(4) The task of epic theatre is therefore to 'uncover' conditions, or to make them 'strange' (*verfremden*). This uncovering (making strange, or alienating) is brought about by the 'interruption' of normal processes. Distance between the audience and stage is created by this interruption of action. These interrupted actions are intended

to counteract any theatrical illusions on the part of the audience that are a hindrance to a theatre attempting to re-arrange reality experimentally (SW2, 778).

(5) In thinking about how this interruption might be achieved, Brecht's rigorous adaptation of montage to theatre draws Benjamin's attention: 'I would like to show you ... how Brecht's discovery and use of the *gestus* is nothing but the restoration of the method of montage decisive in radio and film, from an often merely modish procedure to a human event' (SW2, 778). When employed in epic theatre, montage's distinctive feature lies in its attempt to reveal and unravel certain conditions by the interruption of action: 'The damming of the stream of real life, the moments when its flow comes to a standstill, makes itself felt as reflux: this reflux is astonishment. The dialectic at a standstill is its real object'.[22] Montage technique symbolizes the intersection between theatre and radio, a technique that realizes Benjamin's central idea of dialectical image. In such films as Vertov's *Man with a Movie Camera*, Benjamin finds the similar interrupting effect of montage technique to that of epic theatre.

Benjamin's wholehearted admiration for Brecht is itself, in this analysis, quite astonishing. However, it must be pointed out that Brecht and Benjamin's understandings of montage are not identical and this difference crucially separates their theories of media pedagogy. Whereas Brecht's alienation effect produces and widens the distance between the audience and the stage, Benjamin's montage aims to destroy the gap. Furthermore, while Brecht's epic theatre aims to correct reification and false consciousness, Benjamin's approach to theatrical practice aims to provoke a sensorial awakening. The principal objective of epic theatre is that of 'a theatre of the scientific age'. In epic theatre, Brecht's directorial practice, his insistence on control and precison, and the highly formalized textual basis of his didactic plays, are all far removed from Benjamin's model, which is based on the notion of improvisation. The action of the play itself and children's participation is stressed in Benjamin's model, whereas Brecht's theatre places greater emphasis on rational thinking and the distance between audience and actor. Consequently, while for Brecht reality and play remain clearly distinguished, in Benjamin's account the two melt into each other on a stage. Most significantly, Benjamin's views on theatre are not based on the rationalist approach, which seeks to control the actor's performance. Instead, it is a process of discovery and learning, both for the audience and the actors themselves. More significantly, their principal accounts of communication stand in polar opposition to one another. One emphasizes attention on a cognitive level, while the other prioritizes distraction on a sensual level. Benjamin's view of communication stands in contrast to Brecht's idea of 'distancing', an attitude of cool detachment and critical reasoning grounded on attentive perception. Brecht's famous theatrical concept of 'alienation effect' [*Verfremdungseffekt*] remains instrumentally bound to the emancipatory power of reason and to a critical explanation of society in the rational critique of ideology. As is made clear in his numerous essays, in particular 'Theatre for Pleasure or Theatre for Instruction', Brecht makes a sharp distinction between the role of entertainment and play, and that of education and 'scientific understanding'.[23] This distinction places him closer to the Enlightenment tradition. Benjamin appropriates epic theatre for his own purpose – for his reformulation of theatrical practice for media pedagogy. For this purpose, he endeavours to explore the impact of theatrical practice on physiological process, via a focus on Russian experiments in children's theatre.

Theatre as Play-Space

When he stayed in Moscow for two months, Benjamin learned about Sergei Eisenstein's theatrical experiments, which were being conducted within the agitprop movement *Proletkult*. At the same time, through Asja Lacis, Benjamin also encountered a new composition of children's theatre. Back in Germany, in a period when challenges arising from new forms of communication media such as radio and film were making theatre quickly outmoded, Benjamin drew particular attention to children's theatrical space, much influenced by his own experience in Russia. In late 1928, Benjamin wrote the essay, 'Program for a Proletarian Children's Theatre', the title of which reflects the strong influence of Asja Lacis and Bertolt Brecht. However, this essay is restricted neither to a simple theatrical model, nor to narrow concerns about class interests, as might be assumed from the title. The term 'proletarian' relates less to the production of class-oriented meaning than to the radical alternative to bourgeois culture, a culture that is predicated upon a knowledge of production and transmission. It sketches a radically alternative model of pedagogy, based on and yet going beyond the examples developed in the early Soviet Union, becoming part of the cultural activities of working-class organizations in the Weimar Republic.

Notably, Benjamin's formalistic approach to communication, privileging technical and material form over substantive content, leads him to assert that space is a vital issue in children's everyday lives. In his view, children should be educated 'within a *clearly defined space*', in which their whole life should be engaged and 'framed in all its plenitude' (SW2, 202).

He gives credence to the perspective that the theatre will unleash in children their most powerful and creative future energies. Children's action is considered to be indicative of a process of imaginative creation and aesthetic education: 'For what is truly revolutionary is not the propaganda of ideas . . . What is truly revolutionary is the *secret signal* of what is to come that speaks from the gesture of the child' (SW2, 206). For Benjamin, children's play in a public space like theatre is conceived to be the unifying energy of sensorium and creative practice. Benjamin's original German notion, *Spiel*, can be understood in its multiple meanings as 'play, game, performance and gamble'. As Hansen claims, by means of *Spiel*, Benjamin seeks to create 'an alternative mode of aesthetics on a par with modern, collective experience'.[24]

Benjamin was hardly the first social thinker to grapple with the importance of play in the formation of social and cultural institutions, being fully aware of the German Romanticist tradition of aesthetic education, represented by Friedrich Schiller (1759–1805).[25] Since the publication of the Dutch social historian, Johan Huizinga (1872–1945)'s work, *Homo Ludens: A Study of the Play Element in Culture* in 1938, it had come to be the key reference point in the discussion of play. In this pioneering yet controversial text, Huizinga explored various types of play through history and described the formative role of play in the process of civilization.[26] Nevertheless, his definition of play as a certain type of free and voluntary action totally deprived of any material interest and purpose is too mysterious and too abstract to elucidate human behaviours such as play, work and labour. Huizinga's rather idealist notion of play can hardly grasp the material conditions of human action that involve the development of communications technology, the large scale of metropolitan space, and the propagation of the consumer and entertainment industries. Departing from Huizinga's legacy, Benjamin's contemporary, Roger Caillois (1913–1978), the French social anthropologist and a founding member of the College of Sociology, sought to formulate play and games in a more systematic way from the sociological and anthropological perspective by incorporating social and economic factors into the cultural context of play in his seminal work, *Man, Play and Games* (1958).[27] We will come back to the role of play in retrieving alienated mimetic faculty with respect to cinematic space in more detail later, but it is imperative to underscore how Benjamin's earlier insight into play deriving from his observation on theatrical space provides some crucial motifs for formulating the main contours of media pedagogy.

First, the liberating function of play helps to reverse the decline of the mimetic faculty. Children's play is not 'imitation', but enables correspondence with objects: 'A child wants to pull something, and so he *becomes* a horse; he wants to play with sand, and so he *turns into* a baker; he wants to hide, and so he turns into a robber or a policeman' (SW2, 115, emphasis added). For Benjamin, the supremacy of Chaplin's acting lies in its corresponding relation between himself and the object. As exemplified in Chaplin's act, children's mimesis is in this way able to mediate between subjective and objective experience.

> When the urge to play overcomes an adult, this is not simply a regression to childhood. To be sure, play is always liberating. Surrounded by a world of giants, children use play to create a world appropriate to their size. But the adult, who finds himself threatened by the real world and can find no escape, removes its sting by playing with its image in reduced form. (SW2, 100)

Second, Benjamin's media pedagogy requires the receptive role of the set of sensation. The fulfilment of childhood arises primarily from the liberation of the whole sensory apparatus. As such, children's mimetic behaviour is based not on contemplative and rational communication but on sensorial and corporeal engagement. It is important to reiterate the theoretical assumptions underpinning Benjamin's argument that creative practice is exactly proportional to receptive perception in children's theatre. Children's experience of colour exemplifies the undoing of alienated sensory perception as a whole through their sense of touch. As such, in Benjamin's account, children's experience of colour is not restricted to optical perception but involves whole sensory perception.

Third, in Benjamin's account, the role of a teacher in the theatre is to 'observe' children with 'unsentimental love'. Observation, whether distanced, indifferent or non-empathetic, is the starting point of education because it is through this distance that every childhood action becomes a 'signal'. In this way, Benjamin opposes the traditional view of a disciplinary education. Children's play rejects the hierarchical relation between adult/teacher and children/students. He seems to be oriented towards the orthodox Marxist view of education, as exemplified in his 1929 essay 'Communist Pedagogy' (SW2, 273–5). However, his position is yet more radical than this; his critique is directed towards the rationalized modern education system itself. In Benjamin's view, while meek educators still cling to Rousseauesque idealist dreams that we are inherently born good, others like writer Joachim Ringelnatz (1883–1934) and painter Paul Klee (1879–1940) have aptly grasped 'the despotic and dehumanized element in children' (SW2, 101). For Benjamin, children's creativity is oppressed by old European humanist approaches to education, which give credence to disciplinary and rational behaviour. A child's despotic character is not behaviour to be rectified or trained, but the primal symbol

of the liberated human sensorium. Almost every childlike
gesture is a 'command' and a 'signal'. Like a collector, children control the world of objects from which the adult is
alienated. The task of the teacher is the same as that of the
observer – 'to release children's signals from the hazardous
magical world of sheer fantasy and apply them to materials' (SW2, 204). For Benjamin, children's despotic character
marks essential virtues of man, that is, 'the destructive character' (SW2, 541). This character entails being 'young and
cheerful' and 'always blithely at work' and seeing 'no image
hovering before him' and 'nothing permanent' (SW2, 541–
2). Benjamin praises the destructive character of a child as
'an Apollonian image of the destroyer' (SW2, 541).

Fourth, Benjamin contends that children's play is
grounded on 'improvisation', which is central to children's
theatrical action. Children's play also corresponds with
modern urban life, consisting as it does of instantaneous
fragments: 'But, childhood achievement is always aimed not
at the "eternity" of the products but at the "moment" of the
gesture. The theatre is the art form of the child because it is
ephemeral' (SW2, 204). The fragmented yet instantaneous
improvisation of children's gesture brings forth spontaneous
and unpredictable attributes of carnivalesque stage.

> The performance is the great creative pause in the process
> of upbringing. It represents in the realm of children what
> the carnival was in the old cults. Everything was turned
> upside down; and just as in Rome the master served the
> slaves during the Saturnalia, in the same way in a perfor-
> mance children stand on the stage and instruct and teach
> the attentive educators. (SW2, 205)

Children's theatre becomes a space of festival through the
wild liberation of a child's imagination.[28]

Fifth, children's play is bound up with the habitual behaviour of the distracted learning process. In parallel with improvisation, the repetition of movement is the 'soul of play', and gives children great pleasure. Children's play itself is ephemeral improvisation, but the repetition of this behaviour transforms it in an unconscious way into 'habit': 'Not a "doing as if" but a "doing the same thing over and over again", the transformation of a shattering experience into habit – that is the essence of play' (SW2, 120). For Benjamin, children's toys represent a type of technology that is able to mediate images and the body, again reversing the decline of the mimetic faculty. Benjamin considers toys to be an emblem of 'the technological culture of the collective' (SW2, 119). Children's play with toys signifies the interface between technology and the sensorium of human beings. The overcoming of the bourgeois culture is accomplished not through disciplinary education but through habitual behaviour arising from the joyful repetition. Habit is then a paradigm of non-contemplative practical memory, which in turn is executed collectively in a communal space. In Benjamin's view, children's play contains the revolutionary principles that are grounded in the transformation of the sensory apparatus in everyday life and engaged through a play-space.

CONCLUSION

Benjamin's active involvement in radio broadcasting, his numerous radio scripts, and his own formalized radio model, demonstrate his desire to experiment practically with these theoretical concerns, exploring the potential of radio to act as a form of mediated storytelling. However, Benjamin's approach does not aim to construct a nostalgic revival of storytelling as face-to-face communication. His interest in narrative forms of communication relates not only to orality (or onomatopoetic elements of language) in communal communication, but also to concurrent changes in human perception. Benjamin's media pedagogy further seeks a means of realizing the moment of waking and retrieving the alienated and fragmented sensoria. In a public space like theatre, the new collective can be enabled not by knowledge-oriented discipline but by play-oriented communication. Benjamin's interest in the aesthetic public space such as the children's theatre and the cinema posits play as some kind of affective communication beyond goal-oriented rational action.

However, at this point, it is still unclear if Benjamin, who conceives of storytelling as a prototype of communication, understands visual communication interwoven with urban spectacle as inevitably degrading communication. Hence, it should be asked to what extent the principles of Benjamin's radio model, which are drawn from communal communication like storytelling, are applicable to other modes of communication. This aspect of Benjamin's account of communication raises the critical question of how the audience's capacity for critical judgement might be improved in modern society, the dominant modes of which are visual spectacles.

It is still worth asking, and probably important to ask, whether radio's short yet dominating era was finally over in 1940 when television arrived. Radio's death as an old medium has been announced since then, yet we have witnessed that radio has always maintained audiences over the past six decades and has survived in the age of the Internet. This poses a new question: 'Does the interactive, live aspect of streaming define the online listening experience?'[29] Radio has been listened to by individual and private audiences while they are driving, reading, dancing and so on. Digital technology has considerably increased the accessibility of radio via the Internet or podcast and the audiences' participation via simultaneous mutual communication, even in a global scale. The ever increasing power of radio indicates that the 'old' medium has not been easily replaced by new technology. It also applies to the destiny of the book in the digital age. The resilience of radio, in fact, shows the strong power of story-telling, 'the old friend' of human beings, as the British rock band Queen sings.

ART AND POLITICS IN THE AGE

OF THEIR TECHNOLOGICAL

REPRODUCIBILITY

INTRODUCTION

In the 1930s, Benjamin was preoccupied with the role of new visual technology such as photography and film in terms of the unprecedented scale of their effect on human sensory, cognitive capacities and aesthetic practices. The newly rising mass culture engendered by these new technologies seemed fundamentally different from traditional forms of high art like painting, poetry and operas. The rise of the new technological culture and politics prompted him to compose a new theory of art echoing the new technological advancement. His ambition for a comprehensive reflection on the destiny of art was revealed in a letter to Horkheimer of 16 October 1935:

> The issue this time is to indicate the precise moment in the present to which any historical construction will orient itself, as to its vanishing point. If the pretext for the book

is the fate of art in the nineteenth century, this fate has
something to say to us only because it is contained in the
ticking of a clock whose striking of the hour has only just
reached *our* ears. What I mean by this is that art's fateful
hour has struck for us and I have captured its signature in a
series of preliminary reflections entitled 'The Work of Art
in the Age of Mechanical Reproduction'. These reflections
attempt to give the questions raised by art theory a truly
contemporary form. (C, 509)

His reflection was materialized as his magisterial essay 'The
Work of Art in the Age of Its Technological Reproducibility'.
The essay has been hailed as one of the most original contributions to film and cinema studies and has received wide
attention from various academic disciplines such as screen
studies, cultural studies and urban studies, and from those
working in fine arts. Despite its similar reception in various
fields, the Work of Art essay is an unfinished piece, and has
various versions. Having written the first version in Paris in
the autumn of 1935, Benjamin continued to revise the manuscript and left the third and final version in 1939. The second
version was closer to the original structure that Benjamin had
conceived initially and its abridged form was translated into
French and published in the Institute for Social Research's
journal, *Zeitschrift für Sozialforschung* in May 1936. As the
first consideration, the essay brings to the fore the profound
impact of modern technological apparatuses on the human
sensory capacity. However, it uniquely links this impact with
the wider historical transformation of culture, that is, the
displacement of literary culture by the emergence of a new
mass culture within urban capitalist modernity. In doing so,
the essay tries to grasp the emergence of a new mass public
as protagonist in this new media culture, and to assess its
political implications.

There is no doubt that the Work of Art essay is the culmination of his life-long attempt to elaborate a 'materialist'
theory of art. Nevertheless, its work-in-progress character
and the substantial revisions of the various versions provide
complexities of structure. Given its structural complex-
ity, we can draw on Benjamin's own outline in a fragment,
'Theory of Distraction' (SW3, 141–2), which was written
shortly before he started to write the Work of Art essay. In
this writing plan, he integrates three seminal thematic concepts: 'Reproducibility – Distraction – Politicization'. These
three key concepts guide us in reconstructing the essay in a
systematic way and in critically assessing its theoretical relevance for today's media culture.

PHOTOGRAPHIC REPRODUCIBILITY

Key Works
'News about Flowers' (1928)
'Little History of Photography' (1931)
'Paul Valéry' (1931)
'The Rigorous Study of Art' (1932)
'The Present Social Situation of the French Writer' (1934)
'The Work of Art in the Age of Its Technological Reproducibility:
    Second Version' (1936)
'Letter from Paris (2): Painting and Photography' (1936)

Art and Technology

In the Work of Art essay, Benjamin introduces the notion of
'technological reproducibility' as a key aspect of photography, which designates not only the technological capabilities
to copy but also, more importantly, to unravel the nucleus
of historical change: 'What is at stake is not to portray literary works in the context of their age, but to represent

the age that perceives them – our age – in the age during
which they arose. It is this that makes literature into an
organ of history' (SW2, 464). By means of 'technological
reproducibility', Benjamin intends to underscore a potential-
ity of technology that is 'never fully realized or realizable'.[1]
In doing so, he aims to elucidate the intensive reciprocity
between the work of art and historicity, that is, the correspondence between technological development and a specific
historical era. Benjamin derived the idea of the historicity
of the works of art and technology from three prominent
figures. The first is the Austrian art historian Alois Riegl
(1858–1905). Whereas traditional art critics tend to see the
history of art in terms of a rise or fall in artistic standards,
Riegl opposes this conventional formalism and posits the
reciprocity between a particular style of art and art history
with reference to *Kunstwollen*, 'a will to art' or 'an immanent
artistic volition'. In his *Late Roman Art Industry* (1901), he
defines the notion thus: 'The plastic *Kunstwollen* regulates
man's relationship to the sensibly perceptible appearance of
things. Art expresses the way man wants to see things shaped
or coloured, just as the poetic *Kunstwollen* expresses the way
man wants to imagine them. Man is not only a passive, sensory recipient, but also a desiring, active being who wishes
to interpret the world in such a way.'[2] Riegl underscores that
a fundamental intention plays a role to produce a work of
art and to continue the historical transition of art. Viewed
from this point of view, the late Roman art industry is less
akin to a decadent style, as conventional art critics identify it,
than to a certain transitional stage from ancient to modern.
It leads Benjamin to recognize that historicity of art can only
be grasped when certain stages of technological development
are conceived as social and political conditions. In terms of
an artistic volition, Riegl is interested in showing the intersection between sensory organization and cultural expression

and in re-evaluating 'the spatial qualities of visual art around
the time that the new medium of cinema was impressing
its audiences with the apparent physical immediacy of the
moving image'.[3] His distinction between haptic and optical
images helps Benjamin to investigate the physiological nature
of cinematic experience from the perspective of 'mutually
constitutive exchange' between the spectator and images and
from the multidimensional interplay between technology,
body and space.[4] Riegl's emphasis on the beholder's active
corporeal engagement with the reception process provides a
key theoretical motif to Benjamin's analysis of physiological
features of cinematic experience and the rise of a new mode
of collective subjectivity.

Secondly, the central European modernist project in
architecture, which involved Le Corbusier, Adolf Loos and
Siegfried Giedion, stimulated Benjamin's critical imagination on the changing nature of spatial perception. In
particular, Giedion's *Building in France* (1928), a study of the
origins of iron and glass architecture, influenced Benjamin's
understanding of the modernist project in architecture, and
the shift in perception from the individual optic to the collective tactile. As McCole notes, what Benjamin sees in the
architectural avant-garde, then, is 'not a model of rationalization and efficiency but the constructive anticipating a
form of social practice that breaks with bourgeois society'.[5]
From the perspective of the radical reception of technology,
ranging from architectural to communication technologies,
Benjamin is drawn to the enormous potential of technology
and its formative role in changing the nature of aesthetic
practice. For Benjamin, building, the prototype for the work
of art, is appropriated by means of tactile distraction. In his
analysis of the interface between space and the human sensorium, Benjamin brings forth tactile perception as a vital
feature of the experience of place:

Buildings are received in a twofold manner: by use and by perception. Or, better: tactilely and optically. Such reception cannot be understood in terms of the concentrated attention of a traveler before a famous building. On the tactile side, there is no counterpart to what contemplation is on the optical side. Tactile reception comes about not so much by way of attention as by way of habit. The latter largely determines even the optical reception of architecture, which spontaneously takes the form of casual noticing, rather than attentive observation. Under certain circumstances, this form of reception shaped by architecture acquires canonical value. (SW3, 120)

In his view, architecture is an engineering technology that emancipates construction from 'art' by providing a new configuration of spatio-temporal perception that again differs from the optical perception of works of art such as paintings.

Thirdly, the work of the French poet and literary theorist Paul Valéry (1871–1945) leads Benjamin to consider the subordination of intellectual activity to technological advancement and to explore how a materialist art theory corresponds to the deterioration of bourgeois ideals of art, the artist and intellectualism. Benjamin's 1931 essay, 'The Present Social Situation of the French Writer' (SW2, 744–67), emphatically underscores Valéry's distinctive constructivist approach to art, which draws attention to the impact of technology on art itself. While classical humanism attributes the source of creative writing to faculties like genius, inspiration, creativity, eternal value, mystery and spirit, Valéry tries to demystify artistic creativity by identifying the literary work as primarily the result of technical production. In contrast to the responses of Romanticism or reactionary modernism, Valéry's account of the technological nature of art does not attempt to retrieve outmoded humanist ideas of art. Valéry's technical understanding of art leads Benjamin to think of artwork not as a creation and inspiration but as a construction and technique, in which 'analysis, calculation and planning play the principal roles' (SW2, 757). The artist becomes no more than an engineer or producer, an aesthetic or literary engineer.

Fourthly, the Hungarian painter and photographer László Moholy-Nagy (1895–1946) underscores the technological potential of photography for cognitive and perceptual change in terms of production and reproduction. Benjamin was captivated by this modernist's insight into the impact of photography on modernization and rationalization of perceptual and aesthetic response. Moholy-Nagy's seminal essay of 1922, 'Production and Reproduction', characterizes photography as a technological prosthesis, anticipating McLuhan's later idea of the media as extensions of the body. Moholy-Nagy, a prominent professor of design at the famous Bauhaus school in Weimar, strongly advocated the idea of constructivism as a new principle of art and design, arguing that art should be integrated into industry by means of new technology. In his seminal Bauhaus book, *Painting, Photography, Film* (1925), Moholy-Nagy tried to reveal the interrelationship of type, audio and visual perception of all the visual arts from a scientific perspective by utilizing all sorts of creative techniques such as collage, montage and even pictures of X-rays.[6] Following these technological ideas on art, Benjamin intended to show how new media like photography challenged hitherto dominant aesthetic concepts (e.g., beautiful representation, the autonomy of the artist, and the very notion of art itself) and to adduce the new principles of mass culture. The advent of photography designated more than just the improvement of technology; rather, it attested to a deepening crisis in the conventional form of art and coincided with the emergence of a new

socio-political system. In his use of technological reproducibility, the implication of 'technology' is twofold. In a narrow
context, the term designates specific techniques involved in
the reproduction of a work of art, such as etching, printing and lithography. In a broader context, it refers to the
reproduction of 'social relations'. In the age of photographic
reproducibility, the reproduction of art connotes less a plu-
rality, or 'a mere collection of individual occurrences', but
more 'a mass'.[7] While the development of printing technology and newspapers corresponded with the rise of a
bourgeois class and the advent of industrial capitalism, the
progress of photographic technology signalled the rise of
mass society and a crisis in bourgeois culture.

Art-as-Photography

For Benjamin, photography designates the emergence of
both a new art form and a new society. Since the first successful experiment in 1838 by Louis Jacques Mandé Daguerre in
his Paris studio, the advent of photography quickly surpassed
all previous reproduction technologies, and led to an entirely
different stage of media culture. The historical transformation of reproduction technologies moves from founding
and stamping in the Greek era, through the advancement
of xylography, engraving and etching in the Middle Ages,
to lithography at the end of the eighteenth century, which
enabled graphic art to reproduce illustrations of everyday
life; yet photography is the 'first truly revolutionary means
of reproduction', profoundly enhancing the human sensory
apparatus and enabling a new form of aesthetic experience
to stretch across the entire social spectrum. Benjamin's 1931
essay 'Little History of Photography' was one of the first
comprehensive studies of the diverse issues raised by photography. Previously, portraits – painted for and owned only by

the ruling class – had been conceived as symbols of authority and a spectacle of power. Photography made the bourgeois family, and then the masses, owners of their own images. Compared to imposing paintings on and for the aristocracy, photography's honest reflection of reality truly fulfils the aesthetic expectations of ordinary people. The fact that family photos dominated early photography in part indicates that the photographic image itself was still recognized only as a technological substitute for painting, albeit one capable of producing more real yet melancholic images of family. As Pierre Bourdieu indicates, photography as a symbol of middle-brow art 'entirely fulfills the aesthetic expectations of the working classes'.[8] While earlier photographic images produced by daguerreotypes and salt prints were still shrouded in mystique, modernist photographers now began conceiving of photography as a communication technology and began to replace the informational functions of painting with a new reality. The moment that photography overpowers painting is crucial: 'On the rise of photography – Communications technology reduces the informational merits of painting. At the same time, a new reality unfolds, in the face of which no one can take responsibility for personal decisions. One appeals to the lens. Painting, for its part, begins to emphasize color' (AP [Y5,3], 678). In his essay, 'Little History of Photography', Benjamin closely examines prominent modernist photographers of the 1920s and 1930s, who eventually liberated the potential of a new communication technology from the old aesthetic form, that is, the 'fetishistic and fundamentally antitechnological concept of art' (SW2, 508).

Karl Blossfeldt (1865–1932), a German photographer and professor at the Berlin College of Fine Arts, was well known for his close-up photographs of plant anatomy under extreme magnification. In his seminal book, *Originary Forms of Art* [*Urformen der Kunst*] 1928, Blossfeldt seeks to demonstrate that photography enables us to approach nature as a master teacher by imitating forms that recur in the natural world. In 'News about Flowers' (SW2, 155–7), a short review of Blossfeldt's book, Benjamin introduces the issue of photographic reality, arguing that Blossfeldt's photographs unleash the microscopic capability of the camera onto a newly configured reality. The crucial function of photography's close approach to nature demystifies the work of art, but more crucially photography reveals a new reality, that is, a technologically reconfigured reality, which is more natural than nature. As Mertins aptly sums up, Benjamin's analysis of Blossfeldt's photographs registers the link between his various ideas: that 'the most precise technology can give its products a magical value'; that 'the photographic enlargement can reveal a secret within the physiognomic surface of things' and that 'that secret is visible in a tiny spark of contingency with which reality has seared the subject'.[9] In the wake of photographic images, the perception of reality itself began to be profoundly challenged. In similar vein, Benjamin probes the work of August Sander (1876–1974), a German portrait and documentary photographer, whose series 'People of the 20th Century', exhibited portraits of a diverse group of people (a cook, circus people, a banker and so on). Inspired by the New Objectivity [Neue Sachlichkeit] art movement, Sander sought to wrench people's images free from the constricting conventions of bourgeois portraiture. For Benjamin, Sander's photographic image is 'no longer portrait' and 'the tremendous physiognomic gallery' created 'from a scientific view' (SW2, 520). If Sanders photographs unlock the scientific documentation of people from portrait, the French photographer Eugène Atget (1857–1927) decisively liberated photographic reality from the picturesque aesthetic it inherited from painting. At last people disappeared from photos: Atget's images of Parisian streets and surroundings only included empty spaces and discarded objects. His photographic images replaced the 'exotic, romantically sonorous' aspects of early photography with a 'salutary estrangement between man and his surroundings'. He was 'an actor' who 'wiped off the mask and then set about removing the makeup from reality' (SW2, 518). Benjamin linked the function of Atget's photos with the work of the Surrealists. Surrealist literary works endeavoured to blur the boundaries between the mythic and modern characteristics of urban life by integrating familiar objects into unfamiliar situations (e.g., Duchamp's urinal). Atget's photos served to defamiliarize the most familiar objects and awaken the beholder's unconsciousness. What could be more familiar than our streets? Atget's Paris street photos eradicated the mystic images still rooted in 'conventional portrait photography in the age of decline' (SW2, 518), and thereby liberated the photograph as a technological artefact from the thrall of painting.

The theoretical issue that Benjamin underlines here is that modernist photography transforms the relationship between art and technology. We no longer ponder 'the aesthetics of photography-as-art' but the social implications of 'art-as-photography' (SW2, 520). The technological nature of photography reveals not only hitherto unknown realities of nature but also the social dimension of reality itself. At this point, Benjamin's perception of art-as-photography challenges the objectivity of representation by highlighting the slippage of actual reality into the functional. Benjamin ascribes a great deal of credibility to photographic practices that disenchant and demystify the reified world by penetrating reality. In the age of photography, reality is hardly free from technological apparatus and becomes 'the height of artifice'. Recognizing the technological construction of reality, Benjamin thus calls immediate or technology-free reality 'the Blow Flower in the land of technology' (SW3, 115), an imaginary flower that was sought by a medieval poet but never found. Photographic technology renders pointless any conventional questioning of the representation of reality and illusion. Reality becomes an artificially reconfigured object and all experiences, in a sense, become technological, as the term technology itself signifies the artificial organization of perception. The question about the nature of modern aesthetic experience specifically conditioned by photographic technology is not *what* is perceived but *how* the beholder perceives the image.

Likewise, rather than dismissing the photographic image as being a mere representational illusion, Benjamin underscores its role in the construction of social reality itself, providing modern mass consumer society with the reified form of social reality. The advertisement is the necessary outcome created by the photography's capability of aestheticizing social reality. The photographic reproducibility led to the burgeoning of illustrated magazines, and arty journalism and the photographic beautification of the social reality increasingly reified human relations, in other words, 'they are no longer explicit' (SW2, 526). In Benjamin's view, photography provided the material condition for the massive scale of spectacle of commodity culture.

The Decline of Aura

Aura, literarily referring to 'breeze or breath' in Greek, is a central concept in Benjamin's thought of art, technology and experience. This term first appears in the protocols of his experiments with hashish from March 1930 ('Hashish, Beginning of March 1930', SW2, 327–30). From the 'theosophist' perspective, he conceives aura to be an everyday phenomenon, that is, 'an ornamental halo, in which the object or being is enclosed as in a case' (SW2, 328). To underscore its magical rays from daily objects, Benjamin exemplifies Van Gogh's late paintings, where 'the aura appears to have been painted together with the various objects' (SW2, 328). The concept is elucidated in greater depth in 'Little History of Photography' and the Work of Art essay. He links it with the achievement of the modernist photography, in particular, Atget's one: 'He [Atget] was the first to disinfect the stifling atmosphere generated by conventional portrait photography in the age of decline. He cleans this atmosphere – indeed, he dispels it altogether: he initiates the emancipation of object from aura' (SW2, 518). Then, Benjamin offers a quite enigmatic definition of aura:

> A strange weave of space and time: the unique appearance or semblance of distance, no matter how close it may be. While at rest on a summer's noon, to trace a range of mountains on the horizon, or a branch that throws its shadow on the observer, until the moment or the hour become part of their appearance – this is what it means to breathe the aura of those mountains, that branch. (SW2, 518–19)

The notion of aura in his essays on photography and film illustrates a particular way of perceiving a work of art, centring on the reciprocity between the work of art and the beholder. As defined above, the uniqueness of the experience of the mountain involves the conjuncture of a specific time and place, that is, a co-presence (of subject and object) and yet distance (between subject and object) in the now. However, photographic technology does not confine the experience of its image-worlds to a particular temporality or spatiality. In terms of aura, what holds for the experience of nature in the quotation holds for the work of art. Benjamin contrasts the unreproducibility of the work of art with the technologically inherently reproducible photographic image. To be more specific, while the auratic experience relates to unique duration and mythic distance, the experience of the photographic image derives from its ubiquity and transient proximity. The traditional mode of aesthetic experience (that of painting, for instance) is predicated upon an adequate distance between the work of art and the observer – a distance that is the prerequisite for reflection and aesthetic judgement. In contrast, the photographic image is reproduced by the mass's desire to diminish that distance and does not return their gaze. Whereas the decline of aura entails the end of the conventional form of aesthetic autonomy, the collapse of reciprocity between the reproduced photographic image and the beholder constitutes the core foundation of post-auratic mass culture.

> If the distinctive feature of the images arising from *mémoire involontaire* is seen in their aura, then photography is decisively implicated in the phenomenon of a 'decline of the aura'. What was inevitably felt to be inhuman – one might even say deadly – in daguerreotypy was the (prolonged) looking into the camera, since the camera records our likeness without returning our gaze. Inherent in the gaze, however, is the expectation that it will be returned by that on which it is bestowed. (SW4, 338)

The fact that the object at the nascent stage of photographic technology was the portrait (whether of parents, children, lovers or oneself) tells of the desire of the emerging masses to own their images, images hitherto unapproachable and withheld from them, and thereby to destroy the unique and authentic nature of the aesthetic object. Of course, this primary desire persists in the age of the digital camera, or has even been enhanced by personalized digital communication technology. But one thing is certain: in the process of the reproduction, the aura of the original has begun to diminish: 'The peeling away of the object's shell, the destruction of the aura, is the signature of a perception whose sense of the sameness of things has grown to the point where even the singular, the unique, is divested of its uniqueness – by means of its reproduction' (SW2, 519). Here, the notion of aura connotes the unique and unapproachable features of the work of art, that is, the particular spatial and temporal context of the work of art with respect to its originality and authenticity, 'the here and now of the work of art' or 'its unique existence in a particular place' (SW3, 103). The aura cannot be reproduced, copied or duplicated.

Just as the notion of aura is helpful in identifying the quintessence of the conventional work of art such as painting, theatre and music, its decline correspondingly reflects the birth of a new mode of art corresponding to changing social and technological conditions. Locating the concept of the commodity at the centre of his analysis of the intensive reciprocity of art and society, Benjamin employs two analytical concepts from Marx's political-economic approach to the value system of the commodity: 'cult value' (*Kultwert*) and 'exhibition value' (*Ausstellungswert*). While 'cult value' denotes the ritual and magical features of art, 'exhibition value' indicates those technical aspects of art that are on display. The decline of aura signals the displacement of cult value by exhibition value. As with painting, photography in its infancy was surrounded by cult value. As the human subject withdraws from the photographic image, for the first time exhibition value begins to take precedence over cult value. Atget's images of deserted Parisian streets show foremost the waning of aura and the decline of ritual experience.

As Benjamin sees exhibition value replacing cult value, two areas of thematic significance emerge: quantitative changes in art and the qualitative transformation of the nature of art. With respect to quantitative change, cult value refers to the esoteric nature of the work of art and its restricted accessibility to exclusive groups. With the development of technological reproducibility (increasing, for example, the possibilities for transferring art works from place to place), the opportunities for the exhibition of art increase. In this context of the approachability and uniqueness of art works, the emergence of their exhibition value illuminates the heightened public accessibility and visibility of art. As art becomes increasingly more accessible to the masses, the aura of the art work, rooted in its unapproachability, withers. Herein lies the revolutionary function of technological reproducibility, which realizes 'the desire of the present day masses to "get closer" to things, and their equally passionate concern for overcoming each thing's uniqueness by assimilating it as a reproduction' (SW3, 105, original emphasis). The democratization of the reception of visual images is inseparably interwoven with 'the increasing emergence of the masses' and 'the growing intensity of their movements' (SW3, 105), which precipitates the other change in the nature of the art work. The crowd is reproduced, since it encounters itself in the image of the masses.

The rapid advancement of photographic technology accelerated the individual use of the camera in modern culture: 'the camera is getting smaller and smaller, ever readier to capture fleeting and secret images whose shock effect paralyzes the associative mechanisms in the beholder' (SW2, 527). Photography, privatized and individually owned, accelerates 'the literarization of the condition of life' by representing the masses in illustrated magazines or on newsreels, just as newspapers turn the crowd into the reading public. Thanks to individualized photography, we have witnessed the rise of a new public who incessantly record their everyday lives and share these images with other publics. We can easily observe the social implications of the 'literarization of the condition of life' through the contemporary daily use of digital photos constantly shared via social media such as Facebook, Twitter and various image-hosting websites like Flickr. A new kind of media literacy began with the advent of the wide propagation of photographic images. In the age of the photograph (that is, the reproduced image, artificial reality), in which everyone is entitled to produce, own and propagate their own images, 'an illiterate' comes to designate 'the photographer who cannot read his own pictures' (SW2, 527).

As for the qualitative change in art, this is linked to its function. The unique value of the authentic work of art is grounded in ritual. In premodern times, the primary function of a work of art was as an instrument of magic or religion. New media emancipated art from 'its parasitical dependence on ritual', instigating the collapse of the autonomous aspect of art, yet 'the whole social function of art [was] revolutionized' (SW3, 106). The predominance of exhibition value indicates that the social function of art is based on 'politics'. The primary political function of art is to mediate the interplay between 'nature and humanity', that is, to 'train human beings in the apperceptions'. As we shall see, the decline of aura cannot be understood unless careful consideration is given to Benjamin's account of the political attributes of new media. The invention of photography by no means signifies the destruction of aura *per se*; rather, it involves the emergence of technological conditions that disrupt art's cult value. Cult value can be resurrected, albeit discontinuously, by any form of new media: Benjamin sees this in the emergence of the 'Führer cult' in Nazi Germany and the rise of stardom in the Hollywood entertainment industry. In the capacity previously specified in itself, Benjamin's analysis of art and mass culture represents the turbulent political era of the 1920s and 1930s when totalitarian regimes were rapidly emerging across Europe. I will return to the issue of the media and politics in the third section of this chapter.

THE MEDIA CULTURE OF DISTRACTION

Key Works

'On the Present Situation of Russian Film' (1927)

'Reply to Oscar A.H. Schmitz' (1927)

'Chaplin in Retrospect' (1929)

'Mickey Mouse' (1931)

'The Formula in Which the Dialectical Structure of Film Finds Expression' (1935)

'Theory of Distraction' (1936)

'The Paris of the Second Empire in Baudelaire' (1938)

'The Work of Art in the Age of Its Technological Reproducibility: Third Version' (1939)

The Optical Unconscious

In the 1920s and 1930s, the cinematic technologies were swiftly developing and changing the main aspects of the entertainment industries. In 1927, *The Jazz Singer*, the first motion picture with synchronized sound, was premiered, marking the rapid decline of the silent film and the increasing domination of the sound film. In the wake of the arrival of talkies, or 'talking pictures', Benjamin is still preoccupied with the questions about the intersection of the image of silent film and the reception process. His questions ask whether film is the medium of repetition and replication *par excellence* and, if so, does the infinite reiterability of the reception process improve the mimetic faculty? What still fascinates Benjamin is the fact that, in the way the movie camera – whether of the silent film or the sound film – arrests the flow of perception and captures physical movement, everyday lives can be grasped in intricate detail on film. Through his analysis of Blossfeldt's photography of magnified nature, Benjamin investigated the construction of photographic reality. But what is a perceptive dimension of the subject engaging with this image? A new mode of perception emerges in the realm of cinematic reception, where the spatio-temporal organization of experience is artificially reconfigured: 'With the close-up, space expands: with slow motion, movement is extended' (SW3, 117). Interestingly, the movie camera not only extends the comprehension of reality, but also opens up an immense and unexpected field of action. Likening the magician to the painter, Benjamin draws a famous comparison between the function of the surgeon and that of the cameraman. As the surgeon cuts into the patient's body and penetrates it, so the cameraman enters into the web of reality, and offers a technologically reconfigured version of it. The camera's thorough penetration of reality uncovers hidden aspects of the subject.

The new space discovered by the camera corresponds with 'a space informed by the unconscious'. The analogy of psychoanalysis and the unconscious is advanced in connection with the discovery of a new reality. The photographic image world uncovers a new image-space that was hidden not only from the naked eye but also from consciousness. Benjamin underscores the discovery of the optical unconscious thus: 'Photography, with its devices of slow motion and enlargement, reveals the secret. It is through photography that we first discover the existence of this optical unconscious, just as we discover the instinctual unconscious through psychoanalysis' (SW2, 511–12). As psychoanalysis discovers the unconscious instinctual level of our mind and behaviour, photography unearths a hidden dimension of reality. As McQuire underlines, the analogical comparison

between photography and psychoanalysis is more suggestive
than Benjamin thought, revealing 'the fragmented body as
a structure of deep psychic meaning'.[10] In a similar way to
that in which psychoanalysis grapples with the minutiae of
everyday life in the form of 'slips, lapses and insignificant
babble', photography seizes 'trivia, junk and the residues of
daily life'.[11] This comparison emphasizes the fact that both
photographic and psychoanalytic techniques 'emerged in an
historical conjuncture in which older semantic structures
were breaking down in the face of new experiences (urban
industrial acceleration, mechanized warfare)'.[12]

A salient feature of photography as a new medium includes
its capability of configuring a distinct time. For Benjamin,
unlike the subject of paintings, the photographic image primarily comprises the double features of time: pastness and
immediacy. The spontaneous and instantaneous characteristics of the image coincide with the modernist perception of the
quintessence of social reality as 'snap-shots'.[13] Photography
is the emblematic medium corresponding to the dialectical
image, Benjamin's seminal epistemological concept, a flash-
like image at a standstill. The photographic image world
deriving from the moment of the here and now is only recognized after the moment; that is, only in the future. In the
age of photographic and cinematic representation, as Virilio
underscores, the conventional tenses of action (past, present
and future) began to be replaced on a social scale by two
tenses, 'real time' and 'delayed time'.[14] This contingency
distinguishes the photographic image from other traditional
pictorial images reproduced by painting, engraving and
etching. The hidden aspect of reality was the source of the
'magical' value of the image. But, now, thanks to photography, we are capable of grasping the reality by tearing up the
mysterious screen of the image, just as psychoanalysis explains
the 'magical' nature of dreams. The world we have known

is unravelled in a profoundly different way. Herein lies the revolutionary role of technological reproducibility:

> Our bars and city streets, our offices and furnished rooms, our railroad stations and our factories seemed to close relentlessly around us. Then came film and exploded this prison-world with the dynamite of the split second, so that now we can set off calmly on journeys of adventure among its far-flung debris. (SW3, 117)

The optical unconscious yields the effect of disenchantment, and a more rational and mechanical perception of human nature and photographic image worlds shatter the magical and mysterious value surrounding the image. For Benjamin, photographically reproduced images do not simply reflect the reality but construct it, leading to new ways of perceiving, reasoning and awakening.

Shock Experience

For Benjamin, technology had already become the key apparatus of the human body and the increasingly intimate relation between technology and humanity cannot be more evident than in photography. Benjamin's approach to the nature of 'civilization' explores 'the new forms of behaviour' and the 'new economically and technologically based creations' (AP, 14). His main question reflects how the technologization of human action takes place across the entire social spectrum in relation to the development of media. He justifies this idea of the technologization of human action by focusing on changes in haptic and optic experience. For instance, with regard to haptic experience, Benjamin observes that the invention of safety matches in the nineteenth century triggered a variety of innovations that converged in that one abrupt movement

of the hand: for example, the lifting of a receiver, and switching, inserting and pressing of the telephone; the snapping of
the photographer; the use of the typewriter, and so on. We
can easily imagine the progress of this relation all the way to
the use of fingers for today's smartphones with their multifunctional technologies. For the first time in the process of
pictorial reproduction, photography deprived the hand of its
most important artistic functions, which henceforth involved
only the eye looking into a lens. Since the eye perceives
more swiftly than the hand can draw, the process of pictorial reproduction was accelerated so enormously that it could
keep pace with speech.

Significantly, this new media experience corresponds to
the everyday experience of urban spaces: 'The camera gave
the moment a posthumous shock, as it were. Haptic experiences of this kind were joined by optical ones, such as are
supplied by the advertising pages of a newspaper or the traffic
of a big city' (SW4, 328). Following his sociological prede-
cessor Georg Simmel's perceptive insight into the dynamic
rhythm of the metropolitan streets, Benjamin figures the
disrupted perception of urban spectacle as a shock experience and attributes it to the nucleus of the spatio-temporal
register of sense perception of the city. 'Moving through
this traffic involves the individual in a series of shocks and
collisions. At dangerous intersections, nervous impulses
flow through him in rapid succession, like the energy from
a battery' (SW4, 328). As Jonathan Crary points out, while
attention is 'a question of an engagement of the body',
'an inhibition of movement' and 'a state of consciousness
arrested in the present', the emergence of shock experience unravels a noble challenge, a crisis in perception itself,
that is, 'a crisis what is the result of a sweeping remaking
of the observer by a calculated technology of the individual,
derived from new knowledge of the body'.[15] Furthermore,

the way in which shock experience becomes a normal part of everyday life in modern society produces actual physiological changes; the urban experience becomes standardized and consequently collectivized. The Work of Art essay brings forth the interplay of shock experience for the urban dweller and the worker's experience at the machine.

> Thus technology has subjected the human sensorium to a complex kind of training. There came a day when a new and urgent need for stimuli was met by film. In a film, perception conditioned by shock [*schockförmige Wahrnehmung*] was established as a formal principle. What determines the rhythm of production on a conveyor belt is the same thing that underlies the rhythm of reception in the film. (SW4, 328)

For Benjamin, cinema is a distinct urban space that plays a role in training social behaviour among urban dwellers. Working with machines, workers learn to coordinate their own movements with the uniformly constant movements of automation. By means of a close examination of these conditions, Benjamin reaches the critical conclusion that such a subjugation of experience by machinery engenders social discipline and results in the material conditions of collective reception: 'The shorter the training period of an industrial worker, the longer the basic training of a military man. It may be part of society's preparation for total war that training is shifting from techniques of production to techniques of destruction' (SW4, 350). In contrast to the conventional form of aesthetic experience, in the experience of film, Benjamin finds the conditions for a new mode of social experience and the emergence of a new social subject articulated by those new technological experiences. The reception process engendered by film constitutes the radical basis for a new type of social subject. The quintessential feature of the filmic experience in contrast to the perception of painting rests in its 'simultaneous and collective' dimension. Whereas the experience of the authentic art work is conducted solely by an individual within the restricted spatio-temporal context of the here and now, film-watching can be repeated at any time and practised collectively by audiences anywhere around the globe. Yet this collective mode of reception should be differentiated from the one acquired through oral communication, exemplified by storytelling, as discussed in the previous chapter. Cinematic collective reception is no longer rooted in face-to-face interaction or communal communication circumscribed by the here and now, but is primarily mediated by the media spectacle. It differs from the communal experience of storytelling in the sense of its simultaneousness, whereby spatio-temporal differences are no longer significant. If so, the next question concerns as to how cinema audiences or the movie-going public become a new kind of spectator distinct from consumers in the age of mass media and, at the same time, mass consumption.

Distracted Critics

Benjamin argues that cinema as a media space offers a public space where distraction and reflexive judgement are not incompatible. Whereas the decline of aura entails the crisis of individual attentiveness, the standardization of shock experience in urban everyday life involves the establishment of a new mode of perception, distraction. For Benjamin 'distraction, like catharsis, should be conceived as a physiological phenomenon' (SW3, 141). While the art lover still regards the art work as a magical or sacred object, the masses conceive of film as nothing but a means of entertainment and cinema-going as a part of leisure life. In the cinema, 'contemplative' attention is simply impossible; here only the 'distracted' attention of the audience recurs through a succession of shocks and direct stimuli. Distraction is a necessary outcome of the shock experience of film. Benjamin underlines the way in which the fragmentation of film frames tends to impede the viewer's concentration. While a painting invites the beholder to be contemplative, he or she cannot be so before a film frame; while a painting consists of a total vista, the pictures captured by the camera consist of 'multiple fragments': 'No sooner has he seen it than it has already changed. It cannot be fixed on' (SW4, 267). The originality of Benjamin's analysis lies in his argument that critical consciousness is not incompatible with shock-laden visual perception. *'Reception in distraction – the sort of reception that is increasingly noticeable in all areas of art and is a symptom of profound changes in apperception – finds in film its true training ground.* Film, by virtue of its shock effects, is predisposed to this form of reception' (SW3, 120, original emphasis).

The distinguishing feature of Benjamin's account of film, which marks him out from other contemporary Weimar film theorists such as Béla Bálazs (1884–1949), or other cultural critics such as Adorno, is his radical claim that in film these otherwise discrepant perceptions (visual pleasure and critical judgement) are not only inseparable and compatible but even complementary. Benjamin found a middle ground in which education and consumer values correspond in a new kind of media experience. Likewise, shock experience of urban spectacle plays twofold roles, as Gunning points out, not only as 'a mode of modern experience' but also as 'a strategy of a modern aesthetics of astonishment'.[16] The cinema audience's sense of shock derives from 'an unbelievable visual transformation occurring before their eyes, parallel to the greatest wonders of the theatre'.[17] Benjamin locates the emancipatory potential of a distracted mode of reception in its capacity to reorganize human sensorium corresponding to the speedy and abrupt urban rhythm and celebrates a construction of a new mass public whose capability of critical judgement is facilitated through the reception process in distraction.

In his attempt to elaborate the cinematic reception process, Benjamin is deeply influenced by his friend Siegfried Kracauer, who vividly illustrated the rise of a new mass culture and urban experiences in a metropolis like Berlin. Like Benjamin, Kracauer does not lament the disappearance of auratic aesthetic experience. In his 1926 essay, 'The Cult of Distraction: On Berlin's Picture Palaces', Kracauer reveals that contemplation and concentration are just obsolete modes of perception for the rising metropolitan culture. Distraction is a mode that coincides precisely with the city dweller's mode of experience, predicated upon the constant collision of momentary images and spectacles. The spectacle of mass culture requires no concentration and presupposes no intelligence, merely distraction and easy understanding. He illustrates the standardization of distracted reception in urban culture thus:

> There is little room left for the so-called educated classes, who must either join in the repast or maintain their snobbish aloofness. Their provincial isolation is, in any case, at an end. They are being absorbed by the masses, a process that creates the *homogeneous cosmopolitan audience* in which everyone has the same responses, from the bank director to the sales clerk, from the diva to the stenographer. Self-pitying complaints about this turn toward mass taste are belated; the cultural heritage that the masses refuse to accept has become to some extent merely a historical property, since the economic and social reality to which it corresponded has changed.[18]

Drawing upon Kracauer's analysis, Benjamin sees the revolutionary potential of distraction in the emerging new form of mass culture; in his view, distracted perception acquired through cinematic experience potentially coincides with critical judgement, and the mass audience can become a critic, albeit of a quite different kind from the traditional art connoisseur. The cinema audience constitutes nothing less than a 'distracted examiner' (SW4, 269). In Benjamin's view, public audiences are not just passive spectators or consumers; they are critical examiners, too. It is theoretically inapt and historically negligent to identify the audiences of the early cinema only as the inert passive consumers of mass culture. As Gunning felicitously indicates, they were 'not primarily gullible country bumpkins, but sophisticated urban pleasure seekers'.[19] Yet, how can the distracted reception transform these urban entertainment audiences to the critical examiner? Does Benjamin's analysis of distraction have a crucial ambivalence by mechanically and overly combining two incompatible dimensions: critical judgement and distraction? Or as many recent Benjamin scholars critically point out, does his analysis have a serious 'inconsistency' and operate 'in a peculiarly slippery manner'?[20]

The characterization of cinema audiences as distracted critics has given rise to many discussions in the field of media and cultural studies. Since Adorno's scathing criticism, Benjamin has been typically criticized for his overvaluation of 'machinery technology' and his underestimation of a still decisive role of high art.[21] It should be remembered that Benjamin's emphasis on 'the values of distraction' as the conditions of media experience that film provides entails 'the convergence of educational and consumer value in a new kind of learning'.[22] The intersection of these two values shows Benjamin's distinctive insight into the gradual transformation of traditional forms of art by the rise of a new mass culture. But, more importantly, Benjamin asks 'how' these two values can converge. He looks at the way in which distraction brings out a habitual mode of perception and appears to be a social condition of the convergence. Habit, as acquired in and through urban life, is then a paradigm of non-contemplative practical memory, which in turn is executed collectively. Benjamin stresses the critical potential of habitual behaviour acquired through corporeal engagement with surroundings: 'Even the distracted person can form habits. What is more, the ability to master certain tasks in a state of distraction first proves that their performance has become habitual . . . It does so currently in film' (SW3, 120). Whereas the aura embedded in traditional works of art is perceived through the single sense of vision, the new mode of media culture is communicated with an audience via the multiple senses of the body, defined as tactility. In his account, while optical perception is posited as the main cause of the ideological absorption of urban spectacle, tactile appropriation constitutes the core ground for the alternative mode of experience; in his own term, 'profane illumination' (SW2, 209). Distraction indicates less a paying attention elsewhere than a wider engagement of the multiple senses with mass media.

> For the tasks which face the human apparatus of perception at historical turning points cannot be performed solely by optical means – that is, by way of contemplation. They are mastered gradually – taking their cue from tactile reception – through habit. (SW3, 120)

Thus, in modern communications media, the tactile attribute of distraction stands in opposition to the hegemony of visuality. The new mass public is, as Taussig illustrates, 'a distracted collective reading with a tactile eye'.[23] Benjamin's analysis of the entertainment industry, detailed in *The Arcades Project*, is primarily elaborated in relation to these phenomena, that is, the emergence of a new mode of collective tactile perception in connection with the advancement of architectural technology as well as cinematographic technology. The relationship between architecture and spatio-temporal perception is central to Benjamin's account of the replacement of art with industrial production.

For Benjamin, cinema serves as an alternative model to the antiquated notion of the bourgeois public sphere and plays a constructive role in forming a new 'bodily collective' – in Benjamin's own terminology. At this point, Benjamin's insight goes substantially beyond the limitations of the avant-garde movements including surrealism. Cinematic space as a media space comprises multiple modes of space related to body, technology and image, and plays a role in forming a new collective subject. In his view, cinematic space represents the prototype of the entertainment industry received by a distracted mass of people, rather than an attentive individual. Emblematic of the interface between new technology, the spectacular image and tactile perception, cinema in the early twentieth century is capable of offering a 'play-space' [*Spielraum*] (SW4, 265). While play involves a form of mimetic faculty to liberate the restricted and alienated human sensorium, space entails a material condition for corporeal practice. Cinema designates a prototypical form of play-space in which optical image space and tactile space intersect via filmic and architectural technologies.[24] The movie-going experience encapsulates a specifically modern form of collective experience and a technically mediated form of sensory experience. This firmly differentiates the reception of a film from that of literature and the fine arts. It is vital that Benjamin's critical idea of profane illumination is considered from the perspective of the 'bodily collective', in which the cinema is conceived as a form of play-space for sensory, psychosomatic and aesthetic experience. Viewed from this perspective, Benjamin's insight is to have shown how the phantasmagoria of public space has resulted in the anaesthesia of the public body, and why, correspondingly, the objective of media critique should be the synaesthesia of the bodily collective. As we shall see in chapter 5, *The Arcades Project* provides a detailed analysis of the emergence of this new public and the development of the entertainment industry, with particular reference to the phantasmagoria of modernity.

MEDIA AND DEMOCRACY

Key Works
'The Political Groupings of Russian Writers' (1927)
'Theories of German Fascism' (1930)
'The Author as Producer' (1934)
'Hitler's Diminished Masculinity' (1934)
'Theological–Political Fragment' (1938)

Aesthetic Politics

In the context of the interplay of communication technology and politics, early twentieth-century Germany can be defined by the emergence of fascist movements and the rapid growth of new media such as radio and cinema. During the inter-war period, a number of radical German intellectual mandarins raised critical questions and provided insights that still merit careful theoretical consideration today. In the Weimar Republic, both conservative thinkers (such as Ludwig Klages (1872–1956), Oswald Spengler (1880–1936), and especially Ernst Jünger (1895–1998)) and left-oriented liberal intellectuals (such as Kurt Tucholsky (1890–1935), Thomas Mann (1875–1955), and Bertolt Brecht), to name a

few, were fully conscious of the profound transformation of
the bourgeois public sphere and the rise of a new mass culture.[25] Their primary responses to the impact of mass media
on politics, whether lamentations over the 'death' of deliberative politics or the enthusiastic embrace of a new era of
mass politics, converged in the crisis of liberal democracy.
Across the political spectrum, then, these were shared concerns and Benjamin, too, was quick to grasp the changing
dynamics of politics and the rapid growth of mass media
in Western Europe and Russia. Unlike those mandarins –
whether left-wing or right-wing – who were preoccupied
with the ideological and institutional dimensions of politics,
for Benjamin, as described in his 1930 essay, 'Theories of
German Fascism', politics is primarily concerned with identifying ways of organizing experience. Benjamin's media
critique conducts a more penetrating investigation of the
crisis of liberal democracy and the rise of fascism by analysing how aesthetic experiences are interwoven with the
formation of a political public.

Benjamin's insight into the relationship between art and
politics is famously set out in an explicit yet highly enigmatic
passage in the Work of Art essay:

> Humankind, which once, in Homer, was an object of con-
> templation for the Olympian gods, has now become one
> for itself. Its self-alienation has reached the point where it
> can experience its own annihilation as a supreme aesthetic
> pleasure. *Such is the aestheticization of politics, as practised by
> fascism. Communism replies by politicizing art.* (SW3, 122,
> original emphasis)

This concluding remark has led to some overly simplistic
interpretations of Benjamin's insights into the relationship
between art and politics. One of these reductive readings

of 'the aestheticization of politics' identifies fascism as a
quasi-Wagnerian total work of art, while 'the politicization of art' is interpreted as Benjamin's call for another
form of propagandist art that can mirror the aestheticization of politics.[26] These readings limit Benjamin's analysis
to a propagandist approach to art, and consequently miss
the radical context of Benjamin's critique of aesthetic politics. However, if Benjamin's remarks about politics in the
Work of Art essay are examined in conjunction with some
of his other works, his 'Theories of German Fascism'
(1930) and *The Arcades Project*, for example, it becomes
evident that Benjamin's account of the aestheticization of
politics is more than a politically oriented investigation of
the aesthetic dimensions of fascism. Equally, a contextual
reading also shows that 'the politicization of art' means
more than merely making culture a catalyst for communist propaganda. Some readings tend to align the thesis
with the claim that art should provide a particular kind
of vehicle for communist propaganda. True, Benjamin's
somewhat elusive use of the term 'communism' does tend
to invite such a narrow interpretation; but the term communism here actually oscillates between literal-historical
and metaphorical-utopian meanings. By the same token,
Benjamin's call for 'the politicization of art' neither signifies the mere subordination of one discourse (aesthetics)
to another (politics), nor suggests that art must manifest
political ideology or thematic tendentiousness.

The aestheticization of politics represents the focal point
of his account of both the crisis of liberal democracy as a
deliberative and representative political system and the emergence of fascism as a form of direct political communication
between a political power and the public. Benjamin attempts
to find exemplary figures and exponents who have been able
to aestheticize politics and to politicize art: contemporary

avant-garde movements that combine technology and political practice, such as Futurism, New Objectivity, Dadaism, Surrealism, Bauhaus and Brecht's Epic Theatre. The key to understanding the political dimension embedded in the Work of Art essay is to ask why Benjamin devoted himself to an essay that investigated the profoundly changing nature of art in the 1930s, the very period when fascist regimes were rapidly ascending and prevailing over democracies.

Benjamin draws particular attention to the role of technology in the fascist discourse on collective and historic experience. In a collection of essays entitled *War and Warrior* [*Krieg und Krieger*, 1930], edited by Ernst Jünger, right-wing intellectuals presented a mythic picture of the First World War and a heroic image of the 'warrior' by glorifying the experiences of the frontline. From their account, Benjamin elicits the pivotal features of German fascism: the mythification of experience and its subsequent transformation into the collective consciousness. Fascism manifests itself as a political power that is able to manipulate collective experience by identifying defeat in war with the loss of history. It is no coincidence that Jünger endeavours to associate the mythic experience of war with the representation of the masses. Jünger strives to demonstrate that the visual representation of the workers is not conditional or secondary but central to anti-bourgeois politics. This is parallel to Benjamin's discussion of aesthetic politics. Drawing on Jünger's argument, most studies of aesthetic politics conceive of the fascist public sphere as involving 'beautiful illusion' and tend to identify the mode of fascist political communication as the *Gesamtkunstwerk*, the total work of art. However, as Sontag points out, during the Nazi era it was not art that was subordinated to political needs, but politics that appropriated the rhetoric of art.[27] Goebbels asserts that 'politics is the highest and most comprehensive art there is and we who shape modern German policy feel ourselves to be artists . . . the task of art and the artist [being] to form, to give shape, to remove the diseased and create freedom for the healthy'.[28] In this context, Goebbels' speech about the relationship between politics and art signifies the totalitarian view of aesthetic politics and its idea of beauty as physical perfection. If fascist political communication is identified only with certain types of artwork, it restricts an analysis of aesthetic politics to an interpretation of illusion and the false representation of reality. This limited understanding repeats the fallacy of the theory of ideology, and consequently loses sight of the broader context of aesthetic politics, a politics that is inextricably interwoven with the development of the media. In his theory of propaganda, Goebbels devalues the written word due to the implication of reading for time and reflection and utilizes any possible media for sound and image propaganda.[29] Benjamin's analysis is more concerned with *how* fascist communication was able to replace moral and political judgement with aesthetic judgement through political spectacle with the help of the media.[30] His analysis is therefore less akin to the public choreography of political action than to the distinctive ways in which a new form of collectivity is formed and organized through the aesthetic experience of the political spectacle engendered by communication technologies.

Benjamin's essay, 'Theories of German Fascism', reveals how the fascist ideologues endeavour to mythologize the experience of war and to use it for the upheaval of national consciousness. The war experience is mythified through the beautification of the machinery of warfare and the mechanization of the human body. The mythification of war experience reaches its zenith in Filippo Tommaso Marinetti (1876–1944)'s 'Futurist Manifesto', which declares 'war is beautiful' (SW3, 121). This attitude towards war experience entails a

reactionary combination of mythic surrender of individuality to the spirit of war and the heroic identification with the
collective entity. In this vein, Benjamin argues that even very
'objective' images serve to beautify or aestheticize everyday
life, leading to the spectacle of politics. He exemplifies the
work of Albert Renger-Patzsch (1897–1966), a German
photographer of New Objectivity, who advocates straight
photographic realism, rejecting the romanticism of photographers, in his seminal work, *The World is Beautiful* [*Die Welt ist
schön: Einhundert photographische Aufnahmen*, 1928]. Benjamin
aptly indicates how political spectacle operates masquerading
as 'objectivity' in the photographic image: 'For it has succeeded
in transforming even abject poverty – by apprehending it in
a fashionably perfect manner – into an object of enjoyment.
For if it is an economic function of photography to restore
to mass consumption, by fashionable adaptation, subjects that
had earlier withdrawn themselves from it (springtime, famous
people, foreign countries), it is one of its political functions
to renew from within – that is, fashionably – the world as it
is' (SW2, 774–5). As we discussed in a previous section on
photography, Benjamin's analysis of the beautification of the
world underlines the slippage of technologically reproduced
reality into the functional and, in particular, political function. In the age of photography, reality becomes artificially or
technologically mediated, yet perfect, and is hardly ever free
from social and political functions even if the photograph can
be defined as 'objective'. For Benjamin, who gives credence to
the disenchanting function of photography, aesthetic politics
derives not only from spectacular images but also from very
realistic photographic images. Within aesthetic politics, the
political is redefined as the site of authentic experience and
the aestheticization of politics tends to reproduce collective
identification with the powerful by imbuing political figures
with mythic aura. Likewise Benjamin's insight into the aes-

theticization of politics unravels those aspects of the radical anti-modern project that attempt to retrieve the totality of social life, by overthrowing the fragmented and functionally differentiated modern experience.

The Transformation of the Visibility of Power

The aesthetic politics advocated by right-wing intellectuals, including the Futurists, exemplifies the penetration of the political sphere by spectacle, which aims to move the state beyond the liberal democratic code of legality, morality and political emancipation. Their mythic understanding of historic experience involves a political strategy that aligns mythic – yet, lived – experience with political consciousness and action. This particular thematic point is detailed in the Work of Art essay through an exploration of the impact of the media on the crisis of the representative system and the subsequent emergence of fascism. The Work of Art essay raises the central question of whether the increasing visibility of power and new possibilities brought about by communication technology lead to a 'crisis of representative democracy', which is predicated upon the transparent representation of public opinion, rather than more democratization or public engagement: 'The change noted here in the mode of exhibition – a change brought about by reproduction technology – is also noticeable in politics. *The crisis of democracies can be understood as a crisis in the conditions governing the public presentation of politicians*' (SW3, 128, original emphasis). Here, the crisis of bourgeois representative democracy centres on the convergence of politics and popular culture, a convergence that is engendered by communication technology.

Democracies exhibit the politician directly, in person, before elected representatives. The parliament is his public. But

innovations in recording equipment now enable the speaker
to be heard by an unlimited number of people while he is
speaking, and to be seen by an unlimited number shortly
afterward. This means that priority is given to presenting
the politician before the recording equipment. Parliaments
are becoming depopulated at the same time as theatres.
(SW3, 128)

Benjamin associates the collapse of parliamentary democracy with a transformation of the visibility of power; that
is, the representation of the ruler. For Benjamin, this transformation of the visibility of power is part of a broader
transition in the nature of politics.[31] In Western political
discourse, public means 'open to the public', 'performed
in front of spectators', while private, in contrast, is that
which is said or done in a restricted circle of people or,
taken to the extreme, in secret. In this sense, the public/
private dichotomy relates to publicness versus privacy,
openness versus secrecy, visibility versus invisibility.[32]
Benjamin's investigation into these changes in parliament
demonstrates that his analysis of the decay of aura in the
age of the mass media is not restricted to the area of art.
The crisis of representative democracy corresponds to the
emergence of fascism grounded upon the aestheticization
of politics, in much the same way as bourgeois literary culture is replaced by the entertainment industry, bound up
with the sensationalism and commodification of the information industry.

Benjamin believes that increases in the visibility of power
per se, sometimes together with a corresponding growth of
accessibility and openness, do not guarantee more democratization; rather he fears that it may increasingly be possible to
manipulate the representation of the ruler, which results in a
crucial undermining of representative democracy. Benjamin

thinks about the intersection of representation and visibility in three ways in relation to (a) the ruler, (b) the parliament, and (c) the masses:

(a–b) between the ruler and the parliamentary members;
(b–c) between parliamentary members and the masses; and
(a–c) between the ruler and the masses.

First, a–b. Benjamin argues that the omnipresence of the ruler leads 'parliament to be the spectator of the ruler', resulting in 'the theatricalization of parliament', and consequently 'parliaments, as much as theatres, are deserted' (SW3, 128). Right-wing intellectuals attributed the representative system to a distortion of the people's will and considered fascism to be a resolution to this problem. Benjamin, however, argues that fascist politics does not offer a resolution of the crisis of representation, but, in fact, simplifies the issue of representation and precipitates the theatricality of politics. It is increasingly noticeable that in modern politics, the representatives become the spectators and the parliament becomes the spectacle itself.

Second, b–c. As parliament is reduced to a mere audience of the ruler, there is a breakdown of representative democracy and a disempowerment of the people.

Third, a–c. Benjamin associates the rise of fascism with the increased visibility of the ruler. It becomes ever more possible for the ruler to be presented directly to the public with the aid of communication technology. Mass media like radio and film have an important role to play in accelerating the transformation of the visibility of power and of the political public sphere. Rulers are now asked to stand in front of the media and to make themselves public. Benjamin illustrates how media play a decisive role in the changing nature of political spectacle:

Radio and film are changing not only the function of the
professional actor but, equally, the function of those who,
like the politician, present themselves before these media.
The direction of this change is the same for the film actor
and the politician, regardless of their different tasks. It
tends towards the exhibition of controllable, transferable
skills under certain social conditions, just as sports first
called for such exhibition under certain natural conditions.
This results in a new form of selection – selection before
an apparatus – from which the champion, the star, and the
dictator emerge as victors. (SW3, 128)

In Benjamin's view, the wide dissemination of mass media is
the fundament upon which the modern politics of populism
is grounded: the ruler becomes capable of communicating to
people directly, not via their representatives. The function
of politics now substantially hinges upon the performance
of the actor-like ruler, a political event in which all, both
the ruler and the ruled, participate. Benjamin does not imply
that the development of the mass media inevitably serves
to maintain the ruler's dominance, but he observes that its
outcome is the victory of the dictator. In the degeneration
of parliamentary democracy and the growing importance
of the direct relationship between the ruler and the people,
Benjamin sees the dominant dynamic of fascist theatricality:
the victory of Hitler's visibility.

The predominance of exhibition value during the collapse
of bourgeois aesthetic categories, an issue discussed in the
previous section, is associated with the function of political
spectacle. In the first instance, Benjamin characterizes the
fundamental change in the function of the work of art as the
shift from cult value to political value. The replacement of
cult value by exhibition value demonstrates that, from now
on, art's primary function is to be put on 'display'. Above

all, art on display is never separated from 'political function'. If politics depends on the exposure and control of the body (or its image), a function that communication media render possible, then it should be asked whether it is possible to consider the politics of the spectacle or the politics of the visibility of power as being exemplary of all politics in the age of mass media. Here, Benjamin reaches the conclusion that the collective experience of technologically mediated spectacle becomes the dominant mode of political communication. Politics is bound up with the struggle for the visibility of power, even more so in the period following the emergence of electronic communication technology.

The Politics of Media Spectacle

The proliferation of fascist propaganda films in the 1930s leads Benjamin to investigate political spectacle in the light of the reproduction of the masses on the one hand, and the domination of politics by the dynamic of consumer culture on the other. Benjamin's account of political spectacle builds on his specific attempt to interpret the mediated iconography of power and the masses, and to demonstrate the affinity of fascist strategies of political communication with the entertainment industry in the era of high capitalism.

(1) The Reproduction of the Masses

Notably Benjamin's notion of technological reproducibility implies 'mass' reproduction. Mass reproduction relates to the emergence and transformation of the masses themselves: 'Mass reproduction is especially favored by the reproduction of the masses' (SW3, 132). A key feature of filmic technology lies in its crucial affinity with the logic of mass formation. Benjamin brings this issue to the fore: 'In great ceremonial processions, giant rallies and mass sporting events, and in war, all of which are now fed into the camera, the masses come face to face with themselves. This process, whose significance need not be emphasized, is closely bound up with the development of reproduction and recording technologies' (SW3, 132). Communication technology not only affects the visibility of power by virtue of the presentation of the ruler in parliament, but also plays a decisive role in the formation of the masses by means of the presentation of the masses themselves. 'Mass' visual representation technology, capable of crowd scenes and individual close-ups, realizes 'simultaneous mass reception' for the first time. It is this double media quality that makes it possible for film to enable the masses to *experience* themselves and to *enjoy* their own mass movements aesthetically.

> In general, mass movements are more clearly apprehended by the camera than by the eye. A bird's-eye view best captures assemblies of hundreds of thousands. And even when this perspective is no less accessible to the human eye than to the camera, the image formed by the eye cannot be enlarged in the same way as a photograph. This is to say that mass movements, and above all war, are a form of human behaviour especially suited to the camera. (SW3, 132–3)

When describing 'mass movements', Benjamin refers not only to the emergence of fascism but also to the socialist and communist movements of the early twentieth century, all of which are closely associated with the construction of a political public. Benjamin places a particular emphasis on the links between proletarian mass movements and their intersubjective and collective experience in the cinema: 'The proletariat is a collective, just as these spaces are collective spaces. And only here, in the human collective, can the film complete

the prismatic work that it began by acting on that milieu . . .
No other medium could reproduce this collective in motion'
(SW2, 18). Through the experience of seeing its own image,
a crowd recognizes itself as a mass. The representation of the
crowd as possessing a collective subjectivity is not secondary,
but central to politics rooted in mass movements.

(2) The Iconography of Political Spectacle

In a piece written around August 1934, Benjamin offers
a detailed exposition of the image of Hitler, comparing it
with the feminine cast of Charlie Chaplin's character as the
little tramp. This essay, 'Hitler's Diminished Masculinity',
was completed before the release of *The Great Dictator* in
1940. In the Weimar Republic, on the one hand, Chaplin's
film represented 'the perfect compromise between populism and modernism'.[33] Whereas conservative thinkers
viewed Chaplin as 'the personification of cultural and moral
decline', 'a little mongrel without race' and 'the hero of
the sub-human', many avant-garde artists praised him as 'a
great innovator and iconoclast'.[34] In a similar vein to these
artists, Benjamin considers Chaplin to be 'an historical
phenomenon', who uses slapstick comedy to tell the truth
about the fictitious nature of everyday life under capitalism (*Modern Times* and *The Circus*) and fascist politics (*The
Great Dictator*) (SW2, 222). Aware that the problems of contemporary art find their definitive formulation only in the
context of film, he considers Chaplin's films to encapsulate
most of the key issues affecting contemporary film technology (AP [K3,3], 394). Benjamin aligns the exaggerated
mimicry of Chaplin's acting style with this technical potential, observing that Chaplin recuperates the waning mimetic
faculty by mimicking the very fragmentation by which it is
threatened. Chaplin's work exhibits the quintessential features that enable film to open up the optical unconscious

by using various cinematographic devices, such as close-ups and enlargement.[35] Benjamin describes the essence of one of Chaplin's films, *The Circus*, thus: 'The undeniable superiority of Chaplin's films . . . is based on the fact that they are imbued with a poetry that everyone encounters in his life, admittedly without always being conscious of it' (SW2, 222). But, for Benjamin, Chaplin evokes the audience's reaction 'in a more natural way' and more 'effortlessly' than any other avant-garde movements' performances, such as those that the Dadaists and the Surrealists, were able to give (SW4, 280). Benjamin gives a great deal of credit to Chaplin's films for their ability to evoke such a reaction: 'The technological reproducibility of the artwork changes the relation of the masses to art. The extremely backward attitude towards a Picasso painting changes into a highly progressive reaction to a Chaplin film' (SW4, 264). Benjamin draws out 'the progressive reaction' from Chaplin's films, that is, 'an immediate, intimate fusion of pleasure – pleasure in seeing and experiencing – with an attitude of expert appraisal' (SW4, 264). For Benjamin, Chaplin is a pioneer who employs a filmic analysis of assembly-line technology, depicted literally in *Modern Times*. Chaplin 'chops up the expressive movement of the human body into a sequence of minute innervation', a procedure that 'imposes the law of filmic images onto the law of human motorics' (GS I-3, 1040; 1047).

Hitler was taking over the office of *Reichspräsident* after the death of Paul von Hindenburg on 2 August 1934, while officially renouncing the title of president. Benjamin underscores Hitler's communication skills, particularly the image management strategies, in which he maximized the effect of the spectacle in these highly charged political circumstances: 'That happens only once, and never comes again.' Hitler did not accept the title of President of the Reich; his aim was to impress upon the people the singularity of his appearance. This singularity works in favour of his magically transposed prestige' (SW2, 793). It is widely acknowledged that around 1932, under the direction of the opera singer Paul Devrient, Hitler practised his facial expressions in front of a mirror in order to produce a good effect. In Benjamin's view, the central image that Hitler wants to create is that of 'diminished masculinity': 'The fashion keynote for Hitler is not the image of the military man, but that of the gentleman in easy circumstances. The feudal emblems of authority are out of date; there remained only men's fashions' (SW2, 792). Hitler's image is less 'expressive' than 'reflective', as Buck-Morss suggests, giving back to 'the man-in-the-crowd his own image, the narcissistic image of the intact ego, constructed against the fear of the body-in-pieces'.[36] Thus, fascist iconography, according to Koepnick, aims to 'colonize the structure of modern experience, engage popular sentiments and discipline sense perception'.[37]

In parallel with the iconographic analysis of Hitler's image, Benjamin's ideas about changes in the function of spectacle, its shift from ritual to politics, derive from a situation in which the most advanced techniques of contemporary art primarily serve to beautify and propagate the image of power. Benjamin's account of the decline of the 'autonomous sphere of art' reflects the predominance of politics in artistic practice. However, fascist aesthetics is differentiated from other earlier political representations in the sense that it places the masses at centre stage: 'Fascist art is the art of propaganda. It is executed, therefore, for the masses. Fascist propaganda, moreover, must pervade all of social life. Fascist art is therefore executed not only *for* the masses but also *by* the masses' (GS III, 488). Unlike earlier Romanticism, fascist propaganda does not exclude the masses in the process of representing and visualizing power. Rather, it highlights 'the masses' as a beautified hero. This account has close affinity

with Benjamin's contemporary, Siegfried Kracauer's ethno-
graphic description of the 'mass ornament', where he argues
that the masses are enthralled and entranced by their own
spectacular presentation as mass: 'The bearer of the ornaments is the *mass* and not the people [*Volk*] for whenever the
people form figures, the latter do not hover in midair but
arise out of a community.'[38] However, the masses still remain
isolated and marginalized from power. Benjamin emphasizes
this thus:

> Accordingly, one might assume that the masses were in
> control of this art, they could use it as a means of self-
> communication [*Selbstverständigung*], that they were master
> of their own house: master in their theatres and stadiums,
> master in their film studios and their publishing houses.
> Everyone knows that this is not the case. Rather, those who
> dominate over these sites are 'the elite'. And this elite does
> not wish art to provide a means of self-communication for
> the masses. (GS III, 488)

The key feature of the fascist political spectacle is revealed
as the spectacle of pseudo-self-representation.[39] The desires
of the masses are met no more than through image and
representation. Their political and social status remains sub-
stantively unchanged. The masses emerge as a subject of
history within representation, but remain as passive objects
in the political decision-making process.

> The increasing proletarianization of modern man and the
> increasing formation of masses are two sides of the same
> process. Fascism attempts to organize the newly proletari-
> anized masses while leaving intact the property relations
> that they strive to abolish. It sees its salvation in granting
> expression to the masses – but on no account granting them

rights. The masses have a *right* to changed property relations; fascism seeks to give them *expression* in keeping these
relations unchanged. *The logical outcome of fascism is an aestheticizing of political life.* (SW3, 120–1)

As outlined above, the conspicuous distinction between
'proletarianization' and the 'formation of masses' is crucial.
The foremost objective of fascism is to preserve the principle of private property, at once balancing the collectivist
desires of the 'masses' with the desire to 'bring things closer
spatially and humanly', while abandoning representative
democracy. As such, Benjamin's critique of political spectacle does not directly address the expected ideological themes
– nationalism, mythic irrationalism, biological racism – but
rather the structure of communicative dynamics within the
political sphere.[40] In Benjamin's view, fascism is the legiti-
mate heir of the aestheticism of *l'art pour l'art* (Art for Art's
Sake), not because of its ideological claims, but because
they are both based upon the denial of the masses' right
to self-communication (SW3, 122). In accordance with the
scopophilic pleasure of ruler and the masses themselves,
collective experience functions via identification with the
Führer. Through this aesthetic identification, fascist politics
aims to neutralize critical judgement and limit the individual
body's autonomous corporeal pleasure.

(3) The Commodification of Politics

The Work of Art essay also raises the issue of the relationship
between political spectacle and consumer culture as articulated by the entertainment industry. In Benjamin's view, the
aestheticization of politics reflects the broader process of the
aestheticization of everyday life or, in a more specific sense,
'literarization of the conditions of living' (SW2, 742), which
corresponds to the emergence of consumer culture in high

capitalism. For Benjamin, politics is not simply a separate arena. In high capitalism, it is inextricably bound up with consumer culture. The aestheticization of the political spectacle is also connected with the logic of consumer culture and the entertainment industry. The political spectacle is inevitably manifest in certain forms of commodity and created with the help of consumer culture. In Benjamin's view, the commodification of politics signifies that politics has become a marketable object of mass consumption like anything else.[41]

It is notable that a wide range of recent research suggests that even during the Nazi era large sections of the population led a double life, and that everyday culture in Nazi society relied deeply upon leisure activity and private consumption. Politics in high capitalism comes to be a facet of the entertainment industry or, at least, it is increasingly influenced by the pursuit of pleasure that typifies consumer culture. As noted above, fascist political communication is configured as a mass spectacle staged by the state with the help of communication media. As a mass spectacle, fascist politics should be attractive to, and bought and consumed by, the masses. Leni Riefenstahl's films like *The Triumph of the Will* (1935) or *Olympia* (1937) involve a certain form of commodity, and coincide with the main principles of the entertainment industry. In contrast to liberal democracy, which supposedly aims to establish the political arena as autonomous, fascist politics emerges as a system interrelated with capitalism, a marketable item. Here, in the politics of representation, exhibition value is central to political communication between political spectacle understood as commodity, and the masses as consumers. Thus, the more closely politics becomes interwoven with consumer culture, the more closely the logic of political spectacle follows commodity aesthetics. Political spectacle coincides with a form of commodity aesthetics that organizes the consumer's experience in terms of forgetting, fragmentation, anaesthesia, reification and so on. In organizing experience, political spectacle relied on appealing to consumers by presenting them with a carefully designed product. As the flâneur dawdles in the arcades, so the masses look at commodities in the department stores and audiences are enthralled by the cinema. Through his analysis of the aesthetic dimension of political spectacle, Benjamin demonstrates that when visual pleasure replaces rational communication in the political arena, the priority of spectacle over substance and the collapse of the literary bourgeois public sphere accelerate. His account of media politics unpacks the way in which the theatricalization of parliamentary democracy and the emergence of the fascist spectacle derive from the interpenetration of political spectacle and commodity aesthetics.

CONCLUSION

Benjamin's account of the aestheticization of politics illustrates a mass, spectacular and commodified form of modern politics. By capturing the essence of political spectacle as the anaesthesia of the human sensorium, Benjamin is able to explore a particular form of political crisis, which is bound up with the crisis of systems of representation and ocularcentric culture. The emergence of fascism is closely connected with the development of communication technology, but fascism's emergence does not so much involve the resurrection of aura or the re-auratization of power as artificial aura. This illuminates the key feature of political spectacle, that is, an artificial aura reproduced by communication technology. Benjamin's critique of political spectacle is concerned less with the formation of false consciousness than with the alienation of the human sensorium. His analysis further reflects the impact of political spectacle on the crisis of modern experience, a total crisis of perception. Against this backdrop, Benjamin's attempt to politicize art constitutes an attempt to retrieve the isolated and fragmented sensoria of the human body.

Benjamin's insight into the politics of media spectacle is highly relevant for our understanding of politics in today's complex media environment. Of course, the impact of communication technology on democracy and social movements has been a fundamental issue in the fields of social and political theory ever since the mass media, including newspapers, cinema, radio and TV, were institutionally established and came to play a crucial role in articulating and mediating political communications. Yet, it is noteworthy that the recent advent and wide propagation of social media bound up with the Internet, such as social networking sites and blogospheres, tend to go beyond the limits of one-way communication embedded in mass media and to foster reciprocal communication on an unprecedented scale. Since the late 1990s, diverse forms of social media have been engaged in social movements and election campaigns across the globe. Notable examples include: the initial utilization of mobile phones during the anti-globalization demonstration in Seattle in 1999; the enthusiastic employment of Facebook by Barack Obama's election strategists during the presidential election in 2008; and the promulgation through Twitter and YouTube of demonstrations in the wake of the 2009 Iranian elections. More recently, the revolutions in North African and Middle Eastern countries, the so-called Arab Spring of 2011, have engaged with various modes of social media. Hence, there has been a wide range of discussions focusing on the increasing possibilities for the development of grass-roots movements, more systematic representation of public opinion and direct communication between political powers and the public. Yet, many discussions have been overly preoccupied with the quantitative transformation of the public sphere and seem to share both an instrumental perspective on the effective use of social media in political mobilization and an overly optimistic standpoint on the improvement of deliberative democracy, driven by advanced communication technology. Hitherto, a good deal less attention has been paid to a vital question about the changing nature of democracy itself in conjunction with the development of communication technology. Benjamin's analysis of the relationship between media, politics and the masses elaborated in the Work of Art essay offers a more systematic approach to the issue of media and democracy, an issue that has become increasingly significant in the age of social media.

5

THE MEDIA CITY: READING
THE ARCADES PROJECT

The images, my great, my primitive passion.
                                        – Charles Baudelaire

INTRODUCTION

Various forms of the nineteenth-century entertainment industry fascinated Walter Benjamin as exemplary figures of the interface between cutting-edge technologies and urban spectacle. The 1937 Paris World Exhibition caught Benjamin's attention, exiled as he was in Paris from 1933. Paris turned into a huge urban playground and mass festival during the period of the exhibition. Two notable pavilions symbolically faced one another: that of Nazi Germany and that of the Soviet Union. The Eiffel Tower, built as the entrance arch to the 1889 Paris Exposition, stood as a symbol of old European modernity between newly rising regimes. In the gigantic Nazi Pavilion, designed by Albert Speer (1905–1981), Hitler's favourite architect, international audiences were shown *Triumph of the Will*: Leni Riefenstahl's documentary film of the 1934 Nazi Nuremberg Rally went on to win the Grand Prix for its technological and aesthetic achievements. The 1937 Paris Expo, as we now know it, seemed to Benjamin a prototype of spectacle, unpacking the increasingly close relations between art, technology and politics in the age of high capitalism. The world exhibition is one of the key cultural objects scrutinized by Benjamin in *The Arcades Project*.

Since its publication in 1983, and especially since its translation into English, *The Arcades Project* has increasingly become an indispensable foundation for critical reflection upon contemporary culture and in particular the intersection of media and the city. Once again, two difficulties attend the task of critical interpretation: firstly, Benjamin's extensive discussions of various forms of media are scattered throughout this highly fragmentary text, and, secondly, there is a temptation to generalize and to overemphasize certain themes and concepts without due reference to their historical and political context. *The Arcades Project* is an unfinished project – or one described as a project that was never intended to be complete. In late 1928 Benjamin began to compile the materials on manifold facets of nineteenth-century Paris; after frequent interruptions, he resumed his research from 1934 onwards; and he made the last entries in 1940, just before he fled from Paris. He amassed myriad citations along with his own comments and reflections, and left thirty-six extensive folders to Georges Bataille (1897–1962), who was a librarian at the Bibliothèque Nationale and a founder of the College of Sociology, a group that Benjamin was acquainted with during his period of exile. Benjamin was said to have carried a large briefcase filled with a manuscript while fleeing over the Pyrenees en route to New York City. When asked why he carried it, Benjamin replied: 'It is the manuscript that *must* be saved. It is more important than I am' (AP, 948). Unfortunately, the manuscript was never recovered and we will never know, as has been speculated, if it was even a final version of the project. After the war, the materials left with Bataille were sent to Adorno, whom Benjamin had appointed as an executor of his *oeuvre*, and were published as *Das Passagen-Werk* in 1983, followed by the English edition, *The Arcades Project*, in 1999.

The Arcades Project is by no means a complete 'book'. As Rolf Tiedemann, the editor of the original 1982 edition of *Das Passagen-Werk*, remarks: 'There are books whose fate has been settled long before they even exist as books. Benjamin's unfinished *Passagen-Werk* is just such a case.'[1] Benjamin left only an archive, an immense collection of quotations and notes divided into different sections (where we can continue to conduct his research). Benjamin's collecting practice in a dark reading room at the Bibliothèque Nationale resembles an activity known as *tikkun*, the Jewish mystic work of the holy man in dark times, collecting the pieces of broken vessels and putting them together.[2] This Kabbalistic idea is central to the media critique detailed in his essay 'The Task of the Translator' (SW1, 253–63). It is a task of readers of *The Arcades Project* to collect the scattered fragments and artefacts and reconstruct his project in a similar way, to articulate 'a broken vessel'. We might say this is the purpose of his project, inviting readers into the process of collecting, interpreting and awakening.

As his interest increasingly focused on the intersection of modern urban experience and technology, Benjamin began to probe into the spectacular aspects of commodity culture, interwoven with the emergence of the entertainment industry. His original intention was to write a short newspaper article entitled 'Parisian Arcades. A Dialectical Fairy Play [*Féerie*]' (C, 322). It is noteworthy that the term *Féerie*, literally meaning fairyland, began to be used in Paris in the early 1820s to indicate 'a form of theatrical spectacle'.[3] Whatever his original plan, Benjamin's detailed analysis meant that the single essay on the genealogy of the Paris arcade expanded into a far larger book project on the primal history of modernity. Benjamin revealed the importance of the project thus: 'it is the theatre of all my conflicts and all my ideas' (C, 359).

Bearing in mind the grand scale and scope of the project, the main aim of this chapter is to help read *The Arcades Project* in a systematic way from the perspective of media studies, which requires engaging with other interdisciplinary approaches, in particular urban and cultural studies. For this purpose, this chapter reconstructs *The Arcades Project* with particular reference to phantasmagoria, a concept that Benjamin himself locates in the centre of his project. In discussing his analysis of modernity as phantasmagoria, this chapter tries: (1) to draw out the methodological implications of *The Arcades Project* for his media critique; (2) to illuminate literary montage as a particular media practice adopted by Benjamin for the project; and (3) to clarify his distinctive idea of profane illumination, as awakening from the dream world of high capitalism.

PHANTASMAGORIAS OF MODERNITY

Key Works
'Paris, the Capital of the Nineteenth Century' (1935)
'Paris, Capital of the Nineteenth Century' (1939)
'On the Concepts of History' (1940)
Related Convolutes in *The Arcades Project*:
[N], 'On the Theory of Knowledge, Theory of Progress'
[p], 'Anthropological Materialism, History of Sects'

Dialectical Image

As we discussed in the previous section, the photographic construction of reality leads Benjamin to grasp the fleeting nature of modernity by means of image itself. In his view, history in the age of technological reproducibility becomes imagistic. Benjamin elaborates two distinctive analytical concepts in *The Arcades Project*: one the dialectical image; the other, phantasmagoria. While Benjamin propounds the concept of the dialectical image as the epistemological core of his media critique in tackling the historicist approach to culture, he utilizes the notion of phantasmagoria to go beyond shortcomings embedded in the Marxist study of culture and art.

The ephemeral character of modern experience raises a crucial methodological issue concerning the object of social and cultural studies: the object of study is itself transitory. It is a fundamental issue of aesthetic modernism, stemming from Charles Baudelaire's definition of ephemeral modernity. In the city, the objects that we are looking at are caught up in a state of flux and in ceaseless movement. Methodologically, we have to ask: how can we grasp the ephemeral dynamic of cultural and social relations while avoiding abstract generalization and quasi-scientific quantification? By locating the notion of dialectical image at the centre of his approach to modernity, Benjamin tries to grapple with this vital methodological question imposed by modernity itself. Benjamin defines the dialectical image as 'an image that emerges suddenly, in a flash' (AP [N9,7], 473). The notion of the dialectical image corresponds to the ephemeral character of urban spectacle in motion. He outlines key components of historical materialism thus:

On the elementary doctrine of historical materialism. (1) An object of history is that through which knowledge is constituted as the object's rescue. (2) History decays into images, not into stories. (3) Wherever a dialectical process is realized, we are dealing with a monad. (4) The materialist presentation of history carries along with it an immanent critique of the concept of progress. (5) Historical materialism bases its procedures on long experience, common sense, presence of mind and dialectics. (AP [N11,4], 476)

The foremost epistemological issue stems from the fact that the ephemeral feature of urban spectacle can only be grasped by image, no longer by a story. His emphasis on the dialectical image as an object of historical materialism reflects the crisis of bourgeois literary criticism, a criticism that is based on rational and dialogic communication. As we discussed in chapter 2, on the crisis of communication and the rise of the information industry in nineteenth-century Western European cities, Benjamin seeks to find a new form of criticism corresponding to the crisis of the old mode of communication and to the emergence of the new mode of communication. In his earlier work, *One-Way Street* (1928), in which the influence of Surrealism is evident, he pioneered a new form of aesthetic practice under the rubric of 'thought-image' (*Denkbild*), a practice involving the presentation of aphoristic fragments. In an age when abundant information prevails over unique individual stories, an object of historical, cultural and social investigation breaks down into discrete fragments, and no longer forms an integrated whole. Those attempts to reconstruct social reality as an organic whole appear to be no more than a conservative approach to history, an approach that petrifies and consequently reifies the past in the name of objectification. 'An object of history' in Benjamin's historical materialism, as Michael Jennings notes, designates neither 'an isolated historical event, fact, artefact, or person' nor 'the discrete bits of evidence marshalled to build an argument'; but 'something *constituted* in the act of writing history or criticism'.[4] Benjamin's practice of collecting historical objects in *The Arcades Project* is an engineering practice and aesthetic attempt to integrate a past historical object into a present constellation (AP [N10a,3], 475).

Benjamin's criticism of the holistic reconstruction of historical reality by means of the notion of dialectical images is consonant with his distinctive perception of Now-Time (*Jetztzeit*). He opposes the evolutionary view of time exemplified by Hegel's philosophy of history as 'the homogeneous, empty time' (SW4, 396). Calling the materialist view of time 'Now-Time', he identifies the synchronous relation between the past and the present, between continuity and discontinuity, and between the abiding and the momentary. As emphatically stated in his reflection on history, 'On the Concept of History' (1940), 'historicism offers the "eternal" image of the past; historical materialism supplies a unique experience with the past' (SW4, 397). This thesis encapsulates the core aspect of his historical materialism. The main doctrines of historicism in cultural historicism and of positivism in social sciences lie in their belief in the reconstruction of history as a total reality. In their views, history is only conceived by an event in the past. In contrast, for Benjamin, history is only and always recognized by today's experience: 'The past can be seized only as an image that flashes up at the moment of its recognizability [*Augenblick seiner Erkennbarkeit*], and is never seen again' (SW4, 390). Thus, his media critique abandons the epic element in history but reconstructs and thereby 'redeems' history as 'the specific epoch, the specific life and the specific work'. History is never seen again and the work of art is never appreciated again, unless they are retrospectively captured as an image and retrieved as an image of 'now'. Images of history appear to be no less than 'sudden flash' and 'momentary illumination'. Benjamin found an example in Monet's impressionist painting, *Cathedral of Chartres*.

> The daily sight of a lively crowd may once have consti-tuted a spectacle to which one's eyes needed to adapt. On the basis of this supposition, one may assume that once the eyes had mastered this task, they welcomed opportunities to test their newly acquired ability. This would mean that the technique of Impressionist painting, whereby the image is construed from a riot of dabs of colour, would be a reflec-tion of experiences to which the eyes of a big-city dweller have become accustomed. A picture like Monet's *Cathedral of Chartres*, which looks like an image of an ant-hill of stone, would be an illustration of this hypothesis. (SW4, 350)

Monet's painting catches the transient moment at a stand-still as ambiguity and the figurative appearance. In a similar way, historical materialism aims to present history as imag-istic by constructing the historical and cultural objects as figural fragment. In revealing multifaceted aspects of time and space, historical materialism holds the significance of a 'rescue-operation' of history.

For Benjamin, the main task of critique is to unfold and fulfil the incomplete meaning of the work of art in a narrow sense, and of history in a broader sense. Media critique as an immanent critique encompasses Benjamin's particular idea of history as the dialectical image. An historical object exists as a monad, indicating not only an aesthetic object but also 'history in miniature': 'Thinking involves not only the move-ment of thoughts, but their arrest as well. Where thinking suddenly comes to a stop in a constellation saturated with tensions, it gives that constellation a shock, by which thinking is crystallized as a monad' (SW4, 396). The historical object conceived as the monadological fragment brings to the fore the importance of inconspicuous and instantaneous objects, which have been disregarded in the idealist philosophy of art and history.[5] The world is represented not by abstract concepts (Hegel's *Spirit* or even Marx's *Capital*) but by the minutiae of mundane everyday life. Seemingly insignificant tiny objects and unrelated fragments are ones waiting to constitute a constellation. Benjamin's fascination with the small things and ruins illustrates the subversive character of his media critique against any form of abstract generalization of history, philosophical system or universal historicism. As his friend Kracauer points out, Benjamin's critique propounds the 'discontinuous multiplicity of the image' against the continuity of the system of ideas, concerning 'to demonstrate that big matters are small and small matters big'.[6] Viewed in this light, *The Arcades Project* appears as critical constellations of fragmented objects, objects that separated in the past but become authentic historical truth by the encounter with readers. History can only be rescued when present readers are engaged with its construction.

Montage

How, then, did Benjamin conduct his media critique in *The Arcades Project*? Benjamin conceives montage as the core method of the historical materialism, that is, a way of dealing with the dialectical image. He proposes montage as a specific media practice corresponding to the ephemeral character of modernity, a practice that actively intervenes in the flow of history or progress and aims to unearth and release an object from continuous history:

A central problem of historical materialism that ought to be seen in the end: Must the Marxist understanding of history necessarily be acquired at the expense of the perceptibility

of history? Or: in what way is it possible to conjoin a heightened graphicness [*Anschaulichkeit*] to the realization of the
Marxist method? The first stage in this undertaking will be
to carry over the principle of montage into history. That
is, to assemble large-scale constructions out of the smallest
and most precisely cut components. Indeed, to discover in
the analysis of the small individual moment the crystal of
the total event. (AP [N2,6], 461)

Montage is not an overarching theory but a specific practice, corresponding with immanent critique and being
rooted in ideas about the communicability of tradition and
past experience. Benjamin's conception of montage derives
from his earlier preoccupation with quotation. While working on *The Origin of German Mourning Drama*, he boasted of
a systematic collection of over 600 quotations. In his early
essay, 'Goethe's Elective Affinities' (written in 1919–22),
quotation is already regarded as more than a technique and
central to discovering new ways of dealing with the past.
Benjamin underscores the implication of literary montage:
'To write history thus means to *cite* history' (AP [N11,3],
476). As Hannah Arendt notes, Benjamin 'became a master
when he discovered that the transmissibility of the past had
been replaced by its citability'.[7] By dislocating the historical objects, he aims to interrupt the context of a text and to
redeem history itself.

Benjamin was aware that a media product is no longer
created as an organic whole and is only put together from
fragments. The works of Karl Kraus, Bertolt Brecht, the
Surrealists, John Heartfield and Sergei Eisenstein are
regarded as precedents for Benjamin's idea of montage. For
them, montage is a noble technique corresponding to technological advancements in newspapers, theatre, photography
and film. The way that newspapers are edited is a prime

example of montage: fragmented stories are put together without a context. Benjamin draws particular attention to the destructive power of quotation embedded in Kraus' satirical critique in his newspaper (SW2, 453). Like the well-timed 'gesture' in Brecht's epic theatre, Benjamin emphasizes, a well-placed citation serves to interrupt the flow of a text, disturbing the reader's absorption. Furthermore, the surrealist literary montage has led to the changing nature of literary representation in association with the illustrative way of seeing. In conjunction with his epistemological concept, 'picture-thought', Benjamin adapts 'picture writing' from Surrealism as a new form of 'three dimensional writing' (SW1, 456) to present history via the dialectical images. While the Surrealists' 'artistic attempt' to represent urban reality by means of photography has 'failed', Heartfield's work successfully grasps 'the social impact of photography' (SW3, 241).[8] While collaborating with Brecht and being influenced by his idea of 'functional transformation', Heartfield tries to utilize a fully photographic montage technique for a new mode of aesthetic practice. The interplay between image and document in Heartfield's photomontages is recognized as an exemplar of the 'politicization of art' and offers Benjamin a constructive motif to conduct the Arcades research from the perspective of montage.

Benjamin's conception of montage is further elucidated under the influence of Russian avant-garde film movements, in particular, Eisenstein's theory of film. In the 1920s and 1930s the key characteristic of Russian film-making can be described as a '*technē*-centred trend', given the dominance of Constructivist movements.[9] Aware of the centrality of technical experiments, Benjamin was fascinated by technique-oriented Russian film-making during the period: 'everything technical is sacred here, nothing is taken more earnestly than technique'. The Russian word *montazh* literally means 'machine assembly' in the sense of 'mounting' a motor.[10] Montage as a film technique seems to Benjamin to be an important tool that can be used in 'aesthetic engineering', that is, a core aspect of modern media practice. Given its typically extensive use of editing, the Russian Constructivists linked to this machine-based meaning of montage a sense of 'assembling materials in a way that generates a degree of friction among them'.[11] It is unsurprising, therefore, that Benjamin tries to make the most of its possibilities in his practice in *The Arcades Project*. He does not endeavour to 'explain' the meaning of history. He adapted montage technique to let the meaning of history reveal itself when it is presented as a constellation.

> Method of this project: literary montage. I needn't say anything. Merely show. I shall purloin no valuables, appropriate no ingenious formulations. But the rags, the refuse – these I will not inventory but allow, in the only way possible, to come into their own: by making use of them. (AP [N1a,8], 460)

The Arcades Project is an outcome of his montage practice to reconstruct the primordial history of modernity by means of fragmented images. It is a literary montage, or 'an idiosyncratic method of the archaeology of the debris',[12] in which Benjamin presents the prototype of urban spectacle by superimposing fragments onto the text. Drawing on these principles of montage, one can see the reason why we should consider Benjamin's approach to media in *The Arcades Project* as constituting not a theory of media as such but a media practice. Benjamin did not attempt to formulate a comprehensive, systematic and abstract theory of media culture. Rather, *The Arcades Project* itself is a constellation of fragmented images, characterized by a series of ideas and insights that emerge at different times and in different texts and historical and political contexts.

Phantasmagoria

In *The Arcades Project*, Benjamin actively applies the notion of phantasmagoria to his analysis of nineteenth-century Paris, a city that is conceived to be an emblem of 'technological civilization' to use his own terminology. The metropolis – Paris, for example – becomes 'a study of the kind of aesthetic conservation that had been the subject of some of Benjamin's earlier writings on the philosophy of art'.[13] Benjamin reveals in a letter to Gretel Adorno of March 1939 his great eagerness to explicate more profoundly the concept of phantasmagoria: 'I have busied myself, as well as possible in the limited time, with one of the basic concepts of the "Arcades", placing at its core the culture of the commodity-producing society as phantasmagoria' (GS V, 1172). Benjamin began to draw attention to the Marxist theory of commodity culture as bound up with the concepts of reification and fetishism, the tenets developed by Georg Lukács in *History and Class Consciousness* (1923). Many commentators have considered the notion of phantasmagoria to be merely another term for what Lukács called commodity fetishism; yet Benjamin seeks to apply the epistemological character of the dialectical image into the area of commodity culture in terms of phantasmagoria:

> The property appertaining to the commodity as its fetish character attaches as well to the commodity-producing society – not as it is in itself, to be sure, but more as it represents itself and thinks to understand itself whenever it abstracts from the fact that it produces precise commodities. The image that it produces of itself in this way, and

that it customarily labels as its culture, corresponds to the concept of phantasmagoria. (AP [X13a], 669)

Thus constructed, Benjamin's interest in the notion of phantasmagoria is closely linked to his critical assessment of the theoretical blind spots in the conventional Marxist analysis of art and culture. In Benjamin's view, whereas the conventional historicism of art tends to uproot the object of cultural studies from social relations, the Marxist theory of art reduces cultural objects to the ideological super-structure, which is determined by economic relations. For Benjamin, the cultural objects explored in *The Arcades Project* are neither autonomous from material conditions nor mere products entirely determined by the commodity exchange system; rather they are the objects that express the collective wish image bound up with the certain level of technological development in a historical epoch.

In Adorno's view, however, Benjamin's approach to the collective wish images in terms of phantasmagoria is too dangerously associated with the 'reactionary theories' of Carl Jung's psychology and Ludwig Klages' social anthropology. In a letter to Benjamin of 2 August 1935, Adorno ascribes Benjamin's approach to the dialectical image and the dream-ing collective to his 'overvaluation and uncritical acceptance of machine technology' (ABC, 110). While Adorno sees Benjamin's use of phantasmagoria as the subjectification of cultural phenomena uprooted from their material condition, in particular, commodity relations, Benjamin maintains that the notion of phantasmagoria designates a kind of undergo-ing illumination, in particular, a collective wish image of a society. In the revised 1939 exposé, he even expanded the use of phantasmagoria, locating it at the centre of his analysis of modernity:

Our investigation proposes to show how, as a consequence of this reifying representation of civilization, the new forms of behaviour and the new economically and technologically based creations that we owe to the nineteenth century enter the universe of a phantasmagoria. These creations undergo this 'illumination' not only in a theoretical manner, by an ideological transposition, but also in the immediacy of their perceptible presence. They are manifest as phantasmagorias. (AP, 14)

The term phantasmagoria literally means a gathering of ghosts in public space and is defined as 'a shifting series or succession of phantasms or imaginary figures, as seen in a dream or fevered condition, as called up by the imagination, or as created by literary description'.[14] The term was frequently used as a literary metaphor by later Romantic and symbolist writers such as Edgar Allan Poe, Arthur Rimbaud and Charles Baudelaire to illustrate 'delirium, loss of control, the terrifying yet sublime overthrow of ordinary experience'.[15] The term phantasmagoria also indicates the ghost show premiered in Paris in 1797. These shows were illusionist exhibitions, a type of public entertainment in which ghosts were produced with the use of magic lanterns, or *lanterna magica*. For Benjamin, the ghost show seems to indicate the prototypical relationship between visual technology and the nineteenth-century European entertainment industries and the primal mode of spectators' experience of them. From the phantasmagorical experience, Benjamin draws out a key aspect of modern communication: the decline in the communicability of experience. The phantasmagoric experience reveals a transformation from communication involving copresence to communication with an absent other, such as a ghost.[16] The shocking experience of the spectators designates the demise of narrative communication through bourgeois literary media such as the novel. As Kittler notes, the magic lantern turns the *camera obscura* 'inside out'.[17] The transformation of visual technology from *camera obscura* to *lanterna magica* shows 'a dramatic epistemological shift from apparatically-produced subjectivity to a "corporeal subjectivity", where the body was "the active producer of optical experience".[18] The phantasmagoric experience leads Benjamin to grasp the emergence of mediated communication and the congruent changing nature of the collective experience of the spectacle. Viewed in this way, the phantasmagoria of the entertainment industry holds manifold theoretical implications.

At the epistemological level, the experience of phantasmagoria raises doubts about the supposedly rational nature of the human subject. In the experience of phantasmagoria, the Cartesian divide between subject and the objective world becomes questionable. Benjamin finds that the experience of phantasmagoria coincides with a very central attribute of the modern experience of the spectacle, one which specifically depicts the shock penetrating into everyday life and the subsequent breakdown of communication. The shock experience involves feelings of terror and the loss of control. The experience of phantasmagoria is neither the 'false' consciousness nor mere 'illusion', but rather a real entity made material 'in space, objects and practices'.[19] The experience of phantasmagoria is neither partial nor transient but rather a general mode of modern experience arising from the expansion of the spectacle into all social communications.

At the level of social theory, Benjamin seeks to avoid the crucial limitation of the Marxist approach to art and culture. On the one hand, for Benjamin the fundamental limitation of Marxist theories is rooted in the tenet of ideological superstructure, which results in 'a deductivist aesthetic'. Here, Benjamin shares with critical theorists common criticisms of a causal relationship between superstructure and base. In the vulgar Marxist theory, the work of art is reduced to nothing but a commodity. The deductivist aspect is derived from the fundamental failure of Marxism to acknowledge the changing relationship between reality and representation. The Marxist theory of ideology analogically derives from the outdated model of visual representation technology, the *camera obscura*, which directly reflects optical inversion. It takes for granted the stable and honest reflection of objects and presents the world upside down, leading to misrecognition.[20] In this vein, Marxist theory differs little from the theory of knowledge that underpins the Enlightenment project. For Benjamin, the optical analogy of ideology stemming from the *camera obscura* gives rise to a fundamental problem in the theory of knowledge in the age of technological reproducibility and, furthermore, renders questionable the Marxist notion of critical activity, or the foundation of revolutionary activity. A Marxist theory of ideology based on trust in the reflection of reality cannot explain *how* a true or objective world could be represented or recognized. The relationship between seeing and believing is a point that Benjamin critically challenges in terms of phantasmagoria. He questions those understandings that hold that the outside world is reflected in the subject's consciousness in the same way as an image is reflected in a *camera obscura*. Benjamin, who was familiar with varied illusionist technologies at the time, such as diorama, panorama and cinema, considers the mirroring function of the superstructure to be doubtful. The initial question posed by phantasmagoria is not 'what' is to be represented and perceived but 'how' an object is to be represented and perceived.

At the level of cultural theory, some Western Marxist theorists such as Georg Lukács sought to revise Marx's notion of ideology in connection with commodity fetishism, as developed in *The Capital*. Benjamin was aware of the fact that the notion of fetish appears in Marx's account as a way of illustrating problems of representation and conscious-ness against the backdrop of the development of a complex capitalist system. As the notion of fetish originally refers to the etic attribution of inherent value or power to an object, Benjamin draws from Marx's emphasis on fetishism in *The Capital* the idea that the perception of commodity culture is less akin to 'mechanical' reflection than to 'ambiguous' imagistic attributes. Benjamin finds that the imagistic aspects of commodity fetishism correspond with a key tenet of his dialectical image. As Jay indicates, the term phantasma-goria is used to disguise 'the social-psychological genesis' of cultural and historical objects by making them appear to be derived from 'natural sources'.[21] Yet, more importantly, Benjamin goes further to reconstruct substantially, rather than to revise, the theory of commodity fetishism. Opposing the architectural analogy of superstructure as the reflection of the base, Benjamin offers his own formula, emphasizing the expressive role of the superstructure:

On the doctrine of the ideological superstructure. It seems, at first sight, that Marx wanted to establish here only a causal relation between superstructure and infrastructure. But already the observation that ideologies of the super-structure reflect conditions falsely and invidiously goes beyond this. The question, in effect, is the following: if the infrastructure in a certain way (in the materials of thought and experience) determines the superstructure, but if such determination is not reducible to simple reflection, how is it then – entirely apart from any question about the originating cause – to be characterized? As its expression. The superstructure is the expression of the infrastructure. The economic conditions under which society exists are expressed in the superstructure – precisely as, with the sleeper, an overfull stomach finds not its reflection but its expression in the contents of dreams, which, from a causal point of view, it may be said to 'condition'. The collective, from the first, expresses the conditions of its life. These find their expression in the dream and their interpretation in the awakening. (AP [K2,5], 392)

In this formulation, expression denotes the relatively autonomous character of the superstructure as opposed to its inversion or mechanical reflection. At this point, it is fair to say that Benjamin's idea of phantasmagoria is deeply influenced by commodity fetishism but is not entirely reconcilable with the conventional Marxist understanding of ideology. In Benjamin's modified version, the role of the base is to 'condition' the expression – not by means of mechanical power of production but by 'technological reproducibility', which reproduces the masses through a transformation of the collective experience of the spectacle. Likewise, phantasmagoria in *The Arcades Project* illuminates those imagistic aspects of collective experience that are expressed in the commodity and conditioned by a certain historical and cultural level of technology.

MEDIA SPECTACLE AND URBAN SPACE

Benjamin's analysis of the phantasmagoria of modernity in *The Arcades Project* is primarily concerned with the process of the formation of a new public and the constructive role of the various forms of the entertainment industry. In the fragments of 'Central Park', written as preliminary studies for his Baudelaire studies, Benjamin traces the emergence of the new collective subject with particular reference to 'the multitude', locating it between the 'crowd' and 'the masses' (SW4,

187). He sees the new collective subject as 'the multitude' as differentiated from the conventional modes of the collective: the crowd, the masses, the working class and so on. The emergence of the new collective subject is bound up with the issue of the advances in architectural technology accessible to the entertainment industry and concomitant changes in urban experience. As we examined in chapter 4, the decline of aura explicated in the Work of Art essay reveals how collective behaviours are rationalized, standardized and disciplined during the process of modernization and urbanization. Various forms of the entertainment industry explored in *The Arcades Project* constitute the new modes of collective experience such as tactile distraction engendered by cutting-edge architectural and communication technologies. Benjamin's analysis of the interaction between the entertainment industry and urban experiences is particularly relevant for an understanding of today's mediascape, where the boundaries between the real and the virtual are blurred and media spectacle and urban spaces are inextricably intertwined. The categories that Benjamin provides in his two exposés, written in 1935 and 1939 respectively, outline key aspects of the entertainment industry. The first exposé, 'Paris, the Capital of the Nineteenth Century', was written for the Institute of Social Research to propose a sponsored research project and to offer broad structural outlines of the project. [22] The six thematic sections of the first exposé were intended to represent corresponding convolutes in *The Arcades Project*:

I.   Fourier, or the Arcades
II. Daguerre, or the Panoramas
III. Grandville, or the World Exhibitions
IV. Louis Philippe, or the Interior
V.   Baudelaire, or the Streets of Paris
VI. Haussmann, or the Barricades

Those six main objects in the exposés are dispersed as monads or as an urban allegory from A to Z throughout the files of convolutes. The exposés show how *The Arcades Project* is planned as a constellation of historical objects illustrating phantasmagoria of modernity. The following section introduces *The Arcades Project* according to six key objects outlined in the 1935 exposé. It aims to help read *The Arcades Project* in a methodical way by drawing out its relevance for our understanding of today's media culture, in particular, the relationship between media spectacle and urban space.

The Arcade: The Phantasmagoria of the Techno-City

Related Convolutes in The Arcades Project:

A   Arcades, Magasins de Nouveautés, Sales Clerks
B   Fashion
C   Ancient Paris, Catacombs, Demolitions, Decline of Paris
O   Prostitution, Gambling
T   Modes of Lighting
W   Fourier

The Parisian arcade encapsulates the urban space of the nineteenth century; that is, it is an emblem of the spatial alteration accompanying technological innovation and progress. Among general attributes (e.g., access to the interior of a block, public space on private property, a symmetrical street space and skylit space),[23] the most noteworthy feature is 'something between a street and an interior' (SW4, 19). The arcade was originally (around 1800) a large open space with a collection of consumer shops, and became wider, deeper and taller in response to increased consumer demand and the diversification of consumer goods. In the transition, it was gas and iron that brought about the expansion of shops. While gas light provided the solution to restricted business times due to limited light, the application of iron as a construction material offered a solution to space constraints and weather conditions: 'During sudden rain showers, the arcades are a place of refuge for the unprepared, to whom they offer a secure, if restricted, promenade – one from which the merchants also benefit' (AP [A1,1], 31). Benjamin draws particular attention to how the use of iron in the marketplace had a profound impact on the function of the street.

> Trade and traffic are the two components of the street. Now, in the arcades the second of these has effectively died out: the traffic there is rudimentary. The arcade is a street of lascivious commerce only; it is wholly adapted to arousing desires. Because in this street the juices slow to a standstill, the commodity proliferates along the margins and enters into fantastic combinations, like the tissue in tumours. (AP [A3a,7], 42)

The arcade as commercial as well as quasi-public space now plays a main role in reorganizing the structure of Parisian public life. The arcade primarily becomes a 'temple of commodity capital' (AP [A2,2], 37), in which 'customers will find everything they need' (AP [A1,1], 31). For instance, being the first public urban space removed from the disturbances of traffic, the *Palais Royal* served as a multifunctional site of political agitation, a promenade, a luxury market, and a place of education and entertainment.[24]

The arcade serves as a model for other building types, too. For instance, it is mirrored in the architecture of prisons, railway stations and the collective dwellings such as the phalansteries designed by the French utopian socialist, Charles Fourier (1772–1837). In Benjamin's view, Fourier shows an early recognition of the latent capacity of iron and glass construction to affect the unconscious and the affective dimension of communication and to engineer habitual behaviour of the collective. Against the orthodox or 'scientific' Marxists who dismiss Fourier as a 'utopian' socialist and attack the 'immorality' embedded in his thought, Benjamin emphasizes the fact that Marx took a stand against Carl Grün in order to defend Fourier. Benjamin goes on to draw a revolutionary motif for socialism – a society based on a congruous relation between human being, technology and nature – from his very imagination of harmonizing the passions.[25] Fourier is fascinated by the possibility of creating an entirely new mode of communal space with the help of cutting-edge technologies and materials, in particular iron and glass. Fourier designed an ideal community that he called a phalanstère (or phalanstery), and published the details of the model in his work *Theory of the Four Movements and the General Destinies* (1808). The phalanstery, a four-level residential complex, is based upon the structure of a phalanx. The guiding principle of such a community is the spontaneity of the twelve passions, which comprise the five sensual passions (taste, touch, sight, hearing and smell) and the four affective passions (friendship, ambition, love and paternity). Fourier thinks these passions resulted in 810 types of characters, so the ideal number of residents in the phalanstery would be exactly 1,620 people.[26] In this self-contained community, the rich and the poor would live directly next to one another, according to the principles of pleasure. Fourier sees technology to be fundamentally in opposition to the domination and mastery of nature, and conceives labour to be neither fragmented nor isolated from the whole body and senses. Fourier's project comprises a dream of perfect social engineering capable of controlling human passion with the aid of technological advancement.

Benjamin points out that the arcade's accessibility was largely applied in Fourier's utopian projects: 'The arcades, which originally were designed to serve commercial ends, become dwelling places in Fourier' (AP, 16). By transposing the model of the *Palais Royal* into his phalanstery, Fourier wanted to create a massive space, a city composed of interiors where apartments are arranged, as in a hotel, along central galleries, which run along the second floor of the whole building.[27] The phalanstery, for Benjamin, is a city of technology, designed to restore human beings to a system of relationships in which 'morality becomes superfluous' (AP, 16). The phalanstery's key feature imagines 'the collective psychology as a clockwork mechanism', that is, 'human machinery' based on the efficient functioning of society: 'The highly complicated organization of the phalanstery appears as machinery. The meshing of the passions, the intricate collaboration of *passions méchanistes* with the *passion cabaliste*, is a primitive contrivance formed – in analogy with the machine – from materials of psychology' (AP, 5). Praising Fourier for being a harbinger of the new technology, Benjamin is fascinated by his utopian vision of labour opposed to the domination and mastery of nature:

> One of the most remarkable features of the Fourierist utopia is that *it never advocated the exploitation of nature by man*, an idea that became widespread in the following period. Instead, in Fourier, technology appears as the spark that ignites the powder of nature. Perhaps this is the key to his strange representation of the phalanstery as propagating itself 'by explosion'. *The later conception of man's exploitation of nature reflects the actual exploitation of many by the owners of the means of production.* If the integration of the technological into social life failed, the fault lies in this exploitation. (AP, 17, emphasis added)

Benjamin identifies a desire to use technology in the creation of a perfect machinery of human collectivity, arguing that in Fourier's illusionary picture, a man-made mechanism produces 'the land of milk and honey, the primeval wish symbol that Fourier's utopia has filled with new life' (AP, 5). Fourier's utopian view of technology is focused as a precursor of later avant-garde perspectives on machinery, or 'technological reproducibility' in Benjamin's own terminology, whereby the technological apparatus becomes a part of human beings and plays a mediating role in the non-exploitative relation between humans and nature. Nevertheless, it is a city of interiors built according to the engineer's technological construction with no windows and no outside. Being aware that the centralized control of passion relies on the control of seeing, Fourier intends to create optimal conditions for the manipulation of seeing. Likewise, his utopian vision entails the engineering of the whole community by means of technology. At this point Fourier's two impulses collide: his wish image of a classless society in harmony with nature and for us the seemingly dystopian vision of perfectly controlled human passions.[28] Hence, Benjamin considers Fourier's project to constitute a 'reactionary modification' of the arcades into dwellings, simply 'the colourful idyll of Biedermeier inserted into the austere, formal world of the Empire' (AP, 5).

The Panorama: The Phantasmagoria of Techno-Art

Related Convolutes in The Arcades Project:

Q   Panorama

R   Mirrors

S   Painting, Jugendstil, Novelty

Y   Photography

i   Reproduction Technology, Lithography

Benjamin focuses on the panorama as an example that indicates how a conventional art form like painting is doomed to be displaced by the new form of entertainment industry engineered by architectural technology: 'Just as architecture, with the first appearance of iron construction, begins to outgrow art, so does painting, in its turn, with the first appearance of the panoramas' (AP, 5). In the second section of the exposé, Benjamin links the emergence of new techno-art with Louis Jacques Daguerre (1787–1851), the French painter and inventor known for the daguerreotype image process. In 1823, Daguerre invented the diorama, a mobile picture-viewing theatrical device. Benjamin considers him as opening a new horizon for the integration of technology and art. The panorama became popular in the late eighteenth century, most notably during the French Revolution and appeared at almost the same time as the magic lantern show was invented, a period in which various other new visual representation technologies became widely available. The panorama was a 360-degree image painted on the inside of a large cylinder and viewed from a platform at its centre. Invented and patented by Robert Barker in 1787, it was exhibited in Edinburgh, London and other cities around the turn of the century.[29] Most of them used names with the Greek suffix '-rama', which means to 'see'. Benjamin draws particular attention to the then diorama, cosmorama, diaphanorama, navalorama, georama, cinéorama, stereorama, cyclorama and so on. The panoramas, for Benjamin, are a primal type of the modern entertainment industry from which cinema originated: 'The fact that film today articulates all problems of modern form-giving – understood as questions of its own technical existence – and does so in the most stringent, most concrete, most critical fashion, is important for the following comparison of panoramas with this medium' (AP [Q1a,8], 530). Viewed from contemporary media technology, similarities between the panorama and cinema are only found in their architectural characteristics.

The panorama's novelty, from the perspective of the nineteenth century, was the special precautions taken to erase anything that might divert from its illusion.[30] The panorama aimed to create an artificial – yet perfect – reality that foresaw the key aspects of later visual technologies. Benjamin identifies this primeval function thus: 'In their attempt to produce deceptively lifelike changes in represented nature, the panoramas prepare the way not only for photography but for <silent> film and sound film' (AP, 5). The 360-degree painting without border encapsulates the collapse of the classical mode of vision. The panorama is an example of simulacra, in which the boundaries between the real and the represented, the original and the artificial, and the inside and the outside, are blurred. The experience of the panorama arises from the fact that the audience loses all sense of time and space, being overwhelmed by a technologically created artificial totality.

Even though the panorama provided a new corporeal way of seeing things, it also compelled visitors to fix their gaze on the external world of a painted replica. In the panorama, the eye cannot range beyond the frame, because there is no frame in this gigantic visual space. In the sense that the panorama is a means of organizing visual perception, it directs the spectators' gaze as a 'silent and invisible power' of the entertainment industry (SW1, 451). But, the arcade is a building type that is used not only within the entertainment industry, for example in the panorama, but also in institutions such as the prison. The panorama is seen as a means of organizing visual experience based on optics, but, in a sense, it is also paradoxically 'the experience of an interior, and inner-directed gaze'.[31]

The interest of the panorama is in seeing the true city – the city indoors. What stands within the windowless house is the true. Moreover, the arcade, too, is a windowless house. The windows that look down on it are like loges from which one gazes into its interior, but one cannot see out these windows to anything outside. (What is true has no windows; nowhere does the true look out to the universe.) (AP [Q2a,7], 532)

Like Fourier's phalanstery, the panorama lacks windows, being characterized by its dream-like interior. For Benjamin, the transformation of the entertainment industry from the arcade to the panorama epitomizes the constant interplay of optical attention and corporeal distraction. In the essay on his own childhood, 'Berlin Childhood around 1900', Benjamin traces genealogically an issue of the interplay between attention and distraction via his own encounter with the Imperial Panorama [*Kaiserpanorama*]. The Imperial Panorama, located in an arcade, the *Kaisergalerie* in Berlin, consisted of a dome-like apparatus presenting stereoscopic views to spectators seated around it. It had little in common with the panorama, yet was a hybrid of such various visual entertainment technologies as the peepshow, diorama and photography. Moreover, it was an isolated individual's viewing mode amidst a crowd in a public space. Benjamin illustrates a detailed exposition of the Imperial Panorama thus:

One of the great attractions of the travel scenes found in the Imperial Panorama was that it did not matter where you began the cycle. Because the viewing screen, with places to sit before it, was circular, each picture would pass through all the stations; from these you looked, each time, through a double window into the faintly tinted depths of the image. There was always a seat available. And especially toward the end of my childhood, when fashion was already turning its back on the Imperial Panorama, one got used to taking the tour in a half-empty room. (SW3, 346–7)

Moreover, it is one of the noticeable media spaces in which visual consumption is industrialized and the body of the masses and the machine are combined according to the rhythm of a modern factory production system such as Taylorism, a production method that breaks actions into small and simple segments in order to maximize efficiency.[32] The Imperial Panorama also played a role as an educational tool for schoolchildren or the working classes. In *One-Way Street*, Benjamin identifies the power of controlling the gaze by using the Imperial Panorama as an analogical expression: 'For just the same reason the air is teeming with phantoms, mirages of a glorious cultural future breaking upon us over-night in spite of all, for everyone is committed to the optical illusions of his isolated standpoint' (SW1, 453). As the sub-title 'A Tour through the German Inflation' implies, the section on the Imperial Panorama is engaged explicitly with the cultural politics of that time in Germany.

In this vein, one can easily find a great many similarities and differences between two analogies, the panorama developed by Benjamin and the panopticon by the prominent French structuralist philosopher Michel Foucault (1926–1984). Underlining the social implications of the panopticon, Benjamin highlights its close affinity with the panoramas: 'The Wax Museum <*Panoptikum*> a manifestation of the total work of art. The universalism of the nineteenth century has its monument in the waxworks. Panopticon: not only does one see everything, but one sees it in all ways' (AP [Q2,8], 531). Foucault's panoptic model, developed in his seminal work, *Discipline and Punish* (1975), emphasizes the subjective effects of imagined scrutiny and 'permanent visibility on the observed', but is not concerned to explore in any depth 'the subjectivity of the observer'.[33] In contrast to the paradigm of panoptic surveillance, the panorama is a building machine designed to transport rather than confine the moving spectators. While visual perception in the panoptic model primarily hinges upon the capturing of attention, panoramic experience is primarily concerned with corporeal distraction. Benjamin's analysis of visual representation technologies from the diorama via the panorama to the Imperial Panorama reveals that, in the entertainment industry, attention and distraction continuously interchange, and are not wholly incompatible. Attention and distraction should not be thought of as being consistently diametrically opposed. In fact, the shock experience of a spectacle, especially in the form of political propaganda, is a particularly effective means of arousing attentive perception, and distraction is linked more with the interface between spectacle and the body than with isolated optical perception. This being the case, Benjamin pays considerable attention to the tactile dimension of distraction in connection with a media spectacle such as the panorama, being especially concerned with whether it is possible for emancipatory behaviour to be formed by means of corporeal tactility; an experience that has become a dominant mode of modern spectatorship.

The World Exhibition: The Phantasmagoria of the Global Event

Related Convolutes in The Arcades Project:
G   Exhibitions, Advertising, Grandville
K   Dream City and Dream House, Dreams of the Future, Anthropological Nihilism, Jung
U   Saint-Simon, Railroads
Z   The Doll, The Automaton
b   Daumier
'The Ring of Saturn or Some Remarks on Iron Construction'

Benjamin returns again and again in *The Arcades Project* to those utopian visions of modern technology elaborated by such radical social thinkers and revolutionaries as Fourier, Saint-Simon, Blanqui and Marx. While the phalanstery denotes Fourier's utopian idea of a techno-city, the world exhibition epitomizes Saint-Simon's distinctive utopian vision of the globalization of the economy. The modern framework of the entertainment industry was eventually configured by global events, including the modern Olympic Games (1896–), the football World Cup (1930–) and the world exhibition (1851–).[34] These events – whether commercial, industrial or sporting – unpacked the truly global scale of capitalist culture and played a decisive role in spreading out an image of an empire.[35] Among the many, it was the world exhibition, the oldest global event, that captured Benjamin's attention in the context of the primal history of the entertainment industry. As Hinsley senses, the world exhibition of high capitalism and empire indicates 'summary smothering acts of imposed historical interpretation'.[36]

From its inception in London in 1851 to its most recent incarnation in Shanghai in 2010, the world exhibition has been a distinctive form of public culture for global and national spectators and enjoyed seminal status as a modern mass ritual and urban festival. Organizing a world exhibition leads the host city to expedite urban transformation by undertaking high-risk market-driven urban strategies. The spectacle of the world exhibition serves to articulate collective experiences of the spectators and to disseminate the ideas of technology and progress on a global scale. The world exhibition has always been a great social laboratory for the display of cutting-edge technologies by the leading industries of the host nation as well as by key transnational global corporate bodies. For Benjamin, the world exhibition is a symbol of a society of technology and progress, born of 'modern conceptions of steam power, electricity, and photography, and modern conceptions of free trade' (AP [G6; G6a,1], 183). As exemplified in Crystal Palace, built to house the Great Exhibition in London in 1851, the world exhibition demonstrates particular contradictions, arising from the imitation of Renaissance art, realized with new methods of production determined by the machine. The world exhibition represents the urban space in which a new art was born with iron construction (AP [F1a,3], 152), accelerating a 'revolution in artistic forms' (AP [G6; G6a,1], 183–4). In short, the world exhibition shows explicitly that art comes to be transformed into market, and artwork exists only as a commodity form. The world exhibition becomes 'the popular festival', and 'places of pilgrimage to the commodity fetish', arising from the wish: 'to entertain the working classes and becoming for them a festival of emancipation' (AP, 7).

Compared to the great Greek festivals of the Olympics and Panathenaea, the world exhibitions might 'lack poetry', but might make up for this in commodity (AP [G13a,3], 197). World exhibitions also turn out to be 'a training school' in which the working classes, 'their first clientele', forcibly excluded from consumption, are imbued with the exchange value of commodities to the point of identifying with it: 'Do not touch the items on display' (AP, 18). Eventually, Benjamin argues, the entertainment industry makes the identification easier 'by elevating the person to the level of the commodity' (AP, 7). The way in which the masses experience the spectacle in the world exhibition identifies a rise in the level of the new mode of perception, that is, collective distraction: 'World exhibitions glorify the exchange value of the commodity. They create a framework in which its use value recedes into the background. They open a phantasmagoria that a person enters in order to be distracted' (AP, 7). And 'the phantasmagoria of capitalist culture attains its most radiant unfolding in the world exhibition of 1867' (AP, 8).[37]

In the pavilions of the world exhibitions, where purely visual perception is predominant, the principle of advertising is made manifest: 'Look at everything; touch nothing' (AP [G16,6], 201). A primary advertising strategy used by the world exhibition aims to integrate the spectators' desire into the commodity world by separating optic perception from corporeal engagement with the objects. The spectators' experiences of the commodities satisfy their wishes only in the form of images; satisfy their visual hunger but not their stomachs. It becomes evident that the advertising industry is able to provide a new form of aesthetic object, and to develop techniques of rapidly aestheticizing commodities. Traditional ways of producing art works are no longer compatible with these new creative industries (e.g., advertising, fashion and design), which are supported by advancements in technology. Since the establishment of the entertainment industry, it has become commonplace for fashion designers and advertising directors to be the actual agents of social creativity. The advertising industry is responsible for the production of aesthetic objects for the masses. For Benjamin, Grandville is a primal figure of modern graphic design for advertising.

From the late 1920s onwards, the work of Grandville (the pseudonym of Jean Ignace Isidore Gérard, French caricaturist and illustrator, 1803–1847) becomes central to Benjamin's analysis of the way in which advertising had come to form a new mode of art. For Benjamin, Grandville's illustrations in periodicals during the Second Empire demonstrate how advertising synthesizes consumer aesthetics and technology: 'Grandville's works are the sibylline books of *publicité*. Everything that, with him, has its preliminary form as joke, or satire, attains its true unfolding as advertisement' (AP [G1,3],

172). In the age of global consumer culture, in order to capture the masses' attention in a single glance, a work of art
tends to produce sensual images, which consequently bring
about the shock experience of the spectators. Grandville
tries to achieve this effect by showing a topsy-turvy world,
organized according to common laws of the absurd, such as
fish catching men on their lines, a man walked by his dog, a
woman dressing as a man and so on.[38] Charles Baudelaire,
Grandville's contemporary, conceives Grandville to be 'a
morbidly literary artist', who tries to 'project his thought
into the domain of the plastic arts'. Baudelaire found these
images to be 'terrifying'.[39] In fact, Baudelaire's uneasiness
reveals the rise of distinctive images interwoven with the
world of the commodity. Grandville's satirical graphics aim
to turn the rational and orderly world of nature into a hallucinatory and apocalyptic space where the boundaries between
the living and the dead blur. In so doing, Grandville's work,
whether he intended it or not, inverted social relationships
and allowed the oppressed (e.g., of nature, Eros, myth) to
challenge the dominating real world (e.g., of technology,
Enlightenment, rationality). Benjamin grasps the fact that
Grandville's graphic drawings illustrate the transformation of
nature into the phantasmagoria of the commodity. Drawing
on Baudelaire's discomfort, Benjamin considers Grandville's
graphic utopia to be a prototype of the advertisement, which
exposes both the myths and fetishism of commodity culture
in high capitalism. In much the same way that the world exhibition provides the masses with access to phantasmagoria,
Grandville's graphics provide 'the enthronement of the commodity, with its luster of distraction' (AP, 7). Grandville's
illustrations appeal to none other than the masses, that is,
the view of the 'average Frenchman', whose eyes are familiar with advertising in the newspapers and the billboards on
the street. Grandville's illustrations transform the commodity

into the divine, the eternal and the organic, projecting it onto the cosmos: 'World exhibitions propagate the universe of commodities. Grandville's fantasies confer a commodity character on the universe. They modernize it' (AP, 8). Through Grandville's graphic images, 'the phantasmagoria of capitalist culture' penetrates a wide range of spectators.

However, there is another facet of phantasmagoria that Benjamin captures from the utopian character of Grandville's illustrations. Grandville's images appeal to Benjamin because they suggest the emancipatory potential of a carnivalesque world and the material means of awakening from the dream. From Grandville's imagination, Benjamin recognizes that the rationality of technology is combined with the fantasy of art, revealing distinctively the allegories of fragmented and dehumanized experience that characterize commodity culture. Grandville's illustrations do not just follow the same principles as advertising. They lay the commodity bare, debunk the myths perpetuated by capitalism, and reveal the illusion of organic harmony in the world of technology and merchandise. Herein lies the fundamental difference between Grandville's graphic images and the fantasies created by the entertainment industry such as those by Walt Disney. In Benjamin's view, while Disney contains nothing macabre, Grandville's allegorical image is pervaded by a sense of death, *Memento Mori* (Remember you must die!): 'It [Walt Disney] is not in the least morbid. In this it diverges from the humour of Grandville, which always bore within itself the seeds of death' (AP [B4a,2], 72). As Benjamin sharply elucidates in *The Origin of German Mourning Drama*, a Baroque sense of melancholy, exemplified in Albrecht Dürer's *Melancholia I*, views history as a process of decline: 'In allegory, the observer is confronted with the *facies hippocratica* (the death mask) of history as a purified primordial landscape' (OGTD, 166). Benjamin's emphasis on the macabre in Grandville's illustrations testifies to the ephemeral and instantaneous nature of the commodity, or 'the sudden, shocking crystallization of an imagistic experience in absolute graphicness' in stark contrast to its eternal image.[40] In the age of the entertainment industry, Grandville's allegorical images uncover the secret of the dream world created by the entertainment industry by exposing its hidden connection with dark humour: its transience and morbidity.

In this manner, Grandville's work fits well with Benjamin's notion of the dialectical image. The combination of technology and visual animation in Grandville's drawings is not only a precursor of the use of graphics in advertising, but also represents the advent of a new techno-art. For this reason, Benjamin calls Grandville 'a forerunner of Surrealism', particularly of the surrealist film of Méliès (AP [K4,1], 396). In contrast to the Lumière brothers, the founders of the realistic film tradition, Georges Méliès (1861–1938), a professional magician, is recognized as the pioneer of fantasy film-making, a technique based primarily on film-editing. The association between Grandville and Méliès indicates that Benjamin's interest in film centres not on the representation of the outside world, but on the magical or surreal effects created by technologically configured images.

The Phantasmagoria of Private Space

Related Convolutes in The Arcades Project:

D   Boredom, Eternal Return
I   The Interior, The Trace
L   Dream House, Museum, Spa
V   Conspiracies, *Compagnonnage*
g   The Stock Exchange, Economic History
m   Idleness
r   Ecole Polytechnique

While the first three sections of the 1935 exposé concentrate on the emergence of the collective subject, interwoven with the technological advancement, the fourth section, 'Louis Philippe, or the Interior', is devoted to the birth of individual subjectivity bound up with the configuration of the private space. The relationship between private space and individual subjectivity is one of the key themes in his earlier work, *One Way Street* (1928).[41] As also discussed in chapter 2, the formation and meltdown of the bourgeois subjectivity is closely associated with the individualization of the space, a space that is shaped and transformed by the proliferation of the modern novel and the delivery and subscription of newspapers. In the fourth section of the exposé, the interplay between the inner experience of the bourgeois subject and the private space is further investigated in terms of the interior. As Pierre Missac, the French scholar whom Georges Bataille introduced to Benjamin in Paris in 1937, epitomizes, this section intends to link 'the psychological notion of interiority' with 'the sociological notion of the interior'.[42] It is imperative for Benjamin that not until the reign of Louis Philippe (1830–1848), the last French king, did the private citizen of the middle class come into being. The key material condition of the interior is facilitated by the fact that the spread of arcade as a collection of individual shops, occupying a specific place in the development of organized retail trade at the beginning of high capitalism, leads to the emergence of separated space within social space. Herein lies the crucial affinity between arcade and private space: a space without window: 'Arcades are houses or passages having no outside – like the dream' (AP [L1s,1], 406). This newly configured inward private space is separated from the workplace, a private individual is uncoupled from the community, and the bourgeois citizen increasingly heightens the private feature of the space. As Schmiedgen notes, the bourgeois interiority is a twofold space: on the one hand, a space 'within which subjectivity is always forced to be in the closet about itself', and, a space 'to attempt to internalize the other and hence the exterior', on the other.[43] The upholstered bourgeois interiors of the nineteenth century designate the material foundation of bourgeois society: 'From this arise the phantasmagorias of the interior – which, for the private man, represents the universe. In the interior, he brings together the far away and the long ago. His living room is a box in the theatre of the world' (AP, 9). The interior serves as 'the asylum of art', offering the bourgeois individual a psychic refuge from the public realm.

The phantasmagoric feature of private space debunks not only the isolation of the bourgeois subjectivity from the outside world but also its reified and fetishized feature. In a similar way that the aura of the work of art has withered by means of the technological reproducibility and has been replaced by the copies, the genuine authenticity of the individual citizen has been shattered by means of mass consumption, mass communications and mass movements. The individuality, as Cohen observes, exists only as 'modernity's hypostatization of the individual', which is a 'manifestation of reification's subject/object divide', and Louis Philippe is 'not as the agent of dialectical reversal, but rather as the emblem of all its mystifications'.[44] In the Jugendstil (or Art Nouveau) movements and the collector, Benjamin finds some motives of the reversal of the reification of the private individual. In Benjamin's view, on the one hand, Jugendstil's decorative art around the turn of the century completes the individualism by placing ornament in the private house. In doing so, the Jugendstil's ornamentation seeks to liberate the technological potential to transform the interior into nature and to 'reverse the inwardness' of the bourgeois individual. On the other hand, the collector transfigures the ornaments.

Whereas world exhibitions promote 'the universe of commodities' by transforming the object into an entertaining one, the collector has 'the Sisyphean task' – that of divesting the interior of its commodity character by taking possession of it (AP, 9). While in exposés, the bourgeois private collector is characterized as 'the true resident of the interior', who ceaselessly tries to replace the exchange value of commodity with the use value, in his attempt to formulate a practice of media critique, Benjamin ascribes a motive of profane illumination or de-phantasmagorization to collecting.

We will discuss the function of collecting in more detail later in this chapter. But his insight into the spatiality of the bourgeois subjectivity leads us to pose a critical question: to what extent is Benjamin's analysis of the configuration of the private space separated from the community and the construction of the bourgeois subject relevant for examining the interplay between the media space and the users in today's world of digital technology? Do the various forms of personalized media platform (e.g., Internet-connected smartphones and increasingly individualized tech-gadgets like the iPad) that help instantly link people around the globe bring about a collective social subject or, in fact, cause greater isolation of the individual subject from the real public space? Given the ubiquitous character of the current communications technology, it can be said that the formation of bourgeois subjectivity is no longer simply confined within the private space composed of the interior or even a certain form of bourgeois ideology.

The Phantasmagoria of the Street

Related Convolutes in The Arcades Project:

| J | Baudelaire |
| M | The Flâneur |

The transformation of the private citizen in urban space is further analysed in conjunction with the figure of the flâneur on the street. The fifth section of the 1935 exposé, 'Baudelaire, or the Streets of Paris' encapsulates the specific motif in terms of an urban dawdler in the wake of the modern metropolitan culture. Benjamin's lifelong preoccupation with Baudelaire as the flâneur indicates that this French poet is seen as a prototypical writer in the age of commodity culture, epitomizing the meltdown of the old mediascape, in particular, of the bourgeois literary scene. In Benjamin's seminal study of Baudelaire 'the most important motifs of *The Arcades Project* converge' (C, 556). His book project on Baudelaire was never fully completed, yet his extensive notes and comments on Baudelaire survived as fragments in 'Central Park' and Convolute J [Baudelaire].

The new technological space produced by arcades does not simply blur the boundary between the private inside and the public outside. In fact, 'the spatial interpenetration' engendered in the arcade shows 'topographical contradictions like a Möbius strip' as the exterior space is conceived as the interior.[45] As the figure of the flâneur came into being alongside the emergence of arcades as new commercial spaces, the way in which the flâneur dawdles in the arcade illustrates the spatial intersection of the interior and the exterior: 'It is in this world that the flâneur is at home; he provides the arcade . . . with its chronicler and philosopher. As for himself, the arcade provides him with an unfailing remedy for the kind of boredom that easily arises under the baleful eye of a sated reactionary regime' (SW4, 19). The arcade is the place where the bourgeois come to buy and the rest come to look at what they cannot buy. The distinctive character of the flâneur lies in a sense of visual encounter with the metropolis since 'Baudelaire's original interest in allegory is not linguistic but optical' (SW4, 187). The flâneur's activity of observation in the modern city is, as David Frisby illustrates, 'a multifaceted method for apprehending and reading the complex and myriad signifiers in the labyrinth of modernity'.[46] Along with the arcade, the 'mobilized gaze' of the flâneur or window-shopping in a modern sense came into being.[47] The flâneur is less a buyer than a spectator in this theatre of the commodity. 'The flâneur sabotages the traffic. Moreover, he is no buyer. He is merchandise' (AP [A3a,7], 42]). In the arcade, the phantasmagoria of space emerges alongside consumer culture, and the flâneur with optical encounter with the commodities grasps the transitional position of the bourgeois subject into the masses.

For Benjamin, the rise of a new type of consumer experience corresponds to the growth of mass consumption and the end of flânerie as 'the psychotic appropriation of space and time'.[48] Benjamin likens the melting down process of the individual subject to the rise of the commercial space, the department store: 'The crowd is the veil through which the familiar city beckons to the flâneur as phantasmagoria – now a landscape, now a room. Both become elements of the department store, which makes use of flânerie itself to sell goods' (AP, 10). The department store emerges as a corollary of the dramatic changes in urban retail that took place between 1840 and 1870, accelerating the decline of the arcades. The early department store played a prominent role in the development of mass consumer society, by making urban dwellers aware of recent commercial innovations.[49] In the arcades, the main clientele had not been the masses, but a limited section of the privileged class who wanted to be differentiated from the public. With regard to a gender issue, as Benjamin evidently conceives the flâneur only to be a male bourgeois subject, the rise of the department store involves the 'a process of the feminization of the flâneur'.[50] In conjunction with the individuality and the collectivity, the transformation of the arcade to the department store accelerated the decline of the 'private' dawdler and the emergence of the mass consumer. The department store soon served as 'the last promenade for the flâneur' (AP, 10). For Benjamin, for the first time, it is with the establishment of the department store that the crowd becomes the dominant consumer force and consumers 'begin to consider themselves a mass' (AP [A4,1], 43). In the department store, the new collective subjects 'are confronted with an assortment of goods; they take in all the floors at a glance; they pay fixed prices; they can make exchanges' (AP [A12,5], 60). The department stores are temples consecrated to Baudelaire's 'religious intoxication of great cities' (AP [A13], 61). Along with the emergence of collective shopping spaces, the flâneur's joy in watching, previously grounded in contemplative observation, is now easily upset and disturbed. While the existence of the flâneur on the street could be linked to the growth of spaces of consumption, such as arcades, his decline was accelerated by rapid urban planning, that is, the Haussmannization of the Paris street as well as the rise of mass consumer culture generated by department stores.

The Phantasmagoria of Public Space

Related Convolutes in The Arcades Project:
E   Haussmannization, Barricade Fighting
X   Marx
k   The Commune
a   Social Movement

The last section of the exposé, 'Haussmann, or the Barricades', encompasses the rise of the alternative public space within the phantasmagorias of the urban spectacle. Baron Georges-Eugène Haussmann (1809–1891), a French prefect and civic planner under Napoleon III, led the renovation and modernization of Parisian urban spaces in the 1860s by creating twelve grand avenues radiating from the *Arc de Triomphe*. The massive scale of his urban plan was also a political and strategic response to the barricades, aiming to destroy the narrow streets in old Parisian neighbourhoods. Haussmann's urbanism aimed to divide and isolate spaces. His mega-project separated entertainment and leisure spaces from places of work by demolishing many historical sites like arcades built in the early nineteenth century and modernizing public utilities and transportation facilities. As Boyer vividly illustrates, Haussmann seeks to transform Paris into 'a modern city of circulation and flux'. The monuments of the city are isolated from their historical context and uncoupled from 'organic elements of the city's compositional form'.[51] The old Paris as the city of aesthetic pleasure, the corporeal encounter and historical memory is replaced by the city of technological mobility and commodity spectacle. In the wake of this destruction and transformation, the collective memory of history disappeared along with the private citizen as well as the flâneur.

Whereas Haussmann's boulevards consolidate the bourgeois hegemony by demolishing working-class districts, the Paris Commune, or Fourth French Revolution lasting from 18 March 1871 to 28 May 1871 is emblematic of a primal form of the collective public space against the phantasmagorias of the urban spectacle: 'Just as the *Communist Manifesto* ends the age of professional conspirators, so the Commune puts an end to the phantasmagoria holding sway over the early years of the proletariat' (AP, 12). The Commune marks the end of the phantasmagoria of bourgeois modernity by awakening the collective from the dream world of mass consumption and the bourgeois regime and turning the city into a 'play-space' [*Spielraum*] (SW4, 265). While play involves a form of mimetic faculty, which liberates the restricted and alienated human sensorium, space entails a material condition for corporeal practice. In the Commune, Benjamin finds an alternative mode of the communal social relation against the phantasmagoria of the isolated private citizen. As Hansen aptly notes, Benjamin's idea of play-space denotes 'an alternative mode of aesthetic on a par with modern, collective experience, an aesthetics that could counteract, at the level of sense perception, the political consequences of the failed – that is, capitalist and imperialist, destructive and self-destructive – reception of technology'.[52] The Commune shows a critical motif of profane illumination, being awakened from the phantasmagoria of modernity. The play-space, typified in his analysis of the Commune, aims to construct a new form of a mass public via a new form of collective aesthetic and political practice. The Commune reveals 'a utopian and apocalyptic moment of social upheaval in keeping with Benjamin's darkly redemptive political Messianism'.[53] It is evident that Benjamin's vision of a new public space integrates the new principles of solidarity and community into the technological potential of such media as the cinema as a play-space. Yet it is not clear who these new mass publics are, engendered via the sensory, psychosomatic and aesthetic experiences: are they proletariat? Or the multitude?

TACTILITY OF MEDIA CRITIC

Key Works
'The Task of the Critic' (1931)
'The Author as Producer' (1934)

'Eduard Fuchs, Collector and Historian' (1936)

H   The Collector in *The Arcades Project*

Benjamin's imaginative conception of the public space as play-space, as revealed in the section on the Commune, is inspired by surrealist experiments, which try to turn urban space into a playground. The surrealist influence on Benjamin's critique of the humanist elements of bourgeois literary culture is already evident in his 1928 work, *One-Way Street*, a set of aphorisms. The surrealist urban experience typified in Louis Aragon's *Paris Peasant* and André Breton's *Nadja* unearth an unfamiliar experience of familiar objects in the city. The surrealist experiments provide Benjamin with the theoretical means of aligning a distinctive mode of urban experience with the process of aesthetic practice and awakening from the dream world, a process that is conceptualized as 'profane illumination' (SW2, 209). 'Multiple experiences' or 'the surrealist urban sublime' in the surrealist practices is much closer to Benjamin's idea of shock experience of the urban spectacle than Baudelaire's visual observation of Parisian urban reality.[54] However, in his 1929 essay, 'Surrealism: the Last Snapshot of the European Intelligentsia', Benjamin explicitly discredits surrealist practices as 'the sclerotic liberal moral humanistic ideals of freedom' (SW2, 215) and 'an inadequate, undialectical conception of the nature of intoxication' (SW2, 216), attributing their outright failure to their compromising practices when retrieving individual subjectivity. For Benjamin, the theatrical reality and mythic delusion of the city captured by surrealist aesthetic practice are no more than the flâneur's visual pleasure, or 'a gastronomy of the eye', coinciding with the scopophilic observations of the estranged, drained bourgeois male individual. Despite their active employment of cutting-edge technology and radical political manifestation in opposition to the liberal bourgeois regime, the intrinsic shortcomings of the Surrealists derive from their romantic stance on the predominant humanist tradition. The Surrealists remain locked within ocularcentric hegemony and do not relate to the tactile dimension of collective experience, that is, the quintessential – yet overlooked – attribute of profane illumination.

> Nevertheless – indeed, precisely after such dialectical annihilation – this will still be an image space and, more concretely, a body space . . . The collective is a body, too. And the physis that is being organized for it in technology can, through all its political and factual reality, be produced only in that image space to which profane illumination initiates us. Only when in technology body and image space so interpenetrate that all revolutionary tension becomes bodily collective innervation, and all the bodily innervations of the collective become revolutionary discharge, has reality transcended itself to the extent demanded by the *Communist Manifesto*. (SW2, 217–18)

For Benjamin, surrealist aesthetic experimentations are not sufficiently dissociated from conventional humanist practices grounded in the bourgeois public sphere, and fail to engage fully with an alternative mode of public space that increasingly expands social and cultural horizons aided by various forms of technology. Unlike the Enlightenment ideas based on humanist tradition, the profane illumination is less akin to individual rational reflection in the private space than to collective bodily practice in the public space. These 'European intellectuals' remain as 'the private citizen' that '[we] all are trying not to become' (GS VI, 442).

Thus, Benjamin goes on to reject the core aspects of surrealist aesthetic practice, seeing them as rooted in the Romantic understanding of the urban experience. A crucial limitation of surrealist aesthetics lies in their inability to create a form of communicable experience; the experience of their art work is primarily that of the isolated and private individual, not that of the collective masses, whether they be the crowd or the public. For Benjamin, the Surrealists remain in the tradition of 'metaphysical materialism', failing to recognize the new principles of 'anthropological materialism', which is no longer based on individual optical contemplation but on collective tactile distraction that is intertwined with a complex play-space, a space that is constituted in three dimensions: technology, image and the body, as shown in the above quotation. In Benjamin's view, the conventional humanist intellectuals, including the radical Surrealists, have failed to grapple with a new mode of the public, which has already begun to shake and lead to a total crisis of European modernity on an unprecedented scale, whether it be a form of fascism or one of popular culture. The profane illumination from the phantasmagoria is realized not only through the appropriation of critical consciousness, but via the enhancement of habitual behaviour that improves the mimetic faculty of the masses.

Distancing himself from Surrealism, Benjamin envisions an essential faculty of the new intellectual in the wake of the crisis of bourgeois public sphere in the German Marxist historian, Eduard Fuchs' (1870–1940) practice. In his essay, 'Eduard Fuchs, Collector and Historian', Benjamin recognizes that Fuchs distances himself completely from the classical idea of art and historicism, so that conventional bourgeois aesthetic categories play no role in his work: 'neither beautiful semblance [*der schöne Schein*], nor harmony, nor the unity of the manifold' (SW3, 268). While Baudelaire is seen as the allegorist of urban spectacle, Fuchs is conceived as the collector of urban ruins (AP [H4a,1], 211).[55] The collector's behaviour is characterized primarily by bodily engagement rather than attentive contemplation. 'Possession and having are allied with the tactile, and stand in a certain opposition to the optical. Collectors are beings with tactile instincts. Moreover, with the recent turn away from naturalism, the primacy of the optical that was determinate for the previous century has come to an end' (AP [H2,5], 206–7). Collecting indicates a new form of historical and aesthetic practice, that is, 'a primal phenomenon of study' and functions as the most binding of 'all the profane manifestations of nearness' (AP [H4,3], 210 and AP [H1a,2], 205).

Positing an alternative model to ocularcentric subjectivity exemplified by the flâneur, the collector epitomizes the new mode of subject, the one who controls the objective world and transfigures it, 'divesting things of their commodity character by taking possession of them' (AP, 9). By replacing the dominance of 'exhibition value' with 'use value', the collector aims to tear down the phantasmagoria of modernity and to restore the 'dreams of the collective' (AP, 908), dreams that have been fabricated as the spectacle of commodity culture. The collector serves to be engaged publicly with the political struggle for collective memory. While the flâneur as allegorist devotes himself only to visual pleasure, the collector presents historical knowledge according to the image of awakening. Profane illumination as an awakening from the theatrical illusion articulated by various forms of the entertainment industry is prompted by the exemplification of collective remembering. In this vein, the collector is less akin to a theorist than to a practitioner or an aesthetic engineer who engages bodily with the flow of spectacle, the flow of historical obliviousness.

By integrating a 'tactile' element into media practice, Benjamin locates media technology's mimetic possibilities at the centre of the formation of a new mass public. For Benjamin, film is not a visual medium but a tactile one, engendering the bodily collective through a distractive reception process. The aim of revolution is to adapt the tactile feature of media and regroup apperception: 'Revolutions are innervations of the collective – or, more precisely, efforts at innervation on the part of the new, historically unique collective that has its organs in the new technology' (SW3, 124).[56] Benjamin sees tactility as suggesting an alternative to the ocularcentric experience of spectacle, which leads to the anaesthetization of the body. As Tobias Wilke notes, the task of the media critique entails 'the politics of sense' which involves 'sharpening the human faculties of sensation and endowing them, by means of tactical forays into new territory'.[57] The revolutionary politics of Benjamin's media critique aim to give rise to a bodily collective that will be able to transform the phantasmagoric experiences of everyday life by retrieving the alienated human sensorium, reversing the decline of the mimetic faculty, and reconstructing the fragmented body, that is, a synaesthesia of the bodily collective.

CONCLUSION

In this chapter, I have shown that the various forms of public space analysed in *The Arcades Project* are characterized as a social site of collective experience and the living context of the masses. These urban spaces, such as the arcade, the panorama and the world exhibitions, constitute the cultural loci articulated by the aesthetic experience of media spectacle. The meltdown of bourgeois public culture, including the literary public sphere, coincides with the rise of these varied entertainment industries. In my view, the emergence of public space explored in *The Arcades Project* marked the end of the phantasmagorias of bourgeois modernity in three ways: epistemologically, it marked the end of individual rationality; physically, the end of the deliberative public sphere; and symbolically, the end of the culture of the letter. When the dynamics of the pleasure perceived through distraction replaces rational communication bound up with the political arena, then the collapse of the bourgeois public sphere and the crisis of deliberative democracy are accelerated. Herein lie profound differences between the normative model of the deliberative or dialogic public sphere, as developed by Jürgen Habermas, and Benjamin's critical model of the aesthetic public space, that is, a play-space consisting of a three-dimensional complex of image-, technology- and body-spaces. Benjamin tries to find exemplary figures and exponents who have been able to generate a new mode of aesthetic public space, looking to contemporary avant-garde movements such as Surrealism, Brecht's Epic Theatre, the radical movement within Russian children's theatre, Eisenstein's filmic experiment and so on. Benjamin shares with these avant-garde movements the radical critique of the bourgeois public sphere and the humanist tradition of European culture and art, but goes much further by challenging the cornerstone of the modernist project and grasping the constructive role of mass culture in the formation of a new mass public.

Viewed in this light, it is notable that the key features of Benjamin's media critique are diametrically opposed to those of ideological criticism [*Ideologiekritik*] developed by key members of the Frankfurt School, such as Horkheimer, Adorno and Habermas. These differences are particularly relevant for an understanding of the trajectories of contemporary media studies. First, in relation to the object of media studies, ideological criticism considers the object from the perspective of social totality. In contrast, Benjamin's media critique conceives of it as a monadological fragment. Adorno in particular criticizes Benjamin's methodological idea of the dialectical image for its immediacy and lack of conceptual mediation. Second, ideological criticism seeks to analyse the cognitive level of consciousness in the sense of a world-view [*Weltanschauung*], aiming to help the masses to rectify their false consciousness with the aid of self-reflective judgement. In contrast, media critique tries to approach the perceptual level of experience of the subject as expressed in a sense of a world-picture [*Weltbild*]. While ideological criticism regards those spectacular images created by mass media as false representations of the truth, Benjamin's media critique sees them as expressions of collective wishes embedded in their dreams. Third, ideological criticism is a particular form of normative criticism that judges social practice by norms such as freedom, authentic individuality or happiness. In this way, ideological criticism is scathingly criticized by postmodernist theories of culture as being a universal meta-narrative that judges a particular belief system by means of these norms. Benjamin's media critique conversely considers criticism as a manifestation of the historical and cultural object and helps to reconstruct historical meanings rooted in the objects by means of its practice.

On that account, ideological criticism, a core doctrine of the culture industry developed by Horkheimer and Adorno seems barely sustainable as a theory and practice in the context of media spectacle. Despite its profound diagnosis of modern rationality, the ideological criticism of the Enlightenment derived from the pivotal idea that only critical reason is capable of reflecting on and correcting a false belief system. Yet, ideological criticism has paid little attention to the substantial changes in the conditions of the cognitive process and the production of knowledge. Benjamin's media critique does not deny that there is a role for critical reasoning; yet critical reasoning necessitates a certain form of attentive contemplation and the leaving of sufficient distance between the cognitive subject and the object of critical reflection. In a society in which primary collective experiences are bound up with media spectacle, the configuration of time and space is rapidly reshaped by new modes of communication, and the boundary between the cognitive subject and its object comes to be permeated constantly, leading to a breakdown of the sufficient – yet, requisite – distance between the cognitive subject and its object. In the age of media spectacle, it is difficult to distinguish true from false, art from copy, real story from fake drama, and eventually, reality from illusion.

6

CONCLUSION: THE ACTUALITY OF
BENJAMIN'S MEDIA CRITIQUE

In this book, I have tried to suggest that Benjamin's media critique offers unique insights into the development of various modes of communication and into their impact on human sensorium, subjectivity, aesthetic practice and political arena; insights that are highly relevant for today's mediascape. While Benjamin's distinctive account of the media offers many valuable points for contemporary media and cultural studies, there are some aspects that should not be accepted uncritically. It should be asked not only whether his insights can be considered valid in relation to their own historical context, but also whether his analysis of the early stage of communication technologies is sustainable in its original form and applicable to today's more complicated mediascape. In conclusion, I would like to draw out some further theoretical implications of Benjamin's media critique by comparing it with the central doctrine of the Frankfurt School's media theory and further placing it in the context of the work of other more recent media theorists.

CRITICAL THEORY AND
THE CULTURE INDUSTRY

The Frankfurt School has made several contributions to the development of contemporary media studies, yet some of their main doctrines seem barely sustainable today without profound theoretical revisions. For the key members of the Frankfurt School, in particular Horkheimer and Adorno, mass culture – as dubbed 'the culture industry' – plays a central role in a new configuration of the capitalist system, ultimately inducing compliance with dominant social relations via mass media and commodity culture.[1] The theory of the culture industry attributes the self-destruction of Western civilization and the emergence of totalitarianism to the predominance of an instrumental rationality deeply rooted in the Enlightenment project itself. Reflecting on the rapid growth of both political totalitarianism and the Hollywood entertainment industry, they argue that the manipulation and control of the culture industry rendered impossible the communication of authentic experience.[2] Applying Lukács' philosophical concept of reification to the cultural arena, whereby society is understood to be a totality, Horkheimer and Adorno argue that capitalist culture is imposed by the dominant class and that the mass media prove to be nothing more than a means of achieving a totally administered society.[3]

While this radical analysis of the culture industry provides a valuable departure point for the social theory of the media, on its own it constitutes an unsatisfactory basis for an examination of the complex dimensions of the media and modern societies. Unlike media critique, Horkheimer and Adorno's theory of the culture industry is too abstract to be applied to the concrete analysis of media culture. Their approach to the culture industry regards the media foremost as no more than a tool of domination. The oversimplification embedded in their methodology (that is, ideological criticism) led them to exclude any subversive dimensions of popular culture in certain political contexts (e.g., jazz, rock 'n' roll and films), so that they failed to grasp the complex material aspects of modern society that are interwoven with various modes of communication technology.

CRITICAL MEDIA THEORY AND THE PUBLIC SPHERE

Jürgen Habermas' early account of the emergence and transformation of the public sphere made a significant contribution to the development of a critical theory of the media and democracy, albeit in a different vein to the first generation of the Institute. Habermas characterizes the type of criticism elucidated by Benjamin as a redemptive critique, a critique that tends to decipher the history of culture with a view to rescuing it from upheaval and to do justice to the 'collective fantasy images deposited in the expressive qualities of daily life as well as in literature and art'.[4] Habermas explicitly underlines the theological tradition in Benjamin's theory of mimesis, language and communication that underpins his critique, that is, an anti-humanist messianic perspective of history, and a myth-oriented understanding. It seems evident that in many respects the essential features of Benjamin's media critique are opposed to Habermas' theory of communicative action. The incompatibility between Habermas and Benjamin as shown in their respective epistemological perspectives on history and criticism generates more distance between the two theories about the public sphere. Habermas' account of the emergence and the decline of the bourgeois public sphere made a valuable contribution to our understanding of the normative foundation of deliberative or dialogic democracy. Yet, in many respects his theory on the public sphere is unconvincing.[5] Most of all, his work cannot provide a compelling explanation of other dimensions of communication that are less related to the discursive dimension of communication. His notion of the public sphere is less akin to the formative role of the medium of communication – print media in this particular historical context – than to the conversation or discussion as such that were stimulated by print.[6] Not unlike the theory of the culture industry, Habermas conceives the media to be no more than a mere technical device to deliver the message to the receiver. If this is the case, an important question remains unresolved: how might media like print change the very nature of the public in connection with diverse modes of political culture? Habermas overemphasizes the 'model case' of Britain in the late eighteenth century at the expense of other places and periods.[7] Consequently, Habermas' theory of the public sphere is unable to explain the dynamics of other non-bourgeois public spheres as produced by multiple social actors.[8]

Whereas Habermas' theory of the public sphere conceives the public arena to be the formal condition under which an individual could speak and act, regardless of his or her origin and status, Benjamin's analysis of the entertainment industry pluralizes and multiplies a conventional – yet essential – category like the public by presenting a more comprehensive idea of aesthetic public space as a social horizon of collective experience. Varied forms of nineteenth-century public spaces exposed in *The Arcades Project* encompass the cultural and political contexts of everyday lives articulated by affective communication and the aesthetic experience of the popular culture.[9] These features are excluded from Habermas' analysis of the literary bourgeois public sphere, which is based heavily on cognitive rational communication. Benjamin's distinctive account of the public space as a play-space also reveals that in an age when politics is inextricably intertwined with popular culture and the entertainment industry, political participation and social movements are closely bound up with the dynamics of political consumerism and media spectacle.

TECHNOLOGICAL REPRODUCIBILITY IN THE MEDIA GALAXY

In some respects, Benjamin's media critique has formed the foundation of much contemporary media theory, as well as the postmodernization of media culture. It has been claimed that key elements of Benjamin's account of the media have especially marked similarities with the work of Marshall McLuhan (1911–1981) and Jean Baudrillard (1929–2007).[10] Yet these claims tend to oversimplify central tenets of media critique and consequently fail to appreciate its richness. A comparative analysis of theories that are paralleled in their work will clarify some of the important theoretical implications of media critique and its contribution to contemporary media studies.

According to the prominent Hungarian art historian and Benjamin's contemporary, Arnold Hauser (1892–1978), Marshall McLuhan is a theorist who introduces and popularizes Benjamin's seminal aesthetic idea of technological reproducibility in the fields of media and popular culture studies.[11] Viewed from the broader perspective of the mass media, it seems inviting to identify that both Benjamin and McLuhan illuminate the central role of the media in the actual constitution of modern lives.[12] However, any overemphasis on theoretical affinities between the two are no more than superficial and tangential.

As his famous dictum postulates, 'the medium is the message', McLuhan brought to the fore the significance of the form of communication media irrespective of its content.[13] For McLuhan, the communication medium itself has the potential to influence the way a particular medium's content is perceived and to shape cultures dominated by a particular medium. When conventional communication studies were preoccupied with analysing media content in terms of public opinion and propaganda, McLuhan privileged instead the medium over the message, or form over content. A medium can be regarded as any cultural and technological artefact that serves to extend and widen the human senses and limbs by abolishing temporal-spatial limitations. McLuhan conceives of the rise of visuality as one of the key features of the age of modern media communication, the 'Gutenberg Galaxy', as he calls it.[14] With the rise of the printing press, social life shifted from a traditional communal society based upon oral communication to a modern, visual typographic culture that made possible the rise of rational individualism and Western nationalism, as historically probed in terms of the 'imagined communities'.[15] Since then, electronic media such as radio and television have propelled culture into an electronic media society in which communication media themselves have become the central nervous system, leading to the 'global village', as McLuhan famously characterized it.[16] In this respect, McLuhan's analysis of the shift from the oral to the visual and its connection to the uprooting of tradition and the establishment of modern society seems to have close affinities with Benjamin's account of the decline of the communal mode of storytelling and the rise of the individual and private experience of the novel and the predominance of the shock-laden visual perception in the big city.[17]

Nevertheless, the analyses by McLuhan and Benjamin contain significant dissonant elements. McLuhan's understanding of the transformation from traditional to modern society is grounded on so simple a dichotomy between oral and visual perception that it loses sight of the co-existence of various important social formations, as well as obscuring other multiple modes of perception such as distracted tactility. McLuhan still conceives of technology as a neutral apparatus. This is too narrow a concept to appreciate the broader context of technology's social and political functions. It is also too monolithic to grasp other aspects of the media that are institutionally bound up with the distortion and manipulation of communication. While Benjamin's concept of technological reproducibility is deeply rooted in its political and social attributes, McLuhan's understanding of the media is grounded on his view of technology as neutral and instrumental machinery. As James Carey notes, McLuhan appears to be a 'poet of a technological determinism' with one message: 'Yield to the restorative capacity of the modern machine'.[18] On the contrary, Benjamin's thesis of 'politicization of art' shows his media critique aims to politicize the media and, thereby, to bring about a new mass public.

PHANTASMAGORIA, SIMULACRA AND SPECTACLE

Benjamin's startling new insight into the media pre-dated the postmodern turn in media studies typified by the work of Jean Baudrillard. Illuminating the notion of 'mechanical reproduction', Jean Baudrillard praises Benjamin for being the first media theorist to grasp technology as a medium rather than a 'productive force' and as 'the form and principle of an entirely new generation of meaning'.[19] Baudrillard reveals that his theory of simulation draws deeply upon Benjamin's notion of reproduction and McLuhan's idea of the medium as the message: 'The analyses of both Benjamin and McLuhan stand on the borders of reproduction and simulation, at the point where referential reason disappears and production is seized by vertigo.'[20] In the age of postmodern society, he argues, the new media-saturated culture becomes predominant over the 'real' world, replacing conventional social relations grounded in industrial political economics. Echoing Benjamin's analysis of the work of art in terms of exhibition value, the use and exchange values of political economy are superseded in the era of postmodernity by sign-value, which reconfigures the commodity as a 'symbol' to be consumed and displayed. With the emergence of cyber-space and new media technologies, production is replaced by reproduction, signs by simulacra, and the real by the hyper-real, in which the traditional distinctions between the real and illusory, subject and object, are obliterated. In this context, Baudrillard considers Benjamin's analysis of the decline of aura to anticipate the theory of simulacra. For Baudrillard, an aura of the work of art is not destined to death. As there is an aura of authenticity about the original, Baudrillard argues, there is both 'authentic simulation' and 'inauthentic simulation'.[21] Benjamin's account of the death of aura seems to Baudrillard to be no more than 'a politically desperate conclusion', leading to 'melancholy modernity'.[22]

Drawing on the endless reproduction of simulacra, the postmodern consumer society enters a universe of hyperreal-ity; in brief, the term hyperreality refers to a situation where the fake is more real than the real.[23] Baudrillard employs the notion of hyperreality to characterize sites of amusement such as Las Vegas and Disneyland, emphasizing the way in which the mass culture of Disneyland causes the aesthetic to be consumed by kitsch. Furthermore, Baudrillard's 'cool culture' also seems connected to Benjamin's (and Kracauer's) characterization of the culture of distraction.[24] Certainly, his analysis of the predominance of hyperreality seems to echo Benjamin's account of the entertainment industry as a perfect, yet technologically reproduced reality.[25]

Baudrillard goes further in connecting Benjamin's idea of
phantasmagoria with the notion of spectacle developed by a
founder of the International Situationist Group, Guy Debord
(1931–1994). In doing so, Baudrillard offers a radical redefi-
nition of the relationship between reality and illusion in
terms of an incessantly self-reproduced reality. The notions
of phantasmagoria, spectacle and simulacra are fundamental
facets of the analysis of modernity as it relates to the complex
intersection of media, commodity and politics. In his seminal
work, *The Society of the Spectacle* (1967), Debord defines the
notion of spectacle not as 'a collection of images' but as
'mediated images' that forge the social relationships between
people.[26] For Debord, spectacle is a materially reconstructed
illusion, which is produced in accordance with the logic of
commodity. In the society of spectacle, the whole of life
is presented as an immense accumulation of spectacle and
becomes mere representation. It is noteworthy that Debord's
visualization of modern culture is not free from Lukács' formulation of reification, fetishism and alienation. It is also
noteworthy that Baudrillard radically sets apart the notion of
spectacle from the dynamics of political economy and commodity fetishism, by claiming that hyperrealism no longer
belongs to false consciousness or representation, the dream
or phantasm, maintained as in the Marxist theory of ideology
or commodity fetishism. Instead, he argues that it signifies a
much more advanced phase insofar as it erases the distinction between the real and the imaginary; it only belongs to
'the hallucinatory resemblance of the real to itself'.

Phantasmagoria and simulacra mark out an area of
common ground for the two authors. Even though
Baudrillard's conceptual pairing of simulacra and sign-value
seems to have close affinity with Benjamin's pairing of phantasmagoria and exhibition-value, there are crucial disparities.
First of all, while Baudrillard covertly distinguishes capital-

ist modernity and postmodernity, Benjamin's account of modernity relies on the dialectical relationship between the old and the new, the past and the present, the continuity and the discontinuity, as epitomized in his term 'Now-Time' (*Jetztzeit*). Secondly, drawing on ideas from political economy, Baudrillard wrongly declares the end of productive relationships, and as such his notion of simulacra grasps only a part of this complex social dimension. By the same token, Baudrillard is incorrect when he claims that we are witnessing the end of perspective and panoptic space and the abolition of spectacle. In contrast, Benjamin's analysis of phantasmagoria entails the co-existence of a panoptic disciplinary dimension and the panoramic entertaining one, revealing a complex interplay of various mechanisms of social control. The varied aspects of the entertainment industry need not be divorced from the larger logic of capitalist modernity, and need not be reduced to ideology or commodity fetishism. Baudrillard's theory is of limited application to a rich analysis of how contemporary advanced media function in various ways to reconfigure perception as well as discipline and entertainment. Thirdly, if Benjamin identifies himself as 'an active nihilist', Baudrillard's postmodern theory appears somewhat 'passive nihilistic' because he cannot see how a collective subject – whether modern or postmodern – might be reconfigured within simulacra. With respect to the formation of a new subject, Baudrillard's notion of the 'inert masses' seems more like a collective flâneur. However, in his view, the human subject is a passive object, which is simply plugged into communication media and lacks both autonomy and the capacity for reflection and critical judgement, a motif that is employed in the Hollywood sci-fi film *The Matrix* (1999), directed by the Wachowski brothers. Here, Baudrillard's theory of simulacra and Horkheimer and Adorno's theory of the culture industry share a perspective on the passivity and the inert nature of the modern masses. In contrast to Baudrillard, Benjamin's analysis of the entertainment industry is concerned to unearth how the phantasmagoric experiences of audiences, spectators and consumers create the dynamics of the formation of the new collective subject. In contrast to Baudrillard's monolithic account of the subject in hyperreal culture, Benjamin's analysis of the rise of a new mass public in a new media public space guides us to grasp key aspects of contemporary digital culture like 'convergence culture' and various forms of media audiences (e.g., fans, bloggers, gamers, social media users, etc.).[27] Benjamin's media critique differs substantially from the postmodern theory of media in its search for the emancipatory potential of the media within the phantasmagoria of modernity.

MEDIA CRITIQUE TODAY

I have sought to show that Benjamin's media critique makes numerous theoretical contributions to the understanding of the development of media and their impact on modern societies. How and why is Benjamin's media critique relevant for us? I think there are once again four aspects for us to consider.

1. Benjamin's media critique is important because it provides a theoretical discussion of the radical transformation and development of new media technologies. He sees these technological innovations as fundamental to the understanding of human communication in the modern age. Benjamin thereby poses the following questions: How do new communication technologies shape modern forms of communication? What new possibilities and new constraints are produced? How are these experienced by audiences, viewers and critics?

2. The question of the human experience of media and how the media themselves transform experiences is fundamental to Benjamin. New media then shape the human perceptual capacities and faculties, and undergird new forms of embodied experience. Media, then, are not simply visual or oral, or literary forms, but reconfigure the entire human body, our sensory apparatus: in other words, media technological transformation, the transformation of the body, and its relation to space and time are intimately interconnected. New media produce new perceptual possibilities, new bodies and new subjectivities.

3. These possibilities are always deeply political in character. New media produce not only body space, and body image, but also a new configuration of public and private spaces. The media create new fora and realms of communication. The media transform the character of communications between the powerful and the powerless, between governments and their electors, and between dictators and the masses. Power is made visible in new ways. The voice of the *Führer* is sent into the domestic private setting. Politics is aestheticized as spectacle. The media are always available to serve the interest of domination, irrationalism, authoritarianism and fascism. Benjamin responded to this danger by demanding the politicization of aesthetics. That is to say, in these new cultural circumstances and in the light of new technological advances, the old aesthetic categories pertaining to painting, to theatrical performance, to musical concerts, to works of art – all these categories of taste – have been transformed. Art's cultic origins are overturned, and a new basis in politics comes to the fore. Aesthetic questions are transformed into political questions, and this politicization of the aesthetic is counter-poised to the aestheticization of politics at the end of Benjamin's Work of Art essay.

4. So, finally, Benjamin is acutely aware of both the dangers and possibilities, both the threats and promises, of new media technologies. Media critique finds its proper place in our world today. Surveying the rapidly changing mediascape of global media communications in the early twenty-first century, a world marked by the proliferation of communications, devices, techniques, technologies and possibilities, we are confronting at every moment the spectacle of culture in the service of commodity, by a world in which political domination and capitalist economic exploitation go hand in hand. Benjamin helps open our eyes to this. But that is not all. He also provides us with sound counsel in reminding us of the hopes that are also embedded in these new technologies. They will enable us: to explore and inhabit our world in new ways by means of opening up the optical unconscious; to gaze upon the world not in terms of auratic submission and mysticism, but with the new, clear-sighted prosthetic capabilities of the camera; and they will augment the possibilities of remembrance in an era threatened with amnesia and barbarism.

Benjamin's media critique engages with the new political questions thrown up by tensions and conflicts between the revolutionary potential of mass communication, traditional aesthetics and fascist propaganda. Benjamin's media critique is therefore concerned to address not merely theoretical issues but an urgent political imperative, illuminating the political orientation, possibilities and dangers of the new media. Benjamin's media critique is not just a theory but a practice that is constantly reconfigured according to the conditions of the contemporary mediascape. It suggests a new approach to communicative practice and political intervention, alive and 'logged on' to ever-changing communication media. Benjamin's media critique helps us to see our world more clearly, to see through deceptions of ideology and power and prompts us to use new media possibilities, new media potentials, to realize a new humanity. Benjamin reminds us:

As long as there is still one beggar around, there will still be myth. (AP [K6,4], 400)

NOTES

CHAPTER 1: INTRODUCING DR BENJAMIN

1 Gershom Scholem, *Walter Benjamin: The Story of a Friendship* (London: Faber and Faber, 1982). On Scholem's own account of Judaic Messianism, liberal Judaism and the notion of redemption, see Gershom Scholem, *The Messianic Idea in Judaism and Other Essays on Jewish Spirituality* (New York: Schocken Books, 1971).
2 Theodor W. Adorno, 'Benjamin the Letter Writer', in Gary Smith (ed.), *On Walter Benjamin: Critical Essays and Recollections* (Cambridge, MA: MIT Press, 1992), pp. 329–37.
3 Siegfried Kracauer, 'On the Writings of Walter Benjamin', in *The Mass Ornament: Weimar Essays* (Cambridge, MA: Harvard University Press, 1995), pp. 259–64.

CHAPTER 2: THE CRISIS OF COMMUNICATION AND THE INFORMATION INDUSTRY

1 Robert Park, 'The Natural History of the Newspaper', *American Journal of Sociology* 29(3) (November 1923): 273.

2 Charles Baudelaire was one of the key literary figures who had preoccupied Benjamin since his translation of selected poems from *Les Fleurs du mal* in 1921. As we shall see in chapter 5, his study of Baudelaire in the 1930s was an important part of his *Arcades Project* and he wanted to write a separate book under the title *Charles Baudelaire: A Lyric Poet in the Age of High Capitalism*, which would comprise three parts: 'Baudelaire as Allegorist', 'The Paris of the Second Empire in Baudelaire', and 'The Commodity as a Subject of Poetry'. The second part was completed in 1938 but received the vitriolic criticism of T.W. Adorno, a criticism directed mainly towards its lack of theoretical perspective. After substantial revision, it was published in early 1940 with a new title, 'On Some Motifs in Baudelaire'. Consisting of three sections, 'The *Bohème*', 'The *Flâneur*' and 'Modernity', the essay 'The Paris of the Second Empire in Baudelaire' offered a detailed exposition of urban culture in the literary field of the Second Empire. These essays have been hailed as Benjamin's seminal literary criticism of Baudelaire in the context of French modernism, yet they also demonstrate his radical critique of the impact of the publishing industry on literary production and the role of newspapers in the transformation of the bourgeois literary field.

3 Gary Smith, 'Thinking through Benjamin: An Introductory Essay', in Gary Smith (ed.), *Benjamin: Philosophy, Aesthetics, History* (Chicago, IL: University of Chicago Press, 1989), p. xii.

4 At university, while studying under one of the leading Kantian scholars, Heinrich Rickert, Benjamin sought to grapple with the epistemological justification of knowledge, that is, the compatibility of rational and metaphysical knowledge, confronted by Kantian philosophy. In his 1918 essay 'On the Program of the Coming Philosophy' Benjamin asserts: 'The task of future epistemology is to find for knowledge the sphere of total neutrality in regard to the concepts of both subject and object; in other words, it is to discover the autonomous, innate sphere of knowledge in which this concept in no way continues to designate the relation between two metaphysical entities' (SW1, 104). For the manifold contexts of the notion of experience as a universal theme in modern Western philosophy, see Martin Jay, *Songs of Experience* (Berkeley, CA: University of California Press, 2005). The Italian philosopher Agamben elucidates Benjamin's motive of the experience thus: '[T]he question of experience can be approached nowadays only with an acknowledgement that it is no longer accessible to us. For just as modern man has been deprived of his biography, his experience has likewise been expropriated. Indeed, his incapacity to have and communicate experience is perhaps one of the few self-certainties to which he can lay claim.' Giorgio Agamben, *Infancy and History: Essays on the Destruction of Experience*, trans. Liz Heron (London: Verso, 1993), p. 13.

5 Walter Ong, *Orality and Literacy* (London: Routledge, 1982), p. 24.

6 Winfried Menninghaus, *Walter Benjamins Theorie der Sprachmagie* (Frankfurt/Main: Suhrkamp, 1980), p. 8.

7 Rainer Rochlitz, *The Disenchantment of Art: The Philosophy of Walter Benjamin* (New York: Guilford Press, 1996), p. 12.

8 Joshua Gunn, 'Benjamin's Magic', *Telos* 119 (Spring 2001): 60–1. Also see, Beatrice Hanssen, 'Language and Mimesis in Walter Benjamin's Work', in David S. Ferris (ed.), *The Cambridge Companion to Walter Benjamin* (Cambridge: Cambridge University Press, 2004), pp. 54–72.

9 Jan Bruck, 'Beckett, Benjamin and the Modern Crisis in Communication', *New German Critique* 26 (1982): 159–71.

10 Miriam Bratu Hansen, *Cinema and Experience: Siegfried Kracauer, Walter Benjamin and Theodor W. Adorno* (Berkeley, CA: University of California Press, 2012), p. 147.

11 Hansen, *Cinema and Experience*, p. 147.

12 John McCole, *Walter Benjamin and the Antinomies of Tradition* (Ithaca, NY: Cornell University Press, 1993), pp. 259–60.

13 Ackbar Abbas, 'Walter Benjamin's Collector: The Fate of Modern Experience', in Andreas Huyssen and David Bathrick (eds), *Modernity and the Text: Revisions of German Modernism* (New York: Columbia University Press, 1992), p. 228.

14 Scott Lash, *Critique of Information* (London: Sage, 2002), p. ix.

15 Marshall McLuhan, *The Gutenberg Galaxy: The Making of Typographic Man* (Toronto: University of Toronto Press, 1962).

16 James Carey, 'Walter Benjamin, Marshall McLuhan and the Emergence of Visual Society', *Prospects* 11 (1986): 29–38.

17 Benjamin notes: 'The birthplace of the novel is the individual in his isolation, the individual who can no longer speak of his concerns in exemplary fashion, who himself lacks counsel and can give none. To write a novel is to

take that which is incommensurable in the representation of human existence to the extreme' (SW2, 299).

18 Ferenc Fehér, 'Lukács and Benjamin: Parallels and Contrasts', *New German Critique* 34 (Winter 1985): 125–38.

19 Max Weber, *The Protestant Ethic and the Spirit of Capitalism with Other Writings on the Rise of the West* (Oxford: Oxford University Press, 2008 [1905]).

20 The transmission model of communication devised by Shannon and Weaver defines the notion of information from the mathematical perspective as a quantity that can be measured in bits and defined in terms of probabilities of occurrence of symbols. Claude E. Shannon and Warren Weaver, *The Mathematical Theory of Communication* (Champaign, IL: University of Illinois Press, 1949).

21 Michael Schudson, *Discovering the News: A Social History of American Newspapers* (New York: Basic Books, 1978), p. 119. According to Schudson, while Dewey wrote that the newspaper is 'the only genuine popular form of literature we have achieved', Mead similarly underscores that the role of the newspaper is to fulfil 'an aesthetic function' by engendering 'enjoyability' and 'consummatory value'. See John Dewey, 'Americanism and Localism', *The Dial* 68 (June 1920): 686 and George Herbert Mead, 'The Nature of Aesthetic Experience', *International Journal of Ethics* 36 (July 1926): 390.

22 Walter Lippmann, *Public Opinion* (New York: Macmillan, 1921); Harold Lasswell, *Propaganda Technique in the World War* (London: Kegan Paul, Trench, Truber & Co., 1927) and *Politics: Who Gets What, When, How* (New York: Whittlesey House, 1935). Drawing on Lippmann's analysis of 'the manufacture of consent', Chomsky and Herman later developed the propaganda model deriv-

ing from the monopoly of the information industries. Noam Chomsky and Edward S. Herman, *Manufacturing Consent: The Political Economy of the Mass Media* (New York: Vintage, 1995).

23 Witnessing the total destruction of civilization during the Second World War, Horkheimer and Adorno asked in their groundbreaking work *Dialectic Enlightenment* (1944), 'why mankind, instead of entering into a truly human condition, is sinking into a new kind of barbarism' even though myths are dissolved and knowledge became a substitute for myths. Max Horkheimer and T.W. Adorno, *Dialectic Enlightenment* (London: Verso, 1979), pp. xi and 3.

24 Some forty years later, the famous American sociologist, Alvin Gouldner characterizes news as 'decontextualized communication'. Alvin Gouldner, *The Dialectic of Ideology and Technology* (New York: Seabury Press, 1976).

25 Jürgen Habermas, *The Structural Transformation of the Public Sphere* (Cambridge: Polity, 1989). For a comprehensive introduction to the notion of the public sphere and its relation to the contemporary media studies, see Alan McKee, *The Public Sphere: An Introduction* (Cambridge: Cambridge University Press, 2004) and Richard Butsch (ed.), *Media and Public Spheres* (London: Palgrave Macmillan, 2009).

26 Among the first generation of the Frankfurt School, an exception is Leo Löwenthal, who paid substantial attention to the role of popular culture in the process of rationalization. He is one of the few theorists to analyse in a concrete way the rise of mass culture in conjunction with the development of mass communication in his work: *Literatur und Massenkultur* (Frankfurt/Main: Suhrkamp, 1980); *Critical Theory and Frankfurt Theorists* (New Brunswick, NJ: Transaction Books, 1989);

'Sociology of Literature in Retrospect' and 'Historical Perspectives on Popular Culture', in Stephen E. Bronner and Douglas M. Kellner (eds), *Critical Theory and Society: A Reader* (London: Routledge, 1989), pp. 40–51 and pp. 184–98.

27 Richard Burton, *The Flâneur and His City: Patterns of Daily Life in Paris 1815–1851* (Durham: University of Durham, 1994), p. 15.

28 Russell Berman, 'Writing for the Book Industry: The Writer under Organized Capitalism', *New German Critique* 29 (1983): 39–56.

29 Franz Hessel, *Spazieren in Berlin* (1929), cited in David Frisby, 'The *Flâneur* and Social Theory', in Keith Tester (ed.), *The Flâneur* (London: Routledge, 1994), p. 81. In his 1929 essay 'The Return of the *Flâneur*' (SW2, 262–7), Benjamin gives a detailed review of Hessel's book.

30 Charles Baudelaire, *The Painter of Modern Life* (London: Phaidon, 1995).

31 Baudelaire, *The Painter of Modern Life*, p. 12.

32 Baudelaire emphasizes: 'By no one as by Daumier has the bourgeois been known and loved (after the fashion of artists) – the bourgeois, that last vestige of the Middle Ages, that Gothic ruin that dies so hard, that type at once so commonplace and so eccentric.' Baudelaire, *The Painter of Modern Life*, p. 177. Benjamin quotes this passage in AP [b1a,3], 741.

33 Baudelaire, *The Painter of Modern Life*, p. 171.

34 As many feminist critics rightly point out, in his analysis of the gaze of the flâneur, Benjamin takes into account only that of the European male bourgeois. Other kinds of gaze, including that of women, are excluded. Benjamin's only allusion to women in his account of flânerie is to prostitutes, but this account still conceives of the female as an object of commodity spectacle, not as the subject

of observing. For more criticisms of Benjamin's male-oriented perspective, see Janet Wolff, *Feminine Sentences: Essays on Women and Culture* (Cambridge: Polity, 1990); Mica Nava, 'Women, the City and the Department Store', in Pasi Falk and Colin Campbell (eds), *The Shopping Experience* (London: Sage, 1997), pp. 56–91; Deborah Parsons, '*Flâneur* or *Flâneuse?* Mythologies of Modernity', *New Formations* 38 (Summer 1999): 91–100; and Patrice Petro, *Joyless Streets: Women and Melodramatic Representation in Weimar Germany* (Princeton, NJ: Princeton University Press, 1989).

35 Susan Buck-Morss, 'The *Flâneur*, the Sandwichman, and the Whore: The Politics of Loitering', *New German Critique* 39 (1986): 99–140.

36 For more details about the historical and social context of Kraus' association with *Die Fackel*, see Edward Timms, *Karl Kraus. Apocalyptic Satirist: Culture and Catastrophe in Habsburg Vienna* (New Haven, CT: Yale University Press, 1986).

37 Christopher Thornhill, 'Walter Benjamin and Karl Kraus: The Construction of Negative Language', *New Comparison* 18 (1992): 42–56.

38 In the wake of the globally networked information world, Benjamin's diagnosis of the emergence of the public journalists or mass authors has been vindicated by varying examples like the decline of the news-'paper' industry, the diminishing traditional role of the professional journalist in agenda setting and gatekeeping, and the rapid growth of participatory journalism via social media. See Adrienne Russell, *Networked: A Contemporary History of News in Transition* (Cambridge: Polity, 2011).

39 Benjamin's analysis of Brecht's theory of epic theatre will be discussed in more depth in chapter 3. Here I focus

more on Brecht's idea of the role of intellectuals and the impact of technology on the intellectual practice.

40 A free-floating intelligentsia is a term coined by the German sociologist Karl Mannheim, 'The Problem of the Intelligentsia, An Enquiry into Its Past and Present Role', in Bryan S. Turner (ed.), *Essays on the Sociology of Culture* (London: Routledge, 1992), pp. 91–170.

41 Pierre Lévy, *Collective Intelligence: Mankind's Emerging World in Cyberspace* (New York: Basic Books, 1999).

42 Howard Rheingold, *Smart Mobs: The Next Social Revolution* (Cambridge, MA: Basic Books, 2003).

CHAPTER 3: RADIO AND MEDIATED STORYTELLING

1 Anton Kaes and Martin Jay (eds), *The Weimar Republic Sourcebook* (Berkeley, CA: University of California Press, 1994), p. 594.

2 John Potts, *Radio in Australia* (Sydney: New South Wales University Press, 1989), p. 103.

3 Sabine Schiller-Lerg, 'Walter Benjamin, Radio Journalist: Theory and Practice of Weimar Radio', *Journal of Communication Inquiry* 13 (1989): 45.

4 The original script does not exist, but his other essays, written in a similar period, help follow his journey to Moscow and his analysis of Russian political and cultural milieu, which include 'The Political Groupings of Russian Writers' (SW2, 6–11), 'Moscow' (SW2, 22–46), and *Moscow Diary* (Cambridge, MA: Harvard University Press, 1996).

5 Arno Schirokauer, 'Art and Politics in Radio' (1929), in *The Weimar Republic Sourcebook*, p. 609.

6 The widespread availability of 'dance music' through radio broadcasting and two-sided records led to concerns

over 'jazz fever' and the Americanization of German culture. Kurt Weil, a composer and a collaborator with Brecht, acknowledged the implications of the mechanization of music (Kurt Weil, 'Dance Music' [*Tanzmusik*] (1926), in *The Weimar Republic Sourcebook*, p. 597).

7 Bertolt Brecht, *Brecht on Theatre: The Development of an Aesthetic* (London: Methuen Drama, 1974), p. 51.

8 Brecht, *Brecht on Theatre*, p. 52.

9 Sabine Schiller-Lerg's extensive work is the most informative resource for the study of Benjamin's radio activities so far; it includes an extensive listing of the dates of Benjamin's programmes as well as their technical details. The analysis of Benjamin's radio programmes is indebted to her scrupulous study. Sabine Schiller-Lerg, *Walter Benjamin und der Rundfunk: Programmarbeit zwischen Theorie und Praxis* (Munich: K.G. Saur, 1984). Buck-Morss provides her comments on Benjamin's radio scripts with a focus on the importance of childhood memory. Susan Buck-Morss, '"Verehrte Unsichtbare!": Walter Benjamins Radiovorträge', in Klaus Doderer (ed.), *Walter Benjamin und die Kinderliteratur: Aspekte der Kinderkultur in den zwanziger Jahren* (Weinheim: Juventa Verlag, 1988), pp. 93–119. Jeffrey Mehlman offers a highly literary analysis of Benjamin's radio scripts for the children's programmes in his *Walter Benjamin for Children: An Essay on His Radio Years* (Chicago, IL: University of Chicago Press, 1993).

10 The related plays are: 'Robber Bands in Old Germany', 'Bastille, the Old French State Prison', 'Caspar Hauser', 'Dr. Faust', 'Cagliostro', 'Borsig' and 'Theodor Hosemann'. These are only available in German.

11 'The Bootleggers or the American Alcohol Smugglers', 'Stamp Swindlers' and so on.

12 'The Downfall of Herculaneum and Pompeii', 'The

Mississippi Flood of 1927', 'The Railway Disaster at the Firth of Tay' (SW2, 563–7), 'The Canton Theatre Fire', 'The Lisbon Earthquake' (SW2, 536–40) and so on.

13 'Demonic Berlin' (SW2, 322–6), 'Moscow' and 'Naples'.

14 'Myslovitz-Braunschweig-Marseilles: The Story of a Hashish Trance' (SW2, 386–93).

15 'The Cold Heart'.

16 'True Dog Stories'.

17 'Children's Literature' (SW2, 250–6), 'Bert Brecht' (SW2, 365–71), 'Unpacking My Library: A Talk about Book Collecting' (SW2, 486–93) and 'Franz Kafka: *Beim Bau der Chinesischen Mauer*' (SW2, 494–500).

18 Schiller-Lerg, 'Walter Benjamin, Radio Journalist', p. 46.

19 Unlike most radio researchers engaging with content or textual analysis in the 1920s and 1930s, T.W. Adorno, a musicologist by training, actively investigated the impact of radio on music and tried to formulate a theory of radio with particular reference to 'radio physiognomics', by which he means 'the study of the elements of expression of the "radio voice"' (T.W. Adorno, *Current of Music: Elements of a Radio Theory* (Cambridge: Polity, 2009), p. 49). Adorno's analysis of the culture industry in 'On the Fetish Character in Music and the Regression of Listening', famous as a polemic against Benjamin's Artwork essay, is also a report from his research activity as the Musical Director of the Princeton Radio Project led by Paul Lazarsfeld (1901–1976, the Austrian sociologist) between 1938 and 1941.

20 Bertolt Brecht, 'Radio as an Apparatus of Communication', *Screen* 20 (Winter 1979/1980), pp. 24–5.

21 Elizabeth Wright, *Postmodern Brecht* (London: Routledge, 1989), p. 76

22 Walter Benjamin, 'What Is Epic Theatre? [First

Version]', in *Understanding Brecht* (London: Verso, 1998), p. 13.

23 Brecht, *Brecht on Theatre*, pp. 69–77. On Brecht's strong emphasis on the role of media in social transition to socialism, see Roswitha Mueller, *Bertolt Brecht and the Theory of Media* (Lincoln, NE: University of Nebraska Press, 1989), pp. 28–9.

24 Miriam Hansen, *Cinema and Experience: Siegfried Kracauer, Walter Benjamin and Theodor W. Adorno* (Berkeley, CA: University of California Press, 2012), p. 183.

25 Friedrich Schiller, *On the Aesthetic Education of Man in a Series of Letters* (1794). In the tradition of the Frankfurt School, Herbert Marcuse focused more attention on the role of play and aesthetic education in the advanced capitalist society from the perspective of social psychology. Herbert Marcuse, *Eros and Civilization: A Philosophical Inquiry into Freud* (Boston, MA: Beacon Press, 1974) and *The Aesthetic Dimension: Towards a Critique of Marxist Aesthetics* (New York: Beacon Press, 1978).

26 Following Schiller, Huizinga defines play: 'Summing up the formal characteristics of play we might call it a free activity standing quite consciously outside "ordinary" life as being "not serious", but at the same time absorbing the player intensely and utterly. It is an activity connected with no material interest, and no profit can be gained by it. It proceeds within its own proper boundaries of time and space according to fixed rules and in an orderly manner. It promotes the formation of social groupings which tend to surround themselves with secrecy and to stress their difference from the common world by disguise or other means.' Johan Huizinga, *Homo Ludens: A Study of the Play-Element in Culture* (Boston, MA: The Beacon Press, 1950), p. 13.

27 During the period of his exile in Paris, Benjamin

became acquainted with the members of the College
of Sociology, a group of French intellectuals based in
Paris, centring around the journal *Acéphale*, who analysed
social existence from their particular theoretical perspective of sacred sociology and underlined the significance
of ritual and communal life. Leading figures included
Georges Bataille and Pierre Klossowski as well as Roger
Caillois (Denis Hollier (ed.) *The College of Sociology
1937–39* (Minneapolis, MN: University of Minnesota
Press, 1988)). Benjamin's famous essay 'The Work of
Art in the Age of its Technological Reproducibility' was
first published in French, translated by Klossowski, in
1936. Benjamin frequently attended gatherings organized by the group and was interested in their critiques
of the surrealist overemphasis on the fantasy of urban
life. While analysing a phantasmagorical representation
of urban space in *The Arcades Project*, Benjamin referred
to Caillois' work, such as 'Pairs, Myth Modern' (1937)
(AP [M11a, 5] and [M12,1], 439) and 'The Praying
Mantis: Investigations into the Nature and Meaning of
Myth' (1937) (AP [Z2a,1], 696). In his attempt to formulate a notion of 'mimetic faculty', Benjamin draws on
Caillois' work on mimicry in the anthropological and
sociobiological contexts (Hansen, *Cinema and Experience*,
p. 147). However, Benjamin's overall response to this
closed and esoteric circle was not highly positive, fearing its affinity with 'pre-fascist aestheticism' (Pierre
Klossowski, 'Between Marx and Fourier', in Gary Smith
(ed.), *On Walter Benjamin: Critical Essays and Recollections*
(Cambridge, MA: MIT Press, 1988), p. 368). Benjamin,
under a pseudonym, wrote a scathingly critical review
of Caillois' essay, 'L'Aridité' (GS III, 549–52). For
more details about the relationship between Benjamin
and the College of Sociology, see Michael Weingrad,

'The College of Sociology and the Institute of Social Research', *New German Critique* 84 (Autumn 2001): 129–61.

28 Noteworthy is that Terry Eagleton, the British literary critic, conjures the close affinity between the Russian literary critic Mikhail Bakhtin's analysis of carnival and Benjamin's idea of children's play. Eagleton, *Walter Benjamin or Towards a Revolutionary Criticism* (London: Verso, 1981), esp. 'Carnival and Comedy: Bakhtin and Brecht', pp. 142–72.

29 Geert Lovink, 'Radio after Radio: From Pirate to Internet Experiments', in *Networks Without a Cause: A Critique of Social Media* (Cambridge: Polity, 2011), p. 122.

CHAPTER 4: ART AND POLITICS IN THE AGE OF THEIR TECHNOLOGICAL REPRODUCIBILITY

1 Samuel Weber, 'On Benjamin's '-Abilities', *Dædalus* (Spring 2007): 140.

2 Alois Riegl, 'The Main Characteristics of the Late Roman Kunstwollen' (1901) in Christopher S. Wood (ed.), *The Vienna School Reader: Politics and Art Historical Method in the 1930s* (New York: Zone Books, 2003), pp. 94–5.

3 Laura Marks, *The Skin of the Film: Intercultural Cinema, Embodiment, and the Senses* (Durham, NC: Duke University Press, 2000), p. 164.

4 Vivian Sobchak, *The Address of the Eye: Phenomenology and Film Experience* (Princeton, NJ: Princeton University Press, 1992), p. 93.

5 John McCole, *Walter Benjamin and the Antinomies of Tradition* (Ithaca, NY: Cornell University Press, 1993), p. 185.

6 Giuliano Bruno, *Atlas of Emotion: Journeys in Art,*

Architecture and Film (London: Verso, 2002), p. 23. Benjamin underlines Moholy-Nagy's insight into the relationship between old media (painting) and new ones (photography) by offering a lengthy extract from his seminal book *Painting, Photography, Film*: 'The creative potential of the new is for the most part slowly revealed through old forms, old instruments and areas of design that in their essence have already been superseded by the new. These, as they take shape are driven to a euphoric efflorescence. Thus, for example, futurists' (structural) painting brought forth the clearly defined problem of the simultaneity of motion, the representation of the instant, which was later to destroy it – and this at a time when film was already known but far from being understood. Similarly, some of the painters (neoclassicists and verists) today using representational–objective methods can be regarded, with caution, as forerunners of a new representational optical form that will soon be making use only of mechanical, technical methods' (SW2, 523).

7 Samuel Weber, *Mass Mediauras: Form, Technics, Media* (Stanford, CA: Stanford University Press, 1996), p. 84.

8 Pierre Bourdieu, *Photography: A Middle-Brow Art* (Cambridge: Polity, 1990), p. 79.

9 Detelf Mertins, 'Walter Benjamin and the Tectonic Unconscious: Using Architecture as an Optical Instrument', in Alex Coles (ed.), *The Optic of Walter Benjamin* (London: Black Dog Publishing, 1999), p. 217.

10 Scott McQuire, *Visions of Modernity* (London: Sage, 1998), p. 51.

11 McQuire, *Visions of Modernity*, p. 51

12 McQuire, *Visions of Modernity*, p. 52.

13 Elissa Marder, 'Flat Death: Snapshots of History', *diacritics* 22: 3–4 (Fall–Winter 1992): 128–44. Benjamin uses the temporal analogy of 'snapshot' in his 1929

essay 'Surrealism: The Last Snapshot of the European Intelligentsia' (SW2, 207–21).

14 Paul Virilio, *The Vision Machine* (Bloomington, IN: Indiana University Press, 1994), p. 67.

15 Jonathan Crary, 'Spectacle, Attention, Counter-Memory', *October* 50 (Autumn 1989): 103.

16 Tom Gunning, 'An Aesthetic of Astonishment: Early Film and the (In)Credulous Spectator', *Art and Text* 34 (Spring 1989): 128.

17 Gunning, 'An Aesthetic of Astonishment', p. 119.

18 Siegfried Kracauer, *The Mass Ornament* (Cambridge, MA: Harvard University Press, 1995), p. 325.

19 Gunning, 'An Aesthetic of Astonishment', p. 117.

20 Howard Eiland, 'Reception in Distraction', *boundary2* 30: 1 (2003): 52.

21 Adorno's letter to Benjamin dated 2 August 1935 (ABC, 110).

22 Eiland, 'Reception in Distraction', p. 57.

23 Michael Taussig, *The Nervous System* (New York: Routledge, 1992), p. 142. For the recent discussion of tactile dimension of and embodiment in cinema, see Jennifer M. Barker, *The Tactile Eye: Touch and the Cinematic Experience* (Berkeley, CA: University of California Press, 2009).

24 For a discussion of the notion of space in Benjamin's analysis of cinema, see Gertrud Koch, 'Cosmos in Film: On the Concept of Space in Walter Benjamin's "Work of Art" Essay', in Andrew Benjamin and Peter Osborne (eds), *Walter Benjamin's Philosophy: Destruction and Experience* (London: Routledge, 1994), pp. 205–15.

25 Jeffrey Herf, *Reactionary Modernism: Technology, Culture and Politics in Weimar and the Third Reich* (Cambridge: Cambridge University Press, 1984).

26 Rainer Stollmann, 'Fascist Politics as a Total Work

2

of Art: Tendencies of the Aestheticization of Political Life in National Socialism', *New German Critique* 14 (Spring 1978): 41–60. Ansagar Hillach, 'The Aesthetics of Politics: Walter Benjamin's "Theories of German Fascism"', *New German Critique* 17 (Spring 1979): 99–119.

27 Susan Sontag, *Under the Sign of Saturn* (New York: Vintage, 2001), p. 92.

28 Quoted from Sontag, *Under the Sign of Saturn*, p. 92.

29 Crary, 'Spectacle, Attention, Counter Memory', p. 104.

30 Martin Jay, '"The Aesthetic Ideology" as Ideology; or, What Does It Mean to Aestheticize Politics?', *Cultural Critique* (Spring 1992): 41–61.

31 John B. Thompson, 'The New Visibility', *Theory, Culture and Society* 22 (2005): 31–51.

32 Norberto Bobbio, *Democracy and Dictatorship* (Cambridge: Polity, 1989), p. 17.

33 Sabine Hake, 'Chaplin's Reception in Weimar Germany', *New German Critique* 51 (Fall 1990), p. 91.

34 Hake, 'Chaplin's Reception in Weimar Germany', p. 92. For various accounts of Chaplin's film by contemporary European intellectuals, including Kurt Tucholsky, Franz Kafka, Béla Balázs, Henri Lefèbvre among others, see Dorothee Kimmich (ed.), *Charlie Chaplin: Eine Ikone der Moderne* (Frankfurt/Main: Suhrkamp, 2003).

35 As Hake points out, the technical perfection of Chaplin's slapstick comedies, supported by the most advanced Hollywood film techniques, made them look far superior to the German ethnic and rustic comedies, and demanded serious attention from audiences (Hake, 'Chaplin's Reception in Weimar Germany', p. 91). Eisenstein expressed his desire to use whatever methods were most effective, remarking that 'we prefer Charlie's

arse to Eleonora Duse's hands' (*The Film Factory*, ed. R. Taylor and I. Christie, p. 59).

36 Susan Buck-Morss, 'Aesthetics and Anaesthetics: Walter Benjamin's Artwork Essay Reconsidered', *New Formations* 20 (Summer 1993): 142.

37 Lutz Koepnick, *Walter Benjamin and the Aesthetics of Power* (Lincoln, NE: University of Nebraska Press, 1999), p. 4.

38 Kracauer, *Mass Ornament*, p. 76.

39 Adorno later elaborates the dynamics of propaganda and the transformation of the masses with particular reference to identification, idealization and the technique of personalization. T.W. Adorno, 'Freudian Theory and the Pattern of Fascist Propaganda', in J.M. Berstein (ed.), *The Culture Industry* (London: Routledge, 1991), pp. 114–35.

40 Russell A. Berman, 'The Aestheticization of Politics: Walter Benjamin on Fascism and the Avant-Garde', in *Modern Culture and Critical Theory* (Madison, WI: University of Wisconsin Press, 1989), p. 37.

41 Mike Featherstone, 'Postmodernism and Aestheticization of Everyday Life', in Scott Lash and Jonathan Friedman (eds), *Modernity and Identity* (Oxford: Blackwell, 1992), pp. 265–90.

CHAPTER 5: THE MEDIA CITY: READING *THE ARCADES PROJECT*

1 Rolf Tiedemann, 'Dialectics at a Standstill: Approaches to the Passagen-Werk', in AP, 929.

2 Margaret Cohen, 'Benjamin's Phantasmagoria: The Arcades Project', in David S. Ferris (ed.), *The Cambridge Companion to Walter Benjamin* (Cambridge: Cambridge University Press, 2004), p. 210. On Benjamin's Judaic

Messianism, see Irving Wohlfarth, 'On the Messianic Structure of Walter Benjamin's Last Reflections', *Glyph* 3 (1978): 148–212.

3 Margaret Cohen, 'Benjamin's Phantasmagoria', p. 203.

4 Michael W. Jennings, *Dialectical Images: Walter Benjamin's Theory of Literary Criticism* (Ithaca, NY: Cornell University Press, 1987), pp. 204–5.

5 The term 'monad' is a metaphysical concept elucidated by the German philosopher and mathematician Gottfried Wilhelm Leibniz (1646–1716), referring to the ultimate, irreducible element of the universe. On the epistemological influence of Leibniz's monadology on Benjamin's philosophy of knowledge discussed in *The Arcades Project*, see Peter Fenves, 'Of Philosophical Style – from Leibniz to Benjamin', *boundary 2* 30:1 (2003): 67–87.

6 Siegfried Kracauer, 'On the Writings of Walter Benjamin', in *The Mass Ornament* (Cambridge, MA: Harvard University Press, 1995), pp. 261–2.

7 Hannah Arendt, 'Introduction', in Walter Benjamin, *Illuminations*, ed. Hannah Arendt (London: Fontana, 1973), p. 43.

8 Benjamin met Heartfield in Paris in the Spring of 1935, when the German artist visited for an exhibition of his photomontage. In a letter to Alfred Cohn of 18 July 1935, Benjamin states that he had 'a really good conversation with him [Heartfield] about photography' (C, 494).

9 David Bordwell, 'Montage in Theatre and Film', in *The Cinema of Eisenstein* (Cambridge, MA: Harvard University Press, 1993), p. 120.

10 Bordwell, 'Montage in Theatre and Film', p. 120.

11 Bordwell, 'Montage in Theatre and Film', p. 121.

12 Gyorgy Markus, 'Walter Benjamin or The Commodity as Phantasmagoria', *New German Critique* 83 (Spring/Summer, 2001): 13.

13 Kevin McLaughlin, 'Virtual Paris: *Benjamin's "Arcades Project"'*, in Gerhard Richter (ed.), *Benjamin's Ghosts* (Stanford, CA: Stanford University Press, 2002), p. 206.

14 *Oxford English Dictionary*, vol. XI (Oxford: Oxford University Press, 1998), p. 658.

15 Terry Castle, 'Phantasmagoria: Spectral Technology and the Metaphorics of Modern Reverie', *Critical Inquiry* 45 (1988): 48–50.

16 Margaret Cohen, 'Walter Benjamin's Phantasmagoria', *New German Critique* 48 (Fall 1989): 87–107.

17 Friedrich Kittler, *Optical Media* (Cambridge: Polity, 2002), p. 70.

18 Anne Friedberg, *Window Shopping* (Berkeley, CA: University of California Press, 1994), p. 31 and Jonathan Crary, *The Technique of the Observer: On Vision and Modernity in the Nineteenth Century* (Cambridge, MA: MIT Press, 1992), p. 4.

19 Irving Wohlfarth, 'Smashing the Kaleidoscope', in Michael P. Steinberg (ed.), *Walter Benjamin and the Demands of History* (Ithaca, NY: Cornell University Press, 1996), p. 199.

20 Crary, *The Technique of the Observer*, pp. 129–32.

21 Martin Jay, *The Dialectical Imagination: A History of the Frankfurt School and the Institute of Social Research 1932–1950* (London: Heinemann, 1974), pp. 193–4.

22 In contrast to Horkheimer's positive, encouraging response to Benjamin's 1935 exposé, Adorno was severely critical of the exposé. In a letter of 10 November 1938, Adorno poses a particular question about the use of phantasmagoria by linking it to Benjamin's Baudelaire studies:

> It seems to me that this pragmatic introduction prejudices the objectivity of phantasmagoria . . . as much as

the approach of the first chapter reduces phantasmagoria to characteristic types of behaviour in the literary *bohème*. You need not fear that I would suggest that phantasmagoria should simply survive in your text in unmediated form, or that the study itself should assume a phantasmagorical character. But the liquidation of phantasmagoria can only be accomplished in a truly profound manner if they are treated as an objective historico-philosophical category rather than as a 'vision' on the part of social characters. It is precisely at this point that your own conception differs from all other approaches to the nineteenth century. (ABC, 281–2)

Although Benjamin firmly defends his use of phantasmagoria, he partly takes Adorno's advice regarding the structure of his 1935 exposé. In the 1939 exposé, Benjamin added more comprehensive remarks on phantasmagoria in the introduction and greater emphasis on Blanqui's radical utopianism in the conclusion, while removing the second section, 'Daguerre, or the Panoramas'. For this reason, I use the 1935 exposé as an outline closer to Benjamin's original thought.

23 Johann Friedrich Geist, *Arcades: The History of a Building Type* (Cambridge, MA: MIT Press, 1983), p. 12.

24 Geist, *Arcades*, p. 60.

25 Michael Hollington, 'Benjamin, Fourier, Barthes', in Gerhard Fisher (ed.), *'With the Sharpened Axe of Reason': Approaches to Walter Benjamin* (Oxford: Berg, 1996), pp. 116–17.

26 Charles Fourier, *The Utopian Vision of Charles Fourier: Selected Texts on Work, Love, and Passionate Attraction* (Columbia, MI: University of Missouri Press, 1983).

27 Fourier, 'The Ideal Community', in *The Utopian Vision of Charles Fourier*, p. 243.

28 John McCole, *Walter Benjamin and the Antinomies of Tradition* (Ithaca, NY: Cornell University Press, 1993), p. 285.

29 Stephan Oettermann, *The Panorama: History of a Mass Medium* (New York: Zone Books, 1997), pp. 15–16.

30 M. Christine Boyer, *The City of Collective Memory: Its Historical Image and Architectural Entertainment* (Cambridge, MA: MIT Press, 1996), p. 253.

31 Graeme Gilloch, *Walter Benjamin: Critical Constellations* (Cambridge: Polity, 2002), p. 121.

32 Jonathan Crary, *Suspensions of Perception: Attention, Spectacle and Modern Culture* (Cambridge, MA: MIT Press, 2001), p. 138.

33 Friedberg, *Window Shopping*, p. 20.

34 Maurice Roche, *Mega-events and Modernity: Olympics and Expos in the Growth of Global Culture* (London: Routledge, 2000). The world exhibition is also called 'a world's fair', 'world exposition', 'universal exposition' or just 'expo'.

35 On the necessity of the shared image of an empire, Edward Said acutely points out: 'For the enterprise of empire depends upon the *idea of having an empire*, as Conrad so powerfully seems to have realized, and all kinds of preparations are made for it within a culture; then in turn imperialism acquires a kind of coherence, a set of experiences, and a presence of ruler and ruled alike within the culture.' Edward W. Said, *Culture and Imperialism* (New York: Alfred A. Knopf, 1993), p. 11.

36 Curtis M. Hinsley, 'Strolling through the Colonies', in Michael P. Steinberg (ed.), *Walter Benjamin and the Demands of History* (Ithaca, NY: Cornell University Press, 1996), p. 120.

37 On the politics of the exhibitions in early nineteenth-

century France, see Patricia Mainardi, *Art and Politics of the Second Empire: The Universal Expositions of 1855 and 1867* (New Haven, CT: Yale University Press, 1987).

38 Michele Hannoosh, *Baudelaire and Caricature: From the Comic to an Art of Modernity* (University Park, PA: The Pennsylvania State University Press, 1992), p. 159.

39 Charles Baudelaire, *The Painter of Modern Life* (London: Phaidon, 1995), pp. 180–1.

40 Max Pensky, *Melancholy Dialectics: Walter Benjamin and the Play of Mourning* (Amherst, MA: The University of Massachusetts Press, 1993), p. 215.

41 Benjamin's analysis of the bourgeois interior and the urban individuality is illustrated in the following sections of *One-Way Street*: 'Breakfast Room' (SW1, 444–5); 'Cellar' (SW1, 445); 'Dining Hall' (SW1, 445–6); 'This Space for Rent' (SW1, 476); and 'Betting Office' (SW1, 484–5).

42 Pierre Missac, *Walter Benjamin's Passages* (Cambridge, MA: MIT Press, 1995), p. 112.

43 Peter Schmiedgen, 'Interiority, Exteriority and Spatial Politics in Benjamin's Cityscapes', in Andrew Benjamin and Charles Rice (eds), *Walter Benjamin and the Architecture of Modernity* (Melbourne: re.press, 2009), p. 149.

44 Cohen, 'Benjamin's Phantasmagoria', p. 214.

45 Tom Gunning, 'The Exterior as *Intérieur*: Benjamin's Optical Detective', *boundary* 2 30: 1 (2003): 106.

46 David Frisby, 'The *flâneur* in social theory', in Keith Tester (ed.), *The Flâneur* (London: Routledge, 1994), p. 93.

47 Friedberg, *Window Shopping*, pp. 29–31.

48 Rob Shields, 'Fancy Footwork: Walter Benjamin's Notes on *Flânerie*', in Keith Tester (ed.), *The Flâneur*, p. 73.

49 Rudi Laermans, 'Learning to Consume: Early Department

Stores and the Shaping of the Modern Consumer Culture
(1860–1914)', *Theory, Culture and Society* 10 (1993),
p. 80. Also see Rosalind H. Williams, *Dream Worlds: Mass
Consumption in Late Nineteenth-Century France* (Berkeley,
CA: University of California Press, 1991).

50 Mike Featherstone, 'The Flâneur, the City and Virtual
Public Life', *Urban Studies* 35(5–6) (1998): 914.

51 Boyer, *The City of Collective Memory*, p. 38.

52 Miriam B. Hansen, 'Room-for-Play: Benjamin's Gamble
with Cinema', *October* 109 (Summer 2004): 6.

53 Cohen, 'Benjamin's Phantasmagoria', p. 217.

54 Margaret Cohen, *Profane Illumination: Walter Benjamin
and the Paris of Surrealist Revolution* (Berkeley, CA:
University of California Press, 1995), pp. 213–14.

55 Ackbar Abbas, 'Walter Benjamin's Collector: The Fate
of Modern Experience', in Andreas Huyssen and David
Bathrick (eds), *Modernity and the Text: Revisions of German
Modernism* (New York: Columbia University Press,
1992), pp. 216–40.

56 *The Oxford English Dictionary* describes how the psychological meaning of the term *Innervationsgefühl* was adopted
in the 1880s to refer to the feeling of force exerted by its
supposed cause, efferent discharge. In 1898, it was used
more specifically to designate 'a direct sense of energy put
forth that is independent of any results the putting forth
of energy may produce; this peculiar modification of
sensory consciousness has been called the sense of effort,
or the innervation sense' (*Oxford English Dictionary*, vol.
VII, p. 994.3). In the neurophysiological sense, innervation means 'the neural distribution of and supply to an
organ, gland or muscle' and occasionally denotes 'the
neural excitation of an organ, gland or muscle' (Arthur S.
Reber and Emily Reber, *Penguin Dictionary of Psychology*
(London: Penguin, 2001), p. 355.1). These physiological

understandings originate from William James' theory of emotion, developed in his *Principles of Psychology* (1890). In the context of Benjamin's application of innervation to his analysis of cinematic perception, it is noteworthy that Sergei Eisenstein explicitly refers to bodily movement and its impact on emotion in his theory of montage and attraction. Eisenstein, 'Montage of Attraction', in Richard Taylor (ed.), *The Eisenstein Reader* (London: British Film Institute, 1998), p. 30 and Sergei Eisenstein, 'Notes on Biomechanics', in Alma Law and Mel Gordon (eds), *Meyerhold, Eisenstein and Biomechanics: Actor Training in Revolutionary Russia* (Jefferson, NC: McFarland & Company, 1996), p. 164. If Benjamin's use of innervation is understood as regulating the interplay between humans and the media, then his account of shock experience differs considerably from the surrealist ideas of Sigmund Freud. While 'shock' in surrealist work primarily functions to protect the subject from the external world, the shock-laden distraction in Benjamin's thought serves more constructively to form subjectivity through the provision of a tactile response. For a detailed genealogical analysis of the notion of innervation in Benjamin's theory of film, see Miriam Hansen, 'Benjamin and Cinema: Not a One-Way Street', *Critical Inquiry* 25 (Winter 1999): 306–43.

57 Tobias Wilke, 'Tacti(ca)lity Reclaimed: Benjamin's Medium, the Avant-Garde, and the Politics of the Senses', *Grey Room* 29 (Spring 2010): 44.

CHAPTER 6: CONCLUSION: THE ACTUALITY OF BENJAMIN'S MEDIA CRITIQUE

1 Max Horkheimer and Theodor W. Adorno, *Dialectic of Enlightenment* (London: Verso, 1979 [1944]).

2 Max Horkheimer and Theodor W. Adorno, 'The Culture Industry: Enlightenment as Mass Deception', in *Dialectic of Enlightenment*, pp. 120–67.

3 Theodor W. Adorno, 'On the Fetish Character in Music and the Regression of Listening', in J.M. Bernstein (ed.), *The Culture Industry: Selected Essays on Mass Culture* (London: Routledge, 1991), pp. 26–52.

4 Jürgen Habermas, 'Walter Benjamin: Consciousness-Raising or Rescuing Critique', in Gary Smith (ed.), *On Walter Benjamin: Critical Essays and Recollections* (Cambridge, MA: MIT Press, 1992), p. 118.

5 For the various accounts of the contribution of Habermas' theory of the public sphere, see Craig Calhoun (ed.), *Habermas and the Public Sphere* (Cambridge, MA: MIT Press, 1992) and Bruce Robbins (ed.), *The Phantom Public Sphere* (Minneapolis, MN: University of Minnesota Press, 1993). For Habermas' reply to the criticisms and more recent – yet unchanging – reflections on mass media and democracy, refer to Jürgen Habermas, 'Further Reflections on the Public Sphere', in Calhoun (ed.), *Habermas and the Public Sphere*, pp. 421–61; *Between Facts and Norms: Contributions to a Discourse Theory of Law and Democracy* (Cambridge: Polity, 1996), pp. 359ff; and 'Political Communication in Media Society: Does Democracy Still Enjoy an Epistemic Dimension? The Impact of Normative Theory on Empirical Research', *Communication Theory* 16 (2006): 411–26.

6 John B. Thompson, 'Shifting Boundaries of Public and Private Life', *Theory, Culture and Society* 28: 4 (2011): 49–70.

7 Asa Briggs and Peter Burke, *A Social History of the Media: From Gutenberg to the Internet* (Cambridge: Polity, 2002), p. 73.

8 Influenced by Benjamin's insight, the German social

theorist Oskar Negt and the film director Alexander
Kluge have investigated the much wider range of public
spheres such as proletarian public spheres, in connec-
tion with the development of the electronic media.
Oskar Negt and Alexander Kluge, *The Public Sphere and
Experience* (Minneapolis, MN: University of Minnesota
Press, 1993).

9 Luc Boltanski aptly discusses the moral and political
dimension of the audience's mediated experience in his
Distant Suffering: Morality, Media and Politics (Cambridge:
Cambridge University Press, 1999).

10 Norbert Bolz, 'Walter Benjamin in the Postmodern',
New Comparison 18 (1994): 9–23.

11 Arnold Hauser, *The Sociology of Art* (Chicago, IL:
University of Chicago Press, 1982), p. 614.

12 Richard Cavell, *McLuhan in Space: A Cultural Geography*
(Toronto: University of Toronto Press, 2002).

13 Marshall McLuhan, *Understanding Media: The Extensions
of Man* (New York: Mentor, 1964; reprinted, London:
Routledge, 1997).

14 Marshall McLuhan, *The Gutenberg Galaxy: The Making of
Typographic Man* (Toronto: University of Toronto Press,
1962).

15 Benedict Anderson, *Imagined Communities: Reflections
on the Origin and Spread of Nationalism* (London: Verso,
1982).

16 Marshall McLuhan and Bruce R. Powers, *The Global
Village: Transformations in World Life and Media in
the 21st Century* (Oxford: Oxford University Press,
1989).

17 For critical debates on the relationship between the so-
called Toronto School and the Frankfurt School, see
James Carey, 'Walter Benjamin, Marshall McLuhan and
the Emergence of Visual Society', in *Prospects: An Annual*

of American Cultural Studies 12 (Cambridge: Cambridge University Press, 1987), pp. 29–38; Paul Grosswiler, *Method Is the Message: Rethinking McLuhan through Critical Theory* (London: Blackrose Books, 1998); Judith Stamp, *Unthinking Modernity: Innis, McLuhan and the Frankfurt School* (Montreal: McGill-Queen's University Press, 1995); and Pamela McCallum, 'Walter Benjamin and Marshall McLuhan: Theories of History', *Signature: A Journal of Theory and Canadian Literature* 1 (1989): 71–89.

18 James Carey, 'McLuhan and Mumford: The Roots of Modern Media Analysis', *Journal of Communication* 31 (1981): 176.

19 Jean Baudrillard, *Symbolic Exchange and Death* (London: Sage, 1993), pp. 55–6.

20 Baudrillard, *Symbolic Exchange and Death*, p. 57.

21 Jean Baudrillard, *The Conspiracy of Art* (New York: Semiotext(e), 2005), pp. 108 and 117.

22 Baudrillard, *The Conspiracy of Art*, p. 102.

23 Jean Baudrillard, *Simulacra and Simulation* (Ann Arbor, MI: University of Michigan Press, 1994).

24 Graeme Gilloch, 'The Figure that Fascinates: Seductive Strangers in Benjamin and Baudrillard', *Renaissance and Modern Studies* 40 (1997): 17–29.

25 Baudrillard's characterization of simulation and hyper-reality is influenced by the French media theorist Paul Virilio's schematization of reality, actuality and virtuality. Virilio identifies the 'reality' as the formal logic of traditional pictorial representation, the 'actuality' as the dialectical logic governing photographic and cinematic representation, and the 'virtualities' as the paradoxical logic of the videogram, the hologram or digital image. Paul Virilio, *The Vision Machine* (Bloomington, IN: Indiana University Press, 1994), p. 63.

26 Guy Debord, *The Society of the Spectacle* (London: Verso, 1998), p. 12.
27 Henry Jenkins, *Convergence Culture: Where Old and New Media Collide* (New York: New York University Press, 2006).

FURTHER READING

CHAPTER 1

Bloch, Ernst 1991: 'Recollections of Walter Benjamin', in Gary Smith (ed.), *On Walter Benjamin: Critical Essays and Recollections*. Cambridge, MA: MIT Press, pp. 338–45.

Brodersen, Momme 1996: *Walter Benjamin: A Biography*. London: Verso.

Fittko, Lisa 1991: 'Old Benjamin', in Lisa Fittko, *Escape through the Pyrenees*. Evanston, IL: Northwestern University Press, pp. 103–15.

Gilloch, Graeme 2002: *Walter Benjamin: Critical Constellations*. Cambridge: Polity.

Habermas, Jürgen 1991: 'Walter Benjamin: Consciousness-Raising or Rescuing Critique (1972)', in Gary Smith (ed.), *On Walter Benjamin: Critical Essays and Recollections*. Cambridge, MA: MIT Press, pp. 90–128.

Kracauer, Siegfried 1995: 'On the Writings of Walter Benjamin', in Siegfried Kracauer, *The Mass Ornament:*

Weimar Essays. Cambridge, MA: Harvard University Press, pp. 259–64.

Leslie, Esther 1997: 'The Multiple Identities of Walter Benjamin', *New Left Review* 226 (November–December), pp. 128–35.

Lowenthal, Leo 1983: 'The Integrity of the Intellectual: In Memory of Walter Benjamin', in Gary Smith (ed.), *Benjamin: Philosophy, Aesthetics, History.* Chicago, IL: University of Chicago Press.

Missac, Pierre 1995: *Walter Benjamin's Passages.* Cambridge, MA: MIT Press.

Parini, Jay 1998: *Benjamin's Crossing.* London: Anchor.

CHAPTER 2

Carey, James 1986: 'Walter Benjamin, Marshall McLuhan and the Emergence of Visual Society', *Prospects* 11, pp. 29–38.

Eisenstein, Elizabeth 1968: 'Some Conjectures about the Impact of Printing on Western Society and Thought: A Preliminary Report', *Journal of Modern History* 40: 1, pp. 1–56.

Febvre, Lucien and Henri-Jean Martin 1976: *The Coming of the Book: The Impact of Printing 1450–1800.* London: Verso.

Hayles, N. Katherine 2008: *Electronic Literature: New Horizons for the Literary.* Notre Dame, IN: University of Notre Dame Press.

Jay, Martin 1993: 'Experience without a Subject: Benjamin and the Novel', *New Formations* 20, pp. 145–56.

Lash, Scott 1999: 'The Symbolic in Fragments: Walter Benjamin's Talking Things', in *Another Modernity: A Different Rationality.* Oxford: Blackwell, pp. 312–38.

Lash, Scott 2002: *Critique of Information.* London: Sage.

McLuhan, Marshall 1962: *The Gutenberg Galaxy: The Making of Typographic Man*. Toronto: University of Toronto Press.

Ong, Walter 1982: *Orality and Literacy*. London: Routledge.

Poster, Mark 1990: *The Mode of Information: Poststructuralism and Social Context*. Cambridge: Polity Press.

Rheingold, Howard 2012: *Net Smart: How to Thrive Online*. Cambridge, MA: MIT Press.

Taussig, Michael 1993: *Mimesis and Alterity: A Particular History of the Senses*. New York: Routledge.

Thompson, John B. 1995: 'The Media and the Development of Modern Societies', in *The Media and Modernity: A Social Theory of the Media*. Cambridge: Polity, pp. 44–80.

Thompson, John B. 2005: *Books in the Digital Age: The Transformation of Academic and Higher Education Publishing in Britain and the United States*. Cambridge: Polity.

Virilio, Paul 2000: *The Information Bomb*. London: Verso.

CHAPTER 3

Arnheim, Rudolf. 1936: *Radio*. Trans. Margaret Ludwig and Herbert Read. London: Faber and Faber.

Bergmeier, Horst J.P. and Rainer E. Lotz 1997: *Hitler's Airwaves: The Inside Story of Nazi Radio Broadcasting and Propaganda Swing*. New Haven, CT: Yale University Press.

Brecht, Bertolt 1974: *Brecht on Theatre: The Development of an Aesthetic*. London: Methuen Drama.

Crisell, Andrew 2005: *More than a Music Box: Radio Cultures and Communities in a Multi-Media World*. Oxford: Berghahn Books.

Doderer, Klaus 1996: 'Walter Benjamin and Children's Literature', in Gerhard Fischer (ed.), *'With the Sharpened Axe of Reason': Approaches to Walter Benjamin*. Oxford: Berg, pp. 169–75.

Kittler, Friedrich A. 1999: *Gramophone, Film, Typewriter*. Stanford, CA: Stanford University Press.

Kris, Ernst and Hans Speier (eds) 1944: *German Radio Propaganda: Report on Home Broadcasts during the War*. London: Oxford University Press.

Lazarsfeld, Paul F. 1940: *Radio and the Printed Page*. New York: Arno Press.

Lazarsfeld, Paul F. and Frank N. Stanton (eds) 1941: *Radio Research 1941*. New York: Duell, Sloan, and Pearce.

Mueller, Roswitha 1989: *Bertolt Brecht and the Theory of Media*. Lincoln, NE: University of Nebraska Press.

Nancy, Jean-Luc 2008: *Listen: A History of Our Ears*. New York: Fordham University Press.

Scannell, Paddy 1996: *Radio, Television and Modern Life*. Oxford: Blackwell.

Wizisla, Erdmut 2012: *Walter Benjamin and Bertolt Brecht: The Story of a Friendship*. New Haven, CT: Yale University Press.

Wohlfarth, Irving 1994: 'No-Man's-Land: On Walter Benjamin's "Destructive Character"', in Andres Benjamin and Peter Osborne (eds), *Walter Benjamin's Philosophy*. London: Routledge.

Zipes, Jack 1988: 'Walter Benjamin, Children's Literature and the Children's Public Sphere', *The Germanic Review* LXIII (Winter), pp. 2–5.

CHAPTER 4

Barthes, Roland 1993: *Camera Lucida: Reflections on Photography*. London: Vintage.

Cadava, Eduardo 1997: *Words of Light: Theses on the Photography of History*. Princeton, NJ: Princeton University Press.

Crary, Jonathan 1990: *Techniques of the Observer*. Cambridge, MA: MIT Press.

Hansen, Miriam B. 1987: 'Benjamin, Cinema and Experience: "The Blue Flower in the Land of Technology"', *New German Critique* 40 (Winter), pp. 179–223.

Hansen, Miriam B. 2008: 'Benjamin's Aura', *Critical Inquiry* 34 (Winter), pp. 336–75.

Isenberg, Noah 2001: 'The Work of Walter Benjamin in the Age of Information', *New German Critique* 83 (Summer), pp. 119–50.

Jay, Martin 1993: *Downcast Eyes: The Denigration of Vision in Twentieth-Century French Thought*. Berkeley, CA: University of California Press.

Kaufman, Robert 2002: 'Aura, Still', *October* 99 (Winter), pp. 45–80.

Rancière, Jacques 2009: *The Emancipated Spectator*. London: Verso.

Rodríguez-Ferrándiz, Raúl 2012: 'Benjamin, BitTorrent, Bootlegs: Auratic Piracy Cultures?' *International Journal of Communication* 6, pp. 396–412.

Sontag, Susan 1977. *On Photography*. London: Penguin.

CHAPTER 5

Benjamin, Andrew and Charles Rice (eds) 2009: *Walter Benjamin and the Architecture of Modernity*. Melbourne: re.press.

Buck-Morss, Susan 1989: *Dialectics of Seeing: Walter Benjamin and the Arcades Project*. Cambridge, MA: MIT Press.

Buck-Morss, Susan 2000: *Dream World and Catastrophe: The Passing of Mass Utopia in East and West*. Cambridge, MA: MIT Press.

Friedberg, Anne 2006: *The Virtual Window: From Alberti to Microsoft*. Cambridge, MA: MIT Press.

Frisby, David 1985: *Fragments of Modernity: Theories of*

Modernity in the Work of Simmel, Kracauer and Benjamin. Cambridge: Polity.

Frisby, David 2001: *Cityscapes of Modernity.* Cambridge: Polity.

Gilloch, Graeme 1996: *Myth and Metropolis: Walter Benjamin and the City.* Cambridge: Polity.

Harvey, David 2003: *Paris, Capital of Modernity.* London: Routledge.

Leslie, Esther 2002: *Hollywood Flatlands: Animation, Critical Theory and the Avant-Garde.* London: Verso.

McLaughlin, Kevin and Philip Rosen (eds) 2003: Special Issue: Benjamin Now: Critical Encounter with The Arcades Project, *boundary2* 30: 1 (Spring).

McQuire, Scott 2008: *The Media City: Media, Architecture and Urban Space.* London: Sage.

Patt, Lise (ed.) 2001: *Benjamin's Blind Spot: Walter Benjamin and the Premature Death of Aura.* Topanga, CA: The Institute of Cultural Inquiry.

Wark, McKenzie 2013: *The Spectacle of Disintegration: Situationist Passage out of the Twentieth Century.* London: Verso.

INDEX